BLIND BEASTS:
CHAUCER'S ANIMAL WORLD

BLIND BEASTS

Chaucer's Animal World

by

BERYL ROWLAND

York University
Toronto

Ye blinde bestes, ful of lewednesse!

THE KENT STATE
UNIVERSITY PRESS

Copyright © 1971 by Beryl Rowland
All rights reserved
Library of Congress Catalog Card Number 77-104839
Standard Book Number 87338-095-9

Manufactured in Great Britain
at the press of W. & J. Mackay & Co Ltd, Chatham
Designed by Ruari McLean

First edition

Preface

I N this study of Chaucer's Animal World I have confined myself chiefly to mammals. My observations on birds are of an incidental nature. The limitations I imposed arose originally from the fact that a colleague was about to undertake a study of Chaucer's birds. I have since discovered that my definition is not without precedent. Hildegard of Bingen, the prodigious poet, musician, mystic and scientist of the twelfth century, devoted separate books to birds and animals in her *Physica* (*Patrologia Latina*, CXCVII, cols. 1126–1351); and 'De bestiis et aliis rebus,' a work formerly attributed to Hugh of St Victor (1096–1141), contains a book apiece on birds and animals, as well as two books on more eclectic material (*Patrologia Latina*, CLXXVII, cols. 15–163).

Inevitably, a work of this kind presents problems of organization. My classifications may seem arbitrary and my inclusion of background material excessive. An alternative method of considering Chaucer's animal imagery within the limits of a single work has been most effectively used in some recent articles, and while these papers appeared too late for consideration in the text, I have, where possible, mentioned them in the notes. My own arrangement enabled me to emphasize my original thesis that Chaucer's references to animals usually have a basis in popular tradition or literary convention rather than in the real and observable. At the same time I have sought to show that, despite their origins and despite their traditional application to illustrate human character and behavior, Chaucer's animal images often have a complex significance extending beyond the immediate context to embrace a total portrait or situation.

I began the work as a dissertation under Professor Earle Birney at the University of British Columbia, and I am most indebted to him for his stimulating guidance. Later, by means of a grant from the Canada Council, I was able to study at the British Museum, The Society of Antiquaries, The Warburg Institute, the Bodleian, and other libraries. I am very grateful for this assistance and also for the encouragement given to me both by members of the English Department at the University of British Columbia and of the Pontifical Institute of Mediaeval Studies in Toronto. The book itself has been published with the help of a grant from the Humanities Research Council of Canada, using funds provided by the Canada Council.

BERYL ROWLAND
York University, 1969

ACKNOWLEDGEMENTS

I am obliged to the courtesy of the editors for permission to include material from the following articles:
'Alison Identified,' *American Notes and Queries*, III, 3–4, 20–21, 39; 'Aspects of Chaucer's Use of Animals,' *Archiv für das Studium der neueren Sprachen und Literaturen*, CCI, 110–114; 'Chaucer's "Bukke and Hare",' ' "A sheep that highte Malle",' *English Language Notes*, 11, 6–8, VI, 84–87, 'The *Knight's Tale*, A. 180,' 'The Wife of Bath's Prologue, D. 389,' *Explicator*, XXI, 73, XXIV, 14; 'Chaucer's "Throstil Old" and Other Birds,' 'Chaucer and the Unnatural History of Animals,' ' "Owles and Apes" in Chaucer's *Nun's Priest's Tale*, 3092,' *Mediaeval Studies*, XXIV, 381–384, XXV, 367–372, XXVII, 322–325; ' "Bihoold the Murye Wordes of the Hoost to Chaucer",' 'The Whelp in Chaucer's *Book of the Duchess*,' *Neuphilologische Mitteilungen*, LXIV, 48–52, LXVI, 148–160; 'Animal Imagery and the Pardoner's Abnormality,' *Neophilologus*, XLVIII, 56–60; ' "Wood . . . as an Hare" (*FrT*, 1327),' 'Chaucer's Daisy,' *Notes and Queries*, CCVIII, 168–169, 210; 'Pandarus and the Fate of Tantalus,' *Orbis Litterarum*, XXIV, 3–15; 'The Horse and Rider Figure in Chaucer's Works,' *University of Toronto Quarterly*, XXXV, 246–259.

Contents

I. *The Traditions*

IN Chaucer's day the animal world comprised far less and far more than it
does now. While there was no conception of the infinite variety of forms
which do exist, the imagination invented many which do not: mermaids
— fish, bird or all-woman — who were proficient in song or musical instrument, unicorns which could be tamed only by the sight of a virgin's un-
covered bosom, and werewolves who could be spotted in human guise because their heavy eyebrows met in the middle. These strange creatures and
many others competed for territory on earth, air or sea with the more usual
fauna. They inhabited an animal world which few men observed closely — a
place of terror and wonder, a fantasy kept alive for centuries by the fabulists,
natural historians, homilists, encyclopedists, artists and sculptors as well as by
the folk.

Primitive peoples regarded animals both as replicas of themselves, creatures who once spoke and acted as they did, and as incarnations of spirits,
terrifying and unknowable. The stories they devised about them were originally not in the nature of fiction but a living reality, believed once to have
happened and probably retaining for a long time a counterpart in ritual sacrifices which ultimately died out while the myth lived. When such stories came

to be recorded they were too important in the life of the folk to be presented simply as entertainment. In the *Panchatantra* they were incorporated into a *niti-shastra*, a textbook of wise conduct of life; with Pliny, they served for natural history to illustrate his thesis that all animals were instruments for man's use; in the works of the theologians from the patristic period to medieval times they were facts belonging to the Book of Nature which was an immense cryptogram whereby Man might discover God's truths and become regenerated. In all of them the ascribing of specific traits to certain animals or types of animals, whether as a result of observation or fantasy, persisted, and so lacking was the spirit of scientific enquiry in western Christendom that conventional ideas about animals were reinforced by further fictions.

Among specific works which were part of the popular tradition in Chaucer's time were the fables originating in the East and attributed to Aesop who, according to Herodotus, lived in the sixth century before Christ. These entered the Greek language with Babrius and the Latin with Phaedrus probably in the second or third century of the Christian era. Of the subsequent versions, it was the eleventh-century prose collection of Romulus, based largely on the stories given in brief iambic trimeters by Phaedrus, which became the source of later collections.

Popularized in England from the twelfth century onward by Walter, chaplain to Henry II, Alexander Neckam and Marie de France, stories such as 'The Wolf in Sheep's Clothing,' illustrating the deceptiveness of appearances, and 'Androcles and the Lion,' the classic example of a lion showing gratitude by fawning on his benefactor, circulated so widely that even the briefest allusion must have been understood. Chaucer's Miller in *The Reeve's Tale* (4054–4055) refers to a fable found in the Latin Aesopian collection: ' "The gretteste clerkes been noght wisest men,"/As whilom to the wolf thus spak the mare,' when he plans to outsmart the two young clerks, and the fact that one of the 'lewede' folk should be able to use it so elliptically suggests that the story was part of oral tradition.

Of even greater popular appeal in England was the cycle of animal tales concerned with Renard the Fox. These tales were also of great antiquity, with the trickster hero playing a role similar to that ascribed to the coyote, the great hare and the master rabbit in the American folktale. Coming through the *Panchatantra*, Arabic, Hebrew, Greek and Latin collections with some didactic content, they grew satiric under medieval influence: Renard, like all trickster heroes, represented anarchy against order, individualism against collectivism; he both indulged in and exposed the follies of mankind. By the late twelfth and thirteenth centuries the cycle comprised over twenty branches using the quarrel between Renard the fox and Ysengrim the wolf as the mainspring for the action and showing Renard, still audacious, unscrupulous and resourceful, pitting his wits against a variety of adversaries.

Although versions appeared in German in the late twelfth century and in

Flemish in the early thirteenth, the earliest and fullest development of the beast epic satirizing church, court and society, was in France. There are only two full-length Renard tales extant in England before Caxton but the frequency of the illustrations in homilies, misericords and manuscripts, particularly in the thirteenth and fourteenth centuries, suggest that such tales were well known.

Among the ancient writings which contributed most to the popular animal lore of the Middle Ages are the Bible and Aristotle's *Historia Animalium*. The first expressed many traditional ideas contained in the animal fables and reinforced symbolic concepts. The wolf in sheep's clothing, the dog returning to its vomit, the fierce lion, the stupid sheep, the innocent lamb, the crafty fox and the venomous scorpion are all creatures of common tradition, found in Chaucer's works and accepted even today. Aristotle's great work, known in Chaucer's time through Latin translation, purported to contain a knowledge of animals based on observation. Pliny describes how Alexander ordered some thousands of people throughout the whole of Asia and Greece to become Aristotle's field workers, and report their findings. But there is folklore as well as fact in Aristotle. If he denied the popular belief that the elephant slept standing and could not bend its knees, he was still convinced that the stag was fond of music and that the salamander could not be destroyed by fire.[1]

Pliny, who lived in the period of the great processional zoological shows of imperial Rome, repeated similar fictions: he once burned a salamander to make medicine from its ashes, yet he also declared that the salamander was like ice when it came to putting out a fire. His successor, Aelian, a Roman teacher of rhetoric, must have seen even more exotic zoological shows. On one occasion some four hundred animals, including bears, wild asses, bison, ostriches, cheetahs, lions and leopards, were brought into the arena at one time, bursting forth from a model of a whale washed up on the Italian shores.[2] But if he was almost right when he stated in his Greek treatise on animals that the period of gestation for an elephant was either two years or eighteen months, he too thought that the stag liked music and the salamander fire. Other writers on natural history such as Solinus, his contemporary, Claudian in the fourth century and Cassiodorus in the sixth, extended the number of stories by trying to assemble all extant information from oral and written sources, but still depended mainly on Aristotle and Pliny. Two works which subsequently exercised an immense influence on the Middle Ages, the *Physiologus* and Isidore's *Etymologiae*, repeated the same animal lore without questioning its accuracy.

Although the *Physiologus* seems to have been banned as heretical in 469 A.D., this work of moralized natural history with its enlarged form, the bestiary, was among the best known types of medieval didactic literature. Because of its wide diffusion by translation, its animal lore became common property, passing into general literature, folk ways and art. The title may have originally indicated the Greek pagan author who was dealing with the characteristics (φύσεις) of various animals. Later, when the allegories were added by a Christian writer, it was applied to the book itself. Its use by Ambrose suggests that a Latin version must have existed by 386. The illustrated bestiary, in which the original content of the *Physiologus* was more than doubled, ranked as one of the leading picture books in twelfth-century England, and the popularity of the material is attested not only by the numerous Latin versions but by the French versions of Anglo-Norman poets such as Philippe de Thaon, Gervais, Guilliaume le clerc and Pierre de Beauvais, and by its secular adaptation in Richard de Fournival's *Bestiaire d'amour*. Particularly well known was a Latin version attributed to Theobaldus, Abbot at Monte Cassino, 1022–1035, and the Middle English Bestiary is a free translation of it.

The bestiaries added material drawn from many sources, from the Egyptian Book of the Dead, the Bible, travellers' tales, the works of Herodotus, Aristotle, Pliny, Plutarch and others, and presented little new information on animals. Their most immediate source was the *Etymologiae* of Isidore, bishop of Seville in the seventh century, a textbook for schoolboys in Chaucer's day and twice mentioned in *The Parson's Tale* (89, 551).

Isidore in his twelfth book was peculiarly inventive in explaining the reason for animals' names. There was an etymology to suit the supposed characteristics of each: *canis*, a dog, was derived from *canere*, to sing; *cattus*, a cat, was from *captare*, to seize. Otherwise he repeated much of the information given by earlier writers. The bestiarists often used his etymologies and his stories and they applied the supposed facts of natural history to illustrate moral precepts and theological dogma. None of the writers was interested in stalking a lion to establish whether it did indeed dwell on mountain tops, disguise its spoor with its tail when pursued by hunters, sleep with its eyes open, breathe life on the third day into the cubs which its mate had brought forth dead. The supposed characteristics of the lion were significant only because the lion represented Christ hiding the spoor of his love in high places, the Godhead remaining awake though sleeping in the body after the crucifixion, the Father raising Christ from the dead on the third day.

St Augustine suggested that it was not important whether certain animals existed or not: what was important was their meaning. In *Contra mendacium* he defended Aesop's fables against the charge that they were lies: 'quod utique totum fingitur, ut ad rem quae intenditur, ficta quidem narratione, non mendaci tamen, sed veraci significatione veniatur' (*PL*, XL, col. 538). This was the attitude of the bestiarists, and it was to predominate throughout the medieval period and to encourage the unscientific spirit typical of Alexandrian scholars under the Ptolemies. Pseudo-Hugh of St Victor, the 'Augustus Secundus' of the twelfth century, declared that the whole universe was a book written by God (*PL*, CLXXVI, col. 644). The exegetists furnished glossaries to enable one to read and interpret it symbolically. The fact that an animal could have multiple and very opposite meanings was not considered confusing: the *Allegoriae in*

4

sacram scripturam gave eight symbols for the lion including both Christ and anti-christ (*PL*, CXII, col. 983).

A similar interpretative approach towards animals was adopted by the medieval encyclopedists. Alexander Neckam in the twelfth century, Thomas de Cantimpré and Vincent de Beauvais in the thirteenth, all used natural history to illustrate doctrinal and ethical principles. Although Bartholomew the Englishman's popular *De proprietatibus rerum*, c. 1250, made very little use of obvious moralizing, its purpose as Trevisa, his translator in the fourteenth century, stated in the prologue, was to explain scriptural allegories 'alle thyse propritees of thynges ben full necessary . . . to understonde the obscuretees or derknesse of holy scriptures.'

Of Chaucer's contemporaries the homilists were probably among the writers who referred most frequently to animals. Animal fables, bestiary lore and animals in everyday life all served as subjects for pulpit moralization. The early Christian fathers, Ambrose, Augustine, Leon le Grand and Gregory, used such *exempla* but the vogue reached its height in the thirteenth and fourteenth centuries in such works as Jacques de Vitry's *Sermones vulgares et communes* drawn from many sources including Aesop and the *Roman de la rose* and in the immense collections of the English preachers, Odo of Ceriton, John of Sheppey, priest of Rochester from 1352 to 1363, and the Franciscan, Nicholas Bozon. The fable of the innocent ass sentenced to beating and death by the lion served to demonstrate the fate of those of humble rank; the popular story of Pope Benedict IX appearing after death with the head of an ass and the body of a boar was used to indict the church. The tale of the cheese and the raven became a sermon against vainglory; the story of the singed cat was useful for disciplining wives. If a cat will not stay home, shorten her tail and singe her fur. Similarly with wives, said Odo of Ceriton, with a disapproving glance at the current fashion for long trains or tails to gowns: 'si caude mulierum essent absciendende, capilli tondendi vel comburendi, et sic remanens in domo extra non vagaretur.'³ Some of these homiletic writers vigorously conveyed the sounds and sights of town and country life by adding to such familiar tales as those of the jointless elephant, the lethal basilisk, and the chaste widowed turtledove, new down-to-earth descriptions of the butcher's dog with 'blody mowth,' of the housedog pestering diners until he gets what he wants, of the frog croaking in filthy water.⁴ A wicked daughter is like the 'taille of a cowe whiche, goyng in foule claye, as often as sche moueth hir taille, so often sche defouleth and bys[p]renglith thaim that been nye about hir.'⁵ Similar scatological realism occurs elsewhere, and Chaucer's parson, following the same tradition, refers to the dog eating its vomit (137), the beast in its dung (138), the sow in its dung (157), 'the hyndre part of a she-ape' at full moon (424), and urinating and fornicating dogs (857, 907).

In secular literature honest observation of nature is sometimes more extensive. *The Owl and the Nightingale*, at the end of the twelfth century, despite its use of allegory and dialectic, displays a genuine interest in nature and enumerates eleven mammals as well as many birds and insects. *The Parliament of the Three Ages* gives the poacher's view of the countryside as he stalks a deer:

> Hertys and hyndes · on hillys thay goven,
> The foxe and the filmarte · they flede to the erthe,
> The hare hurkles by hawes, · and harde thedir drives
> And ferkes faste to hir fourme · and fatills hir to sitt . . .
> I sehge ane hert with ane hede, · ane heghe for the nones;
> Alle unburneshede was the beme, · full borely the mydle,
> With iche feetur as thi fote, · for-frayed in the greves,
> With auntlers on aythere syde · egheliche longe.
> (17–28)

Here, and in *Winner and Waster* also, the presentation of the actual scene, conscientiously and sensitively drawn, anticipates the approach to nature which is to reach its finest expression in the medieval period in *Gawain and the Green Knight*.

In *Piers Plowman*, on the other hand, animal allusions are conventional rather than realistic. The setting is predominantly rural but the purpose precludes attention to the kind of detail seen in the works just mentioned. Many references to animals occur simply because they are part of everyday speech. There are more than twenty proverbs and alliterative phrases having to do with animals, such as 'as hende · as hounde is in kychyne' (B. v, 261), 'as much pity as a pedlar has of cats' (B, v, 258), 'bake for Bayarde' (C. ix, 192), 'fisshes in flod' (C, vi, 149), 'a hepe of houndes' (C, vi, 161), and 'as lowe as a lombe' (C, xi, 83). It is important to remember that in literature intended to be read orally animal allusions are likely to occur simply because popular proverbial expressions and alliterative phrases use them extensively. Langland's references to animals are frequently accompanied by moralizations in the homiletic tradition. He uses the Aesopian fable of belling the cat (C, i, 165–215) to show that the burgesses, for all their pretensions, lack the courage and leadership necessary to check Edward III. He cites biblical *exempla* such as that of the wolf in sheep's clothing in order to castigate rich secular or religious bodies (C, xvii, 268–270) and the bestiary lore of the cricket (salamander) who lived in the fire (C, xvi, 243). He briefly alludes to saints associated with animals and he seems to be familiar with the animal symbolism attached to the seven deadly sins because he refers to the lion of Pride (B, xiii, 302, B, xv, 198), the adder of Envy (B, v, 87) and describes Gluttony with 'h us guttes gonne godely · as two gredy sowes' (C, vii, 398).

But in addition to using such conventions, Langland — as is evident even in the last phrase cited — displays a kind of awareness, a feeling for nature pra ctical yet intense and well-suited to an approach which, despite its allegorical method, aimed at immediate effect. The *lyard*, the familiar term for a gray hors e, is the mount for the Good Samaritan (C, xx, 64). Sheep are 'scabbed' and need doctoring with tar (C, x, 262, 264). An image of darting fish is added to the fine alliterative paraphrase of 'Bothe fox and fowel · may fleo to hole and crepe/ And the fisshe hath fynnes · to flete with to reste' (C, xxiii, 44–45), and thoughtful observation gives rise to a sensitive questioning which momentarily brings the poet out of time:

> Briddes ich by-helde · in bosshes maden nestes,
> Hadde neuere weye wit · to worche the leste.
> Ich hadde wonder at wham · where that the pye
> Lernede legge styckes · that leyen in here neste;
> Ther is no wryght, as ich wene · sholde worche here nest to paye.
> If eny mason therto · makede a molde
> With alle here wyse castes · wonder me thynketh!
> ... And siththe ich loked on the see · and so forth on the sterres,
> Meny selcouth ich seih · aren nouht to seggen nouthe;
> Ne what on floures in feldes · and of hure faire coloures,
> How out of greot and of gras · grewe so many huwes,
> Somme soure and somme swete · selcouth me thouhte.
>
> (C, xiv, 156–178)

Other Middle English literature, whether religious or secular, shows a wide use of conventional material on animals. The influence of the bestiaries is to be seen not only in such didactic works as *Jacob's Well, Ayenbite of Inwyt, Cursor Mundi,* and *The Ormulum,* but in *Mandeville's Travels* which dropped the allegorical moralizations while adding to the stock of fabulous beasts. The former works contain bestiary lore of lions, mermaids, whales, elephants and unicorns,[6] as well as commonplace expressions having to do with animals; the latter includes among its travellers' tales such gourmet marvels as the vegetable lamb growing in a gourd-like fruit:

> 'and whan þei ben rype, men kutten hem ato, and men fynden withinne a lytill best, in flesch, in bon, and blode as þough it were a lytill lomb, withouten wolle. And men eten both the frut and the best.'[7]

The romances make use of animal legends having to do with conflicts between man and monster: the dragons killed by Sir Beues and Guy of Warwick are of the same tradition as David's giant, Perseus' sea-monster, Hercules' hydra, Siegfried's giant snake and Beowulf's Grendel. Sometimes such works fuse Biblical and classical stories: the Orphic myth affects the story of David playing his pipe to sheep in *Cursor Mundi,* and Jonah's whale in *Patience* bears some resemblance to the sea-monster (κῆτος) of Lucian, which could hold a city of ten thousand men (IV, ii, 1–2). Equally traditional is the employment of animals by satirists. About 1370 a Latin writer calling himself John of Bridlington used the ancient device of talking animals to criticize the contemporary court. Edward the Black Prince is the *gallus.* Edward III is the *taurus* to whom councillors use honeyed words while disparaging and deceiving him behind his back.[8] Similarly a poet, writing in English in 1399, discussed the intrigues of the day by giving the protagonists their badges or crests, the swan being Gloucester, the horse Arundel and the bear Warwick.[9] An earlier satirist used the story of the fox and the wolf at the court of the noble lion to indict those who exploited the poor. He called his fable a 'vorbisen,' but held out little hope for improved conditions: the poor man was like the innocent ass, powerless to defend himself — 'the lafful man ssal be i-bund / And i-do in strang pine.'[10]

The art and architecture of the period sometimes appear to suggest a close observation of nature. In English churches, on frescoes, pillars and misericords, are life-like hounds, horses, foxes and hares, which have their counterparts in manuscripts of the period and in tapestries. Even an early twelfth-century psalter had a small clear tinted line drawing of oxen at the plough, and *Queen Mary's Psalter* has riding scenes with ferocious dogs rampant for prey. Psalters and books of hours especially, contain vigorous marginal drawings of squirrels, rabbits, hounds in pursuit of stag or hare, which are clearly taken from the contemporary scene. Such works remind us that alongside the unscientific, didactic tradition, there existed the practice of accurately observing nature, and that the attitudes reflected in the avian drawings of Frederick II's *De arte venandi cum avibus* in the twelfth century, and in some of the herbals and in the researches of Albertus Magnus were persistent and influential.[11]

Familiar animals fare better than the exotics: Mary is mounted on a very life-like ass in the early fourteenth-century psalter of Robert de Lisle but the lion at her feet in a subsequent illustration has a shaggy beard and elaborately curled hair; God creates some natural-looking swine in the *Holkham Bible Picture Book* but gives a long neck draped in folds of skin to the camel and horse's hooves to the elephant. In one bestiary a solidly plump Cheshire cat, lightly lined and colored with a ginger wash, looks at a mouse with genuine complacency of life, but for the strange creature with the elongated body below it, turning up his nose in cheeky investigation, the artist seems to have relied mainly on the accompanying description of the weasel.[12] At Sall, Norfolk, a squirrel holds a bunch of grapes instead of the usual nut; a ferocious bear, sullenly squatting on a bench end at Stowlangtoft, Suffolk, has human feet.

It was the great age of copying, not only for writers of encyclopedias and natural histories, and homilists, but for the illustrators of such works, illuminators of psalters, books of hours, bestiaries and Bible picture books, embroiderers, and sculptors. Pattern books of illustrations passed from one cathedral workshop to another. One such model book, the *Harvard Bestiary*, used from 1230–1350, contains seventy-five miniatures, bestiary illustrations enclosed in circular borders which have been pricked for transfer, evidently being reduplicated in large quantities. At the height of the international phase of late Gothic, there were innumerable model drawing books and some of them, such as the so-called 'Carnet Lombards,' had animals as their main subject and appear to have been extensively used. Some of these pattern books simply paraphrased in outline the number of stylized positions which animals could adopt. Others, such as the fourteenth-century *Pepysian Sketch Book*,[13] show that realism was by no means alien to the artistic expression of the period. Just as a Book of Hours may convincingly depict a terrified boar fleeing from the farmer's axe, beside a wholly formal Capricorn, so this sketchbook assembles leaping greyhounds, racing hares, placid cats, and English birds with zodiacal beasts, mermaids, dragons and symbolic pelicans.

Such realistic models were sometimes favored by the English embroiderer, even when he was engaged on ecclesiastical subjects. A cope dated c. 1300, has a long necked landrail with chevron markings, and a striped cat. Another of the same date has thirty-four birds and sixty-six beasts which are all recognizable species. The early fourteenth-century Steeple Aston cope has naturalistic wild animals chasing each other along the border and symbolic devices of animals on its orphrey.[14]

It is frequently stated that the strange animals around cathedral doorways, on capitals of pillars, sidewalls and pews reflect a unique aspect of the medieval mind, demonstrating that their creator was not much concerned with zoological accuracy. But the medieval craftsman may not have been greatly interested in symbolic truth either. The similarity apparent between the animals of manuscript miniatures and those of misericords and other ecclesiastical ornamentation suggest that the carver simply used the copy-book models or the manuscripts themselves. If the foliated ears of the elephant at Exeter Cathedral can identify the animal as an African species and lead us to surmise that the animal presented by Louis IX to Henry III in 1255 may have been the model, even here we see the upstanding tusks of the elephant in the bestiary illustrations, and by the early fourteenth century an elephant in a fine series of misericords in St Katharine's, Regent's Park, with a hog's head, bear's muzzle and telescopic trunk points to an even closer likeness.[15] An equally striking resemblance exists between the camel of misericords and the camel of the bestiaries, both being peculiar, lumpy creatures, often with horse's hocks and cloven feet. In the case of less familiar animals in particular, the designs of open-mouthed panthers, winged lions, pious pelicans plucking at their breasts, and dog-like beavers, are often similar in carving, sculpture, embroidery and manuscript illustration.

Irrespective of their source, however, the most striking quality of these animal illustrations, whether in ecclesiastical sculpture, carving and embroidery, uncolored line drawings, or in illuminations glittering with gold and vivid with color, is vitality. The grey wolf looking at the sheepfold may have a bear's head and the blue spotted animal can only be identified as a tiger because it is examining a glass sphere, but we feel the rapacity of the one and the maternal solicitude of the other. What comes through is the human quality which these animals represent. Hence they are often given human faces or postures, or they are represented in human garb carrying out the functions of man. The fox in a bishop's mitre preaches to birds or, as a doctor, feels the pulse of a patient; or, reversing the normal roles, a human-size hare carries off a boy trussed on his back, a fox rides a dog, or a cock, with lance and shield, rides a fox. It is this kind of humanization which is to be seen in its most exaggerated form in the fifteenth century in Henryson's fables, where much of the humor arises from an incongruous assumption that animals normally perform human rituals. But an awareness of the absurdity of the idea of animals behaving like humans never minimizes the seriousness of the assertion that is being made: in the animal man may see his own characteristics and he can learn. Such is true even in the most symbolic representation. The owl being attacked by other birds is frequently illustrated in manuscripts, in ecclesiastical sculpture and carving. That the scene should be based on ornithological fact is unimportant. But if the owl stands for the Jew, it also stands for the unrepentant heart and provides an exemplum of the nemesis attendant on the betrayal and rejection of Christ.

The symbolic values of animals were also stressed in mummers' performances, pageants and masques. In Jehan de Grise's well-known illuminations in *The Romance of Alexander*, probably made during the years 1339–1344, five mummers hand in hand wear the heads of an ass, a monkey, a goat, an ox and a vulture; a second illustration, in which a dancing boy with tabor and pipe faces another dressed as a stag, shows an interesting survival of the ancient belief sanctioned by Aristotle, Pliny and Aelian that deer like music. In the *ludus dominis regis* held by Edward III in 1347, the players wore heads representing dragons, peacocks and swans.[16] Here again animals were used in such a way as to suggest more primitive rituals when man believed that by wearing the skin of a certain animal he acquired some of that animal's qualities. Such belief certainly persisted consciously until the seventh century, for the *Poenitentials* of Theodore, giving various degrees of penitence for those practising magic, were particularly severe on those who wore animal skins and *assumunt capita bestiarum* (xxvii, 8–22). In the church at Abbots Bromley, Staffordshire, are six sets of reindeer's horns and a hobby-horse used in the annual horn dance when the 'deer' are pursued through the streets by 'riders.' The dance is said to commemorate the restoration of certain forest rights in the reign of Henry III,[17] but it also appears to be a survival of prehistoric hunting rituals.

The animal world with which Chaucer would have been familiar in literature and art was, therefore, a humanized world with animals standing for qualities which were meaningful to man. The fables, the Bible, hermeneutical writings, natural histories, encyclopedias, manuscript illustrations, sculpture and carving, all saw animals as exhibiting human traits, as having conscious motives or even moral standards.

Even in such apparently divergent works as the fables and the bestiaries, the premise was similar, although it differed in scope and in the nature of its application: it ascribed to animals traits already established by long tradition and assumed animal behaviour was inspired by human motives. Expressed in its most extreme form, the premise was that the animal was a human being in disguise. Metamorphosis, such as is seen in the mummers' plays, was in-spired not only by surviving primitive beliefs but by the prevailing concept of the animal in medieval times.

Since the traditional attitude was so strong and unequivocal, it is not surprising that Chaucer, when he considered the animal, thought of its stereotyped characteristics and found it interesting mainly because it provided illustrations of humanity.

II. *Aspects of Chaucer's Use of Animals*

T HE Latin-English vocabularies of the period provide two lists of animals, domestic and wild. All the animals to which Chaucer refers are found on these lists, and there are also some which he omits, such as the unicorn, dromedary, panther, marmoset, ferret, mule, beaver, brock, otter, baboon, onager, cocadryll and mole. The majority that he mentions are indigenous to England: the ass, boar, cat, cow, coney, deer, fox, goat, hare, horse, mouse, ox, pig, polecat, rat, sheep, squirrel, weasel and wolf. The remainder are more exotic creatures such as the ape, bear, camel, hyena, leopard, lion, tiger, whale, elephant and lynx. The two last occur only briefly: the elephant appears with the lynx in the translation of Boethius' *De consolatione philosophiae* (iii, pr. 8, 27, 41) and as 'Sire Olifaunt,' Sir Thopas' Goliath-like enemy, in Chaucer's parody of knightly romances (*Thop*, VII, 808).

Most of these animals, even the more unusual, Chaucer probably saw at some time during his life. The ape to which he refers would be the *macaca sylvanus*, the Barbary ape native to Europe, and from the twelfth century it was a familiar sight in England and on the Continent as a performer exhibited by professional showmen. Bartholomew in his encyclopedia of the thirteenth century claimed that the keeper must tame the ape by beating it and by restraining it with chains and heavy clog (lxxxvi) and it was this kind of relationship which gave rise to the word 'ape-ward' and to numerous proverbial expressions. Skeat, writing in the Victorian era when the animal in respectable knickerbockers and red cap was still the companion of the street-musician in the larger towns, remarked with reference to the Canon-alchemist who made the priest 'his ape' (*CYT*, VIII, 1313) that this expression, meaning 'to lead about at will,' was evidently taken from the fact that showmen used to carry apes about with them 'much as organ-boys do at present.' Two of Chaucer's references to the ape suggest, as we shall see later, that his knowledge may have been derived from close study. In the fourteenth century it was not uncommon for wealthy households to keep apes as exotic pets.

Although I have classified the bear as exotic, it was in fact indigenous to Britain, and baiting it was a favorite sport from Roman times. In 1372 a Parliamentary injunction stated that a fee was to be paid to a certain burgess and his wife by the seneschal of John of Gaunt at Newcastle-under-Lyme for every bear brought to be baited, and the fee was still being paid thirty years later.[1] Bartholomew, as translated by Trevisa, graphically describes the way in which the bear was treated: 'And whan he is take he is made blynde with a bryghte basyn, and ybounde with cheynes, and compelyth to playe' (lxii), and that this blinding was literally done is supported by the Latin 'pelvis ardentis aspectu excaecatur' and by Lydgate's statement in *The pilgrimage of the life of man*, 8494, 'lyk the bacyn that ys brennynge — the Beere yt reveth off hys syht And maketh hym blynd' (8494). In addition to being baited, the bear might be whipped by five or six men encircling him and be required to defend himself, or he might have to dance to music, being trained by having his feet placed on hot plates of iron. If numerous representations serve as a guide, bear-baiting was the most popular pastime. On misericords it appears no less than four times at Beverley Minster alone. It is the subject of many manuscript illustrations,[2] and even today street names in English towns are a reminder of the ancient sport.

Presumably the bears mentioned in medical recipes were the performing kind. The *Regime du corps* finds the cooked flesh of bear unpalatable and lacking in nutriment but strongly recommends it medicinally on the testimony of the Ancients — 'Si com dist Dyacorides, tot li membre de l'ours ont grant vertu de delivrer les maladies des membres ki au cors avient.'[3]

Bears were also of some interest to British kings. Henry I's menagerie at Woodstock only seems to have had lions, leopards, lynxes and camels but Henry II had a bear which sometimes accompanied him on his travels. Henry III was presented with three leopards and a camel by his brother-in-law, the Emperor Frederick II, of ornithological fame, and with an elephant by Louis IX of France, and he housed the animals in the Tower in dens arranged in a semi-circle around a pit used for baiting various animals. He also had a white bear from Norway to which he gave more licence. According to the *Liberate Rolls*, in the fall of 1252, its keeper was given fourpence a day and it was allowed to fish in the Thames, wearing a muzzle and iron chain. Wace, William of Malmesbury and Neckam all refer to the practice of giving spectacular animals, such as leopards, lions and bears, as gifts,[4] and the bear and his warden were often attached to noble households. We may discount John of Garland's claim that even the woods of France contained lions, leopards, tigers, bears and monkeys,[5] but certainly zoological parks such as that at the castle of Visconti became increasingly popular during the next century and Chaucer may have visited some of them. He may also have seen exotic animals which Edward III received from the Black Prince in Gascony and from Italian merchants, as well as the leopard brought back from the east by Henry of Derby in 1393.[6]

Whether Chaucer ever saw a camel, a hyena, a tiger or a whale, is difficult to determine. The hyena and the camel were both imported from North Africa to the South of France, and Chaucer might have seen them in his travels. The stories which were repeated concerning the hyena in medieval times certainly do not indicate any widespread first-hand knowledge of the animal although the fable that the hyena could imitate the human voice may have originated from the similarity of the shrill cry of the spotted hyena, *hyena crocuta*, to that of the African aborigine. Chaucer makes no use of this popular story nor does he refer to the hyena of the bestiaries and sculpture, which devours corpses in their tombs, but he applies an equally fallacious piece of folklore. In 'Fortune' when he says: 'Thee nedeth nat the galle of noon hyene,/ That cureth eyen derked for penaunce' (35–36), he is alluding to the optical benefits which, according to Pliny and Vincent de Beauvais, were derived from the hyena's gall.[7] Bartholomew repeated the story and, as translated by Trevisa, stated that 'this beestys galle is full of medycynall And helpyth moost ayenst dymnesse of eyen' (lxi). Chaucer's single allusion to the camel in the *Envoy in the Clerk's Tale* (IV, 1196) may, as we shall see later, have derived from direct knowledge as well as from a literary source.

Little seems to have been known about the tiger in medieval times, and it is rarely named in collections of medieval arms. The animal which appeared on the arms of Sir John Norwich, a fourteenth-century knight, is supposed to be a tiger but it looks like a lion with a handlebar moustache. Chaucer usually takes it conventionally as the fierce creature described by the natural historians, and even when he is exhorting women to fight like tigers (*Env.* to *Cl.T*, IV, 1199), he is simply applying an epithet common among anti-feminist writers. The unusual epithet in *The Squire's Tale* where the falcon calls her false lover 'this tigre, ful of doublenesse' (543), makes one wonder whether Chaucer saw a tiger. Deceit is the very quality which the tiger exemplifies when stalking its prey. According to one naturalist

the tiger never appears to employ openly that active strength which would seem so sure to attain its end, but creeps stealthily towards the

object, availing itself of every cover, until it can spring upon its destined victim. . . . The tiger has, besides, a curious habit of drawing in its breath and flattening its fur, so as to reduce its bulk as far as possible.[8]
On the other hand, Chaucer may simply be using a conventional attribute. Aldrovandi two centuries later shows that the tiger is traditionally associated with dissimulation (p. 112). The tiger was thought to beguile its victims through the attractive markings of its skin. Robert Greene's apparent reference to Shakespeare in *The Groatsworth of Wit Bought with a Million of Repentance* — 'an upstart crow, beautified with our feathers, . . . with his tiger's heart wrapped in a player's hide' — seems to allude to the same attribute.

As far as whales are concerned, the possibility of Chaucer having seen one is greater. Whales were washed upon the coast of Cornwall in February 1386 and on the coast of Lincoln in 1387, and they seem to have been valued so highly that they were stolen despite the fact that they were royal fish and belonged to the Crown. In some instances the royal ministers had already seized the whales for the king's use, when 'divers evildoers by force took them away'. It seems that royalty were partial to whale meat, particularly as it could be eaten during Lent. Henry III ordered the Sheriffs of London to purchase for him one hundred pieces of the best whale in Lent, and Edward II made handsome payment to three mariners for catching a whale near London Bridge.[9]

Although we think of Chaucer primarily as a man of letters, diplomat, civil servant, court official, we must remember that he was also a Kentish landowner and spent a good part of his time in journeying about the countryside after he gave up his house in Aldgate in 1386. Moreover, his posts as clerk of the King's works and as Deputy Forester must have necessitated an interest in the royal parks and forests, and the descriptions of the country folk in *The General Prologue* and of the village settings of some of the *fabliaux* show a peculiar familiarity with rural living and customs. Yet, as far as nature itself is concerned, he does not seem to draw his inspiration from the fields. He appears to keep his eye steadily on the poetry of others rather than on the object itself. His gardens, whether he is describing the typical castle grounds belonging to Thesus in *The Knight's Tale*, January's stone-walled enclosure designed for quick summer seduction, the Spring garden for picnics and dancing in *The Franklin's Tale*, or the more extensive riverside park in *The Parliament of Fowls*, are all presented in conventional terms with such vague phrases as 'nevere was ther gardyn of swich prys,' and 'so fair a gardyn woot I nowher noon'. The reason is, of course, that Chaucer is not thinking of being 'realistic'. He is using the typical, tropological garden of the month of May, the earthly paradise of *Deduit* which has no geographical location but exists to heighten the symbolic meaning of the action taking place within it. Unless a background serves a specific function, Chaucer does not include it.

In his treatment of nature generally, Chaucer shows the lack of interest in 'scenery' which is characteristic of the period and particularly noticeable in the visual arts, and his scenes themselves are but a back-drop for the human comedy. If we compare his treatment of nature in the Golden Age with Virgil's in the *Fourth Eclogue* and Boethius' in *De consolatione philosophiae* (met. 5, 1–20), we find it is but vaguely idyllic, without Virgil's goats, lions, un-yoked oxen and larks living in an earthly paradise or Boethius' high pine trees shading the contented sleepers. Looking back at an age allegedly un-troubled by 'covetyse' and its attendant evils, Chaucer is interested in the psychological state of primitive man occasioned by the environment, not in the environment itself. If nature is not symbolic, wherever possible it is given a human connotation. His trees, for example, often fit into the iconographical background of the *Roman de la rose*. But where he departs from a source, as in *The Parliament of Fowls* (176–180), he evaluates trees, not for their beauty, but for their use — the oak for building, the elm for coffins to hold carrion, the holm-oak for whip's lash, the shooter yew, and the aspen for smooth shafts.[10]

So consistently does Chaucer rely on tradition or iconography that he has even been unjustly accused of ignorance. According to Lowes, he is guilty of the 'surprising blunder' of ascribing a smell to the daisy in the *Prologue to The Legend of Good Women*:

> As for to speke of gomme, or herbe, or tre,
> Comparisoun may non ymaked be;
> For it surmountede pleynly alle odoures,
> And of ryche beaute alle floures.
>
> (G, 109–112)

Robinson excuses the poet on the plea that he is following the tradition of the 'marguerite poets,' Machaut, Froissart and Deschamps, who transferred to the daisy the quality they admired in the rose. But Chaucer's daisy is presum-ably the short stemmed meadow daisy, *bellis perennis*. If he were referring to the long-stemmed, odorless marguerite he would be under no necessity to kneel down (F. 115). Although Lowes brings authorities to support him.[11] one has only to follow the evidence of one's own nose to realize that here Chaucer is being surprisingly precise. The English meadow daisy has a smell very difficult to define but pleasant, resembling that of newly cut grass, indeed, very much like the fresh, woodland scent of 'gomme, or herbe, or tre.'

Such independent, accurate observation of natural objects is, however, rare, and when he comes to animals he usually appears to present them in terms of the simple, conventional ideas which were already part of popular tradition. When he alludes to the ape as a dupe (*Gen Prol*, i, 706; *MillT*, i, 3389; *RvT*, i, 4202; *CYT*, viii, 1313), a representation of the devil (*FrT*, iii, 1464), a grimacer (*HF*, iii, 1806), an imitator (*HF*, iii, 1212) and a fool (*ParsT*, x, 651; *Tr*, i. 913) and to the bear as a hungry animal (*ParsT*, x, 568) which roars (*HF*, iii, 1589) and causes terror (*NPT*, viii, 2935), he is referring to widely accepted attributes. Some traits are indeed so well known that he does not always state them. In applying the term fox to Pandarus (*Tr*, iii,

1565) or to the canon-alchemist (*CYT*, VIII, 1080), he assumes that his audience is aware of the significance of the metaphor. Even for his fabulous creatures, he relies on popular knowledge and very infrequently seems to resort to specific unnatural history in written sources. For the royal eagle 'that with his sharpe lok perseth the sonne' (*PF*, 331) and his swan, singing 'ayens his deth' (*Anel*, 346–347, *PF*, 342, *LGW*, III, 1355–1366), he did not have to use Alanus' *De planctu naturae*, the most immediate source for his catalogue in *The Parliament of Fowls*. On misericords, pillars, doorways, windows of churches the eagle staring unflinchingly at the sun and forcing his offspring to do the same was a common subject, and the story of the swan singing at its death, although refuted by Pliny (x, 23, 32), was proverbial.

I do not wish to imply that Chaucer's use of tradition was simple or obvious. Traditionally, for example, the eagle was a symbol for St John, who describes his 'flight' to the heavenly city in the Apocalypse 21 :10–11. Similarly, the image of the eagle-sighted Beatrice in Dante's *Paradiso* serves to show, in Bennett's phrase, 'that she can gaze unflinchingly on the supernal glory.' But more ancient still is the symbol of the eagle as artist. For the Greek Pindar, the eagle is the symbol of the poetic mind intensely contemplating higher truth. Pindar's eagle, like St John's inspiration and like Dante's guide to the Empyrean, is close to a central power in creation. It is the 'divine bird of Zeus' and a fitting symbol for an aristocratic kind of poetry. 'Its essence,' as Jaeger reveals, 'is to live in the unapproachable heights of the mind,' disdaining the mere scavengers for truth far below. Thus, in the *House of Fame*, when the poet seeks new inspiration, it comes in the form of a pedantically humorous golden eagle. Here we observe the traditional eagle transmuted by Chaucer's genius. At first glance this eagle hardly seems to be an expression of Chaucer's spiritual nobility, like Pindar's esoteric bird, but when the eagle speaks, it is careful to point out that it is really in the name of Jove that it does so (ii, 606–611). Therefore, the divine messenger which brings Chaucer, as Laurence Shook suggests, 'a new vision of the whole art of poetry,' is part of a very old tradition indeed.[12]

Also traditional is the purpose which the world of animals serves. Chaucer finds animals interesting not as creatures in themselves but as types illustrative of humanity. Such an approach is unscientific, as it had been, with very few exceptions, since Aristotle. It assumes that animals are similar to man and are of significance mainly because they can be used to throw light on man. When Chaucer refers to Wilkyn as a sheep (*WB Prol*, III, 432) and compares those who hope to profit by alchemy to the blundering horse (*CYT*, VIII, 1413–4), he makes conventional ideas serve to illustrate human character and action. Whatever may be the ultimate significance of the birds singing in heavenly harmony in *The Book of the Duchess*, the observation 'ther was noon of hem that feyned/to synge' (317–318) transfers us abruptly from the allegorical to the actual, to the subterfuges of the choristers who have missed rehearsals or of the violinists in the last row.[13] In *The Parliament of Fowls*, the birds are mostly catalogued by traditional tags, and their characters are developed only so far as they throw light on human behavior.[14] Even in *The Nun's Priest's Tale*, where there is sufficient detail to remind us that it is, indeed, a tale of a cock and a fox in that the cock has the habits of a barnyard fowl and the fox follows its natural pursuit, the human characteristics of the protagonists are stressed. The most concrete of references illustrates character. The pilgrims' horses (*Gen Prol*, I, 74, 207, 287–8, 390, 469, 541, 615; *NP Prol*, VII, 2812–3; *CY Prol*, VIII, 559–65) throw light on their riders; the Prioress's dogs (*Gen Prol*, I, 146–9) reveal her sentimentality and her disregard for monastic discipline; the horse chasing wild mares (*RvT*, I, 4080–1), in addition to having a realistic function, emphasizes the proclivities of John and Alayn; the brief reference to Thomas's cat (*SumT*, III, 1775), indicates Friar John's enthusiasm for food.[15]

If Chaucer is typical of his time in regarding animals as possessing stereotyped traits which serve to throw light on human behaviour, equally typical are the conclusions he makes. Although many early civilizations venerated certain animals, the tendency to associate them with the baser aspects of humanity as, for example, in the New Testament when evil spirits were sent into swine, was continued by both pagan writers and the early Christian fathers alike. Plato, in *De respublica* (x, 620c), briefly considered the idea of the souls of men entering the bodies of appropriate animals in the underworld, and Claudian, the last poet of classical Rome, rejoicing in the death of Rufinus, a powerful praetorian prefect torn to pieces by a mob, placed him in hell where the spirits of the cruel entered into bears, of the rapacious into wolves, of the treacherous into foxes, and where those guilty of venery, sloth and gluttony assumed the fat bodies of filthy swine (*In Rufinum*, ii, 483–487).

This equating of various vices to certain traits ascribed to animals became a commonplace in early exegetical writing. Explaining why Moses forbade the eating of swine, the eagle, hawk and raven, Clement of Alexandria saw these creatures as symbols of lust, robbery, injustice, and greed respectively (*PG*, IX, cols. 81, 84), and in the fourth century St Jerome's commentary on Isaiah 11:6–9 (*PL*, XXIV, cols. 150ff), authorized the use of animals to represent the sins. The theriomorphic comparisons most frequently cited were those of Boethius who, giving the story of Circe in *De consolatione philosophiae*, claimed that the vices were even more powerful than the enchantress since they changed the heart instead of simply altering the body. Chaucer translates the passage:

> Than betidith it that, yif thou seest a wyght that be transformed into vices, thow ne mayst nat wene that he be a man. For if he be ardaunt in avaryce, and that he be a ravynour by violence of foreyn richesse, thou schalt seyn that he is lik to the wolf; and if he be felonows and withoute reste, and exercise his tonge to chidynges, thow schalt likne hym to the hownd; and if he be a pryve awaytour yhid, and rejoiseth hym to

ravyssche be wiles, thou schalt seyn hym lik to the fox whelpes; and yif he be distempre, and quakith for ire, men schal wene that he bereth the corage of a lyoun; and yif he be dredful and fleynge, and dredith thinges that ne aughte nat to ben dredd, men schal holden hym lik to the hert; and yf he be slow, and astonyd, and lache, he lyveth as an asse; yif he be lyght and unstedfast of corage and chaungith ay his studies, he is likned to briddes; and if he be ploungid in fowle and unclene luxuris, he is withholden in the foule delices of the fowle sowe. Than folweth it that he that forleteth bounte and prowesse, he forletith to ben a man; syn he ne may nat passe into the condicion of God, he is torned into a beeste. (iv, pr. 3, 101–127)

It was the Boethian view, in which the animals almost exclusively represented the most reprehensible traits of mankind, which was most frequently pressed into the service of moral didacticism by the medieval church. Man, a little below the angels and a little above the brutes, had to be provided with illustrations warning him of what he would become if, instead of elevating his soul, he submitted to the base desires of the body. Since the Aristotelian view that the inner characteristics were exemplified by the outward physical form was widely held, the animal, both by virtue of its position in the Chain of Being and its appearance, served as a most appropriate metaphor for human corruption. Roger Bacon quoted the passage from Boethius in full when he was considering the seven deadly sins, and the *Ancrene riwle*, the first English work to portray the sins as animals, referred to the lion of pride, the serpent of envy, the unicorn of wrath, the bear of sloth, the fox of covetousness, the swine of greediness and the scorpion of luxury.[16]

By the time Mattias Farinator, a Viennese Carmelite, wrote his encyclopedic treatise, *Lumen animae*, in 1330, the connection between animals and the seven deadly sins was an established convention and the sins were frequently depicted as riding in a procession. In *Titulus* 75, Superbia, mounted on a dromedary, has a peacock on her helmet, a lion on her shield and an eagle on her mantle, Luxuria on a bear, has a siren on her shield and a basilisk on her mantle, and the five other deadly sins are appropriately invested. Among Chaucer's contemporaries, Walter Hilton in his mystical work, *The Scale of Perfection* (ii, 14), gives the same attributes to the dog, the ass, the fox and the swine as Boethius does, and Wyclif uses the equation of the animals to the sins to attack, in his unwieldly *Tractatus civili dominio* (iii, 15–16), the basilisk of pride, the adder of envy, the toad of anger, the spider of avarice, the viper of lechery and the serpent of gluttony. Chaucer's friend John Gower in his *Mirour de l'omme* (i, 13ff; ii, 841ff) describes Pride mounted on a lion and holding an eagle, Envy on a dog and carrying a sparrow-hawk, Wrath on a boar with a cock in her hand, Sloth on an ass and holding an owl, Avarice with a hawk and falcon on a horse, Gluttony on a wolf and holding a kite, and Lechery with a dove riding a goat, and similar comparisons are the subject of numerous illustrations in manuscripts, sculpture and tapestries.[17]

In an early fifteenth-century manuscript of *The Canterbury Tales*, an illustration to *The Parson's Tale* shows Gluttony riding a bear and holding a kite feeding on an entrail, Lechery on a goat and holding a sparrow, and Envy on a dog which gnaws a bone.[18]

Chaucer seems to hold the Boethian view. Arcite's speech distinguishing between man and beast suggests that the beast does not share in the Christian plan of redemption: it can follow its animal nature because it has no after-life and reaps no punishment:

> And yet encresseth this al my penaunce,
> That man is bounden to his observaunce,
> For Goddes sake, to letten of his wille,
> Ther as a beest may al his lust fulfille.
> And whan a beest is deed he hath no peyne;
> But man after his deeth moot wepe and pleyne,
> Though in this world he have care and wo.
>
> *(KnT*, I, 1315–1321)

In 'Truth' Chaucer also appears to follow the exegetical writers when he states: 'Forth pilgrim, forth! Forth beste, out of thy stal!/Know thy contree, look up, thank God of al' (18–19). A beast cannot look up. It is man's upright posture which distinguishes him from the beast. Cicero, in *De natura deorum* (II, 56–58), stressed that when the vicious man became a beast, abandoning his reason, he in effect abandoned his upright posture, the symbol of reason. Similar ideas were expressed by exegetical writers such as Lactantius in his *Epitome divinarum institutionum* (PL, VI, cols. 1032–1033). Thus Bartholomew states: 'Whanne an vnresonable beste is perfitliche ymade . . . þe face þerof boweþ toward þe erþe . . . and oonliche to mankynde ordeigneþ vpright stature' (cclviiii).

According to early Christian etymology, ἄνθρωπος meant 'he who looks upwards (to God).' Man alone was capable of raising his face to heaven so that he could see the source of his salvation. Chaucer is presumably making the traditional comparison between man's lower nature and the beast. He probably also uses 'beste' in anticipation of the pun on *vache* in the *Envoy*. Elsewhere he applies the term to the vicious or unbelieving or the helpless. In 'Fortune' men who call Divine Will Fortune are addressed as: 'Ye blynde bestes, ful of lewednesse' (68), and in an *ABC* Chaucer, following Deguilleville, abases himself before the Virgin and states: 'Al I have ben a beste in wil and deede' (45). In the *Second Nun's Tale* (288) the newly converted Tiberius calls unbelievers beasts, and in *The Merchant's Tale* (1280) January deems that if beasts are free they are also insecure and therefore not to be envied. In *The Parson's Tale* beasts provide a powerful excremental image with which to upbraid sinners — 'ye be roten in youre synne as a beest in his dong' (139). They are associated more explicitly with fornication when the ravisher of a virgin is likened to a hedge-breaker and therefore the 'cause of alle damages that beestes don in the field' (870) — a comparison which Chaucer's probable source, Peraldus' *Tractatus de viciis*, does not use.

Chaucer seems to accept the view that the beast exemplified the baser aspects of man's nature. If he does not apply the moral didacticism usually accompanying such an attitude, he most frequently adopts the pejorative symbolism and even reinforces derogatory conventional ideas with equally unfavorable observations of his own. Whereas the writers of the bestiaries have been termed compassionate and have been praised for loving dogs and horses, Chaucer shows little appreciation of the animal world. Except when he is non-committal, he usually finds in the animal qualities similar to the less agreeable qualities in man, and his attitude is consistent whether he is drawing from popular or literary sources, from folklore or from life.

From popular sources Chaucer draws extensively upon the proverbial phrase. His most common animal analogies are those in which he takes some abstract quality, action or physical attribute commonly associated with an animal and makes it serve to illustrate some unattractive aspect of humanity. The human protagonist is fierce like the lion (*KnT*, I, 1598; *SecNT*, VIII, 198), meek as a lamb (*SecNT*, VIII, 199), blindly foolish like Bayard the horse (*Tr.* i, 218; *CYT*, VIII, 1413), as unappreciative as an ass listening to a harp (*Tr*, i, 731). He falls like 'a styked swyn' (*PardT*, VI, 556), groans like a boar (*SumT*, III, 1829), wallows like a pig in a poke (*RvT*, I, 4278), and is drunk like a mouse (*KnT*, I, 1261; *WB Prol*, III, 246). He stinks like a goat if he takes up alchemy (*CYT*, VIII, 886), looks like a wild boar (*SumT*, III, 2160), and has a beard as red as any sow or fox (*Gen Prol*, I, 552). Apart from the lamb with its inescapable religious connotations (*ABC*, 172; *MLT*, II, 452, 459; *PrT*, VII, 581, 584; *ClT*, IV, 538), and the phrases describing Alison, the carpenter's wife, in *The Miller's Tale* (3260) as frolicsome 'as any kyde or calf folwynge his dame,' the proverbial expressions usually give rise to images which are distasteful. Even the lion is applied favorably in proverbial phrase only to Emetreus in *The Knight's Tale* (I, 2171), Troilus in *Troilus and Criseyde* (i, 1074; v, 830), and Jason in *The Legend of Good Woman* (IV, 1605). Elsewhere it shows its proverbial fierceness (*KnT*, I, 1598, *SecNT*, VIII, 198), anger (*KnT*, I, 1656, *SumT*, III, 2152), cruelty in battle (*KnT*, I, 2630) and mercilessness in civil administration (*KnT*, I, 1774–1775). The generosity for which the Noble Lion of the fable is traditionally famous is referred to only once (*LGW*, F, 391–395, G. 377–381), and even this instance is ambiguous. The proverbial faithfulness of the hound is never mentioned, and only derogatory proverbs having to do with its blindness, its stupidity and its snorting are applied to the horse.

In his early works Chaucer often uses traditional ideas perfunctorily for the purpose of swift comparison. In *The Knight's Tale*, independent of his source, he applies the lion and tiger to Arcite — 'as fiers as leon [he] pulled out his swerd' (1598), 'and as a crueel tigre was Arcite' (1657), 'ther nas no tygre in the vale of Galgopheye . . . So crueel on the hunte as is Arcite'

(2626–2628) — the lion to Palamon — 'this Palamon/ in his fightyng were a wood leon' (1655–1656), 'ne in Belmarye ther nys so fel leon . . . as Palamon' (2630–2633) — and the boar to both heroes — 'as wilde bores gonne they to smyte' (1658). He also compares them to hunters of the lion of bear:

> Right as the hunters in the regne of Trace,
> That stondeth at the gappe with a spere,
> Whan hunted is the leon or the bere. . .
>
> (1638–40)

The lack of consistency makes it difficult to accept the view that Chaucer commonly characterizes the lion as 'wood' and the tiger as cruel and crafty, and that he is here suggesting a contrast between the 'mad, instinctive type of fighter' and the one who is a 'crafty rather than an open fighter.'[19] Chaucer appears to be working within a convention, simply using commonplace comparisons in order to stress the fierceness of his heroes.

In his mature works, however, Chaucer's proverbial expressions having to do with animals may assume a significance beyond their immediate context and be applicable to a total portrait or situation. A subtle organic relevance is achieved by means of an oblique extension of a simple figure, which takes into account details of an animal's appearance or behavior, and its popular symbolism.

In the composite picture derived from Robyn in *The General Prologue* and from Symkyn in *The Reeve's Tale*, the Miller is compared to the sow, the fox and the ape with respect to various physical qualities: 'His berd as any sow or fox was reed' (*Gen Prol*, I, 552); he has a tuft of hairs on his wart, which are 'reed as the brustles of a sowes erys' (556), and his skull is 'as piled as an ape' (*RvT*, I, 3935). But his resemblance to the three animals is not restricted to his beard, the hairs on his wart, and his head. The fox is traditionally a crafty animal, a skillful thief; the Miller's adept dishonesty at his trade is not only specifically stressed in *The General Prologue* — 'wel koude he stelen corn and tollen thries' (562) and at the opening of the Tale — 'a theef he was for soth of corn and mele,/ And that a sly, and usaunt for to stele' (3939–3940) — but it accounts initially for the clerks' visit, for the overnight stay, and provides the motive for revenge — 'ther is a law that says thus,/ that gif a man in a point be agreved,/ That in another he sal be releved' (4180–4182). The sow is associated with lasciviousness and defilement (*Bo*, iv, pr. 3, 122–124: *WB Prol*, III, 785; *ParsT*, x, 155); the Miller delights in tales of 'synne and harlotries' (*Gen Prol*, I, 561), and his nose and his weapons appear to suggest that he is lecherous. The ape is another lascivious animal and it has broad shoulders, great strength and a turned-up nose; the Miller is 'short-sholdred, brood, a thikke knarre,' capable of heaving a door off its hinges or of breaking it with his head (*Gen Prol*, I, 549–551), and he has a *camus* nose (*RvT*, I, 3934). The ape, as is indicated in *The Manciple's Prologue* — 'I trowe that ye dronken han wyn ape' (44) — is associated with an advanced stage of drunkenness, and the Miller is both drunk on the pilgrimage — 'the Millere, that for dronken was al pale' (*Mil Prol*, I, 3120) — and at bedtime — 'ful pale he was for dronken' (*RvT*, I, 4150). Finally, Chaucer's use of the simile of the ape foreshadows the denouement of the tale: like the proverbial ape, the Miller becomes a dupe.

An apparently simple proverbial expression — 'as dronken as a mous' — used by the Wife of Bath, also gives depth and significance to human character and situation. The same expression occurs in *The Knight's Tale* (1261), to illustrate that humanity is ignorant of what is best for its welfare — 'we faren as he that dronke is as a mous.' In Arcite's philosophical outburst the image effectively suggests the smallness and helplessness of mankind but it is not particularly characteristic of the speaker. When the Wife upbraids her husband for coming home drunk, the allusion to the mouse is appropriate not only because it occurs in the kind of popular expression which the Wife might be expected to use but because the mouse itself is associated with timidity, a quality which the Wife's tirades evidently induce:

> Thanne wolde I seye, 'Goode lief, taak keep
> How mekely looketh Wilkyn, oure sheep!
> Com neer, my spouse, lat me ba thy cheke!
> Ye shoulde been al pacient and meke,
> And han a sweete spiced conscience,
> Sith ye so preche of Jobes pacience.
> Suffreth alwey, syn ye so wel kan preche.'
>
> (*WB Prol*, III, 431–437)

The figure has two further ironic implications. Earlier, the husband is accused of comparing his wife to a cat (348–54). The Wife herself, commenting on the folly of restricting one's attentions in marriage to one partner, expresses contempt for the mouse which has only one hole to go to:

> For certeinly, I sey for no bobance,
> Yet was I nevere withouten purveiance
> Of mariage, n'of othere thynges eek.
> I holde a mouses herte nat worth a leek
> That hath but oon hole for to sterte to,
> And if that faille, thanne is al ydo.
>
> (569–574)

The images have a cumulative effect, emphasizing Woman's feline, predatory nature. They also convey the earthy vitality of the speaker, particularly when, as in the last illustration, the Wife adds a homely image from her own kitchen world.[20]

Even the most perfunctory proverbial expressions may have complex reverberations. In his *Prologue*, the Pardoner, disclosing his technique as a mob orator, makes an allusion to the dove:

> Thanne peyne I me to strecche forth the nekke,
> And est and west upon the peple I bekke,
> As dooth a dowve sittynge on a berne.
>
> (395–397)

The same proverbial expression is used in connection with Alison (*MillT*, 1 3257–3258) but there the comparison is to the swallow. The difference is significant. In the description of Alison's song as being 'as loude and yerne/ As any swalwe sittynge [*var.* chitering] on a berne,' Chaucer may be alluding to the swallow's twitter, the shrill sound made in excitement or alarm, or he may be thinking of the quality which the swallow sometimes shares with the sparrow and which is remarked upon in 'The Payne and Sorowe of Evyll maryage':

> Wyves been bestes very unstable
> In ther desires, which may not chaunged be,
> Like a swalowe which is insaciable. . . .
>
> (78–80)

In using the dove to describe the Pardoner's gestures, Chaucer may be referring to the dove's habit of inflating and deflating its neck and crop. Its neck has a peculiar pulsating movement, known in pigeon circles as 'pouting'. The Pardoner, distending his neck and nodding, is making a movement which is characteristic of the dove. The dove is also a particularly suitable image for the Pardoner because of its voice. It has a tremulous voice which seems small but has 'far-reaching, echo-like resonance.'[21] The Pardoner's voice has similar qualities. It is 'as smal as . . . a goot' (*Gen Prol*, 1, 688), and yet the Pardoner can sing 'murierly and loude' (*Gen Prol*, 1, 714) and 'rynge it out as round as gooth a belle' (*Pard Prol*, VI, 331). Chaucer may also have been thinking of the symbolism attached to the dove. He claims familiarity with the bestiary (*NPT*, VII, 3271) and in many versions the dove is regarded as a symbol of Christ, the Spirit of God, or the good preacher. One version states that the preacher, symbolic of the dove, refrains from provocative songs and from the fashion of the time.[22] When we consider the description in *The General Prologue*, 'ful loude he soong "Com hider, love to me!"' (672) and 'hym thoughte he rood al of the newe jet' (682), the Pardoner's comparison of himself to the dove appears to be heavily ironical.

In a passage in *The Parson's Tale*, Chaucer not only uses the basic symbolism of the ape as being an imitator and a lecher but he dilates on the physical appearance of the she-ape at *oestrus* to discover the most remarkable resemblances between it and the fashionably dressed man:

> Upon that oother side, to speken of the horrible disordinat scantnesse of clothyng, as been thise kutted sloppes, or haynselyns, that thurgh hire shortnesse ne covere nat the shameful membres of man, to wikked entente./ Allas! somme of hem shewen the boce of hir shap, and the horrible swollen membres, that semeth lik the maladie of hirnia, in the

wrappynge of hir hoses;/ and eek the buttokes of hem faren as it were
the hyndre part of a she-ape in the fulle of the moone./ And mooreover,
the wrecched swollen membres that they shew thurgh disgisynge, in
departynge of hire hoses in whit and reed, seemeth that half hir shameful
privee membres weren flayne.   (422–425)[23]

The Franciscan Friar, Nicholas Philip, compares worldly priests to climbing
monkeys displaying *turpitudinem posteriorum* and arousing derision.[24] St
Bridget, in her *Revelationes Caelestes* says that the worldly bishop resembled
the monkey in four ways: 'quarum prima est, quod praeparantur ei vestes
tendentes ad inferiorem partem, et anteriora velantes sed verecundiora
ejus apparent tota nuda' (fol. 172). Chaucer's image is more extensive in its
implications and certain details concerning the ape are applicable in each
section of the passage cited above. Apes have the habit of turning the hinder
ends of their bodies towards their fellow creatures. The gesture has a sexual
import and is particularly noticeable in the adult female chimpanzee when, in
the phase of her menstrual cycle, she shows sexual skin changes and enlarged
pudendum, and presents herself for copulation.[25] This phenomenon of the four
week menstrual cycle escaped the notice of classical physiologists including
Aristotle and Galen, but it was noticed by St Hildegard of Bingen (*PL*,
CXCVII, cols. 1329ff), and Chaucer certainly appears to be aware of it. His
references to 'wikked entente,' the lunar phase, the *female* ape, and to the
swelling and coloration suggest first-hand knowledge of the appearance and
habits of the animal. Particularly apt is the simile for color. The she-ape's
sexual skin changes to reddish purple, the color of the flesh when the skin is
removed, and very appropriately described as 'flayne.'

The choice of the ape here is appropriate in another respect. Christian
theology assumed that since God had created all things perfect the ape must
have originally had a tail. It must have been deprived of it when it 'fell from
grace.'[26] The tailless posterior of the ape was therefore regarded as an indica-
tion of *hubris*, of pride, of the animal's desire to aspire beyond its station.
Fittingly, the sin with which the Parson is concerned is *superbia*.

The oblique extension of the figure of the she-ape is confined to appearance
and behaviour of limited range. Sometimes more diversified characteristics of
an animal, both physical and psychological, are exploited to give depth to the
human situation and character. The seemingly brief simile of the weasel has
implications of greatest significance in *The Miller's Tale*, and in his indirect
elaboration of the figure Chaucer not only appears to make use of details on
personal observation, as he does in connection with the she-ape, but to take
into account, perhaps not always consciously, the folklore connected with the
animal.[27]

That Chaucer should be familiar with the weasel is not unlikely. The weasel
was domesticated both in ancient and medieval times and took the place of the
cat as a hunter of rats. Probably it was not, like Alison, 'heeld . . . narwe in
cage' (3224) except when it was very wild. The weasel in Neckam's story

seems to have the run of the house, searching for her stolen offspring, poison-
ing the milk and then jumping on the table to upset the bowl when she
realizes her error; and a Latin bestiary made in England in the thirteenth
century shows a brown animal, rather like a small dog, chasing two rats or
mice.[28] In later times, however, in Goldsmith's England and today, weasels
kept as pets are usually caged on account of their destructiveness.

The term weasel is generic and Cuvier applies it to the various members of
the *mustelidae*. In *The Miller's Tale* Chaucer may have been thinking of the
ermine. Trevisa, translating Bartholomew, appears to equate the weasel with
the ermine — 'in some countrees somtyme of the yere all his skynne is whyte,
out take the taylle' (lxxiiii). Except in coloring and size, the ermine (*mustela
erminea*) closely resembles the common weasel in every particular, and
Chaucer would have been familiar with it not only in the fields but on the
gowns of nobility where it appeared as white fur liberally spotted with black
ermine tails or tufts of black lambswool. He may never actually have seen the
ermine alive in its full winter coat, for the complete change, when the animal
is entirely white except for the black tip of its tail, usually occurs only in the
northern parts of Britain. But in describing Alison's attire Chaucer may have
been thinking of the dressed fur:

> A ceynt she werede, barred al of silk,
> A barmclooth eek as whit as morne milk
> Upon hir lendes, ful of many a goore.
> Whit was hir smok, and broyden al bifoore
> And eek bihynde, on hir coler aboute,
> Of col-blak silk, withinne and eek withoute.
> The tapes of hir white voluper
> Were of the same suyte of hir coler.
>
> (3235–3242)

The general color impression is of whiteness with a sprinkling of black. The
particular kind of whiteness of the apron — 'whit as morne milk' — might
well apply to the ermine, for as Goldsmith remarks, 'its fur is more cream than
white.'[29] The coloring and appearance of the ermine's coat are continued in
the lines:

> She was ful moore blisful on to see
> Than is the newe pere-jonette tree,
> And softer than the wolle is of a wether.
>
> (3247–3249)

In winter, the ermine is white like the peartree in bloom and the sheep's
fleece. In summer its coat has a yellowish hue and is described as 'wooly.'[30]
Even the lines 'ful brighter was the shynyng of hir hewe/ Than in the Tour
the noble yforged newe' (3255–3256) suggest the ermine's summer coat and
the sheen on the fur, the glistening appearance peculiar to the *mustela* family.
Alison's song is described as being 'as loude and yerne/ As any swalwe sitt-

ynge on a berne' (3257–3258). The new image does not eliminate that of the weasel, for here we have another creature with white underparts and a noise which is comparable to the squeak of the weasel. Chaucer appears to be alluding to the swallow's high-pitched 'tswee' made in excitement. The swallow's actual song which it utters both on the wing and at rest has remarkably small carrying power and, according to one naturalist, it can only be really appreciated by those blessed with good hearing.[31]

Subsequent details in the portrait of Alison suggest that Chaucer retains the animal image, and gives his heroine further distinctively weasel-like attributes. The description of Alison's eyes implies both the lustful quality commonly attributed to the weasel in folklore, and the actual brightness and color of the animal's eyes:

> And sikerly she hadde a likerous ye;
> Ful smale ypulled were hire browes two,
> And tho were bent and blake as any sloo.
>
> (3244–3246)

'Smale ypulled' is usually interpreted as 'plucked.' Although the anti-feminist writer of *The Book of the Knight of La Tour-Landry* condemned women who 'popithe . . . and paintithe and pluckithe her visage, otherwise thanne God hath ordeined hem', and described the tortures in hell endured by a woman who plucked her hair,[32] eyebrow-plucking became popular in 1370, and Alison is evidently in fashion. Such eyebrows also correspond to the *schnurren*, the sparse, sprouting hairs which the weasel has above its eyes. *Bent* indicates that Alison's eyebrows are arched. The hairs of the weasel are black and because of the darker markings in the fur above the eyes the weasel does appear to have arched eyebrows.

The image of the weasel is still implicit in the description of Alison's youthful animal playfulness, in the references to the country perfume of her mouth, and in the associations with fermented honey, stale ale and stored apples:

> Therto she koude skippe and make game,
> As any kyde or calf folwynge his dame.
> Hir mouth was sweete as bragot or the meeth,
> Or hoord of apples leyd in hey or heeth.
>
> (3259–3262)

For the weasel is a most frolicsome creature; it jumps and gambols, and even when approaching its prey it indulges in playful antics. Furthermore, it may have a 'faintly sweet stink rather like a granary infested with mice,' except when it is annoyed.[33]

Alison has the peculiar habit of 'wynsynge' (3263), starting to one side or wriggling, like a 'joly colt'; but when she is caught in Nicholas' embrace she is like a colt firmly held in the farrier's shoeframe, and she can only writhe her body and turn her head at an angle (3282–3283). The weasel's movements have a peculiar snake-like character. Indeed, so distinctive is its fierce, writhing agility that among the explanations proffered for the phrase 'pop goes the weasel' is that, in the dance, the dancer 'pops' through or under the arms of the other dancers 'in the same sinuous manner as a weasel enters a hole'. Bartholomew, as translated by Trevisa, observes that the weasel, whether wild or tame 'is a swyfte beest of mevynge . . . and plyaunt of body, and full slypper and unstable' (lxxiiii). The animal's characteristic body movement is particularly conspicuous in moments of resistance, and its head is positioned on 'a remarkably long and slender neck in such a way that it may be held at right angles with the axis of the latter.'[34] Although fiercely resistant, however, the weasel can be tamed by being stroked gently and often — if caught young enough.[35]

If the comparison to the mast (3264) hints at a disproportion in the lady's physique, it is one she shares with the weasel. The weasel's body is almost four times as long as it is high. It is also remarkably straight and of the same thickness throughout, and Chaucer's phrase 'upright as a bolt' (3264), meaning 'straight as an arrow,' might well apply to it. In fact, Isidore in his *Etymologies* (xii, 3, 3) uses *telum* to describe the weasel, the significance of the comparison probably lying not so much in the nature of the flight of the weapon as in the appearance of the parallel pattern shaft, which is of uniform thickness from the pile to the nock. If, by association with 'bolt-upright' (*supina*) used by Chaucer in *The Reeve's Tale* (4266) and *The Shipman's Tale* (316) the phrase hints at sexual proclivities, it is applicable not only to Alison but to the weasel in folklore.

In folklore the weasel has a long and conspicuous history. Due, perhaps, to its reputation as an unclean animal in Leviticus 12:29 or to the fable of its unnatural methods of conceiving and giving birth, current even in Egypt according to Plutarch (*De Iside*, 381A), the weasel, in various languages, came to signify a bad young woman. Aelian said that the weasel was once a human being, and was a dealer in spells and sorcery. It was extremely incontinent and was afflicted by abnormal sexual desires. As a result, Hecate in anger transformed it into the malicious creature it now is (xv, 11). Proverbial expressions, such as 'si une fois une fille a fait l'amour, j'aimerais mieux garder un pré rempli de belettes,' imply that the weasel and the young woman have lust and trickery in common, and it is these characteristics which are emphasized in the portrait of Alison. The detailed physical descriptions of her appearance is from the point of view of a seducer. Beginning with a general statement of approval, emphasizing the satisfactory size of her body and its animal likeness, it moves to the striped girdle at her waist, lingers in the folds of the apron around her thighs, and then goes on to her chemise. Of her two suitors, the one embarks on seduction without apparent preliminary courtship, the other offers money for her favors, without fear of giving offence, because, Chaucer explains, 'she was of town' (3380).

Among the alphabetical puzzles in Lady Caroline Kerrison's *Commonplace Book* weasel and woman are grouped together as shrews,[36] and when Nicholas urges John to prepare for a Deluge comparable to the Flood, his ploy for separating Alison from her husband is to compare her obliquely to Noah's Wife, a famous shrew in popular tradition. The weasel was also a well-known shapeshifter,[37] and in Chinese and Japanese tales its shapeshifting often involved sexual trickery. One of the weasel's favorite forms was that of a witch, and it is interesting to note that the name Alison was allegedly one of the most common witch names.

Not only does Alison's general character conform to that of the weasel in folklore but she is associated with other elements peculiar to the weasel in popular superstition. Like the weasel in Aelian's proverb: γαλᾶι δὲ ὑποτρίζουσαι . . . Χειμῶνα ἔσεσθαι συμβάλλονται ἰσχυρόν. (vii, 8). — 'when the weasel squeals the winter reels,' and the French proverb 'quand on voit courir les belettes le long des chemins ou des haies, elles annonçent la pluie ou l'orage,' she presages a deluge, and like the weasel in both ancient and modern folklore, she brings ill-luck. Even today among brides in Greece the weasel is propitiated by flattering words and honey[38] — a diet not recommended by Goldsmith, who tells of a weasel who died from it, nor by the sportsman Daniel who advises rubbing the animal's teeth with garlic to tame it.[39] Absolon observes a similar ritual, 'what do ye, hony-comb, sweete Alisoun/ My faire bryd, my sweete cynamome?' (3698–3699), and offers fermented honey among his gifts — 'he sente hire pyment, meeth, and spiced ale' (3378).

Finally, the weasel's traditional reputation for δίκη, for giving judgement,[40] is also exemplified in Alison. By cheating her husband 'for al his kepyng and his jalousye' (3851), causing Absolon to kiss 'hir nether ye' (3852), and Nicholas to be 'scalded in the towte' (3853), she metes out a form of rough justice.[41] In order to dispense such justice she also makes use of *osculum a tergo*, an indispensable part of *homagium Diabolo*, an unsophisticated, animal-like observance singularly appropriate to a weasel-witch.

In the weasel, Chaucer selects an attractive little animal, playful even with its intended victim, a creature of ill-omen, associated with lust, trickery and witchcraft, and his indirect elaboration of the physical and psychological aspects of his original figure gives depth to the portrayal of his heroine. The weasel serves as an appropriate symbol for the desirable yet wanton young woman of the *fabliau*, whose animal nature brings discomfort to others but remains itself sportive (3740), tricky (3832–3833), and untamed (3850–3851).

In using simple and conventional ideas about animals to throw light on human nature, Chaucer is following a tradition. It is a tradition, found in the sacred books, fables, expository writings of many kinds, encyclopedias, natural histories, homilies, popular lore as well as in art and architecture, which assumes that the animal behaves like Man, that it may usefully illustrate him, and that it has certain unvarying characteristics. He also follows the tradition, abundantly supported by theological exegesis, that if animals represent the infinite variety in human nature, they also stand for the less admirable attributes. But in some of his most effective animal figures he is original: we have seen that even when he uses a simple proverbial phrase his treatment may reflect the animal's actual habits as well as its popular symbolism or even a combination of these two aspects with the animal's folklore. In such instances he obliquely explores the various implications of the figure and extends its significance beyond the original reference in order to make a graphic disquisition on his subject.

III. *Animals Mainly from Tradition*

DESPITE the variety of animals which Chaucer uses, the aspect which he selects is usually the same in each case. With few exceptions, he takes images which reveal the animal in an uncompromising light and applies them to human situations equally unpleasant in character. His practise is consistent whether he draws from traditional lore or fable, or from material apparently derived from personal observation.

Allusions to the ass and the ape are almost always pejorative, and owe something to popular tradition and something to direct literary sources. Sometimes the source is stated: in *The Nun's Priest's Tale* (3312) the fox, extolling the wisdom of cocks, refers directly to Nigel Wireker's *Burnellus* or *Speculum Stultorum*:

> I have wel rad in 'Daun Burnel the Asse,'
> Among his vers, how that ther was a cok,
> For that a preestes sone yaf hym a knok
> Upon his leg whil he was yong and nyce,
> He made hym for to lese his benefice.
>
> (3312–3316)

In *The Monk's Tale*, for the account of Samson and the miraculous 'asses cheke' which enabled him to slay a thousand men and to quench his thirst, the Monk cites the Book of Judges:

> Whan they were slayn, so thursted hym that he
> Was wel ny lorn, for which he gan to preye
> That God wolde on his peyne han some pitee,
> And sende hym drynke, or elles moste he deye;
> And of this asses cheke, that was dreye,
> Out of a wang-tooth sprang anon a welle,
> Of which he drank ynogh, shortly to seye;
> Thus heelp hym God, as *Judicum* can telle.
>
> (2039–2046)

Proverbial expressions are common: in *Troilus and Criseyde* the metaphor of the ass listening to the harp is given by Pandarus when he seeks to arouse Troilus from his despondency. The same Greek proverb, to denote lack of comprehension or appreciation occurs in Boethius' *De consolatione philosophiae* (i, pr. iv, 3).

The motif of the ass with the lyre or harp is popular in medieval art. It originated in Chaldean art and came into the Middle Ages through the fables of Phaedrus. In most instances the ass is not supposed to dislike music. One preacher says that the ass likes music but is so stupid that he tramples on the instrument; another cites Bartholomew as his authority that the ass may lift his head out of his feeding trough to listen to a pipe or trumpet, but when the music stops 'he putteth down is hed ageyn to is mete and thenketh no more thereof. Forsothe ryght so itt fareth by a synnefull man, thow he listen never so well goddes worde. . . .'[1] Pandarus, on the other hand, in his sententious explanation of the metaphor, denies the animal any appreciation:

> 'What! slombrestow as in a litargie?
> Or artow lik an asse to the harpe,
> That hereth sown whan men the strynges plye,
> But in his mynde of that no melodie
> May sinken hym to gladen, for that he
> So dul ys of his bestialite?'
>
> (i, 730–735)

The ape is the proverbial dupe (*Gen Prol*, i, 706; *MillT*, iii, 3389; *RvT*, iii, 4202; *CYT*, viii, 1313), and it is an animal of grimaces and tricks (*HF*, iii, 1806; *ParsT*, 651). There are also God's apes in *Troilus and Criseyde* (i, 913), Devil's apes in *The Parson's Tale* (651), and the ape in the hood (*Intr.PrT*, vii, 440) and these require explanation. God's ape was the Devil, the imitator of God: the Devil copied the Trinitarian concept, ruling a kingdom, holding a Sabbath which caricatured the Holy Mass, and possessing twelve disciples. When Pandarus uses the expression he is thinking of the Devil not as the

epitome of evil but as a fool. He is reminding Troilus how he used to scorn
the behavior of lovers and call them fools.

> 'How often hastow maad thi nyce japes,
> And seyd that Loves servantz everichone
> Of nycete ben verray Goddes apes;
> And some wolde mucche hire mete allone,
> Liggyng abedde, and make hem for to grone;
> And som, thow seydest, hadde a blaunche fevere,
> And preydest God he sholde nevere kevere.'
>
> (i, 911–917)

In *The Parson's Tale* the Devil's apes are the imitators of the Devil. Here the
indictment is serious: the Parson is saying that those who are *japeres*, trick-
sters, perform the function of the Devil and encourage people in a life of sin:

> After this comth the synne of japeres, that been the develes apes; for
> they maken folk to laughe at hire japerie as folk doon at the gawdes of an
> ape. Swiche japes deffendeth Seint Paul./ Looke how that vertuouse
> wordes and hooly conforten hem that travaillen in the service of Crist,
> right so conforten the vileyns wordes and knakkes of japeris hem that
> travaillen in the service of the devel./ Thise been the synnes that comen
> of the tonge, that comen of Ire and of othere synnes mo./
>
> (651–653)

Chaucer's purported source, Paul in his letter to the Ephesians 5:1 does not
use the image when condemning levity, but he does urge his readers to become imitators of God.

The ape in the hood in an expression used by the Host at the conclusion of
The Shipman's Tale. The Host warmly appreciates the story of a monk who
seduced a merchant's wife by paying her with one hundred francs which he
had borrowed from her husband. He says:

> 'Wel seyd, by *corpus dominus*,' quod oure Hoost,
> 'Now longe moote thou saille by the cost,
> Sire gentil maister, gentil maryneer!
> God yeve the monk a thousand last quade yeer!
> A ha! felawes! beth ware of swich a jape!
> The monk putte in the mannes hood an ape,
> And in his wyves eek, by Seint Austyn!
> Draweth no monkes moore unto youre in.'
>
> (435–442)

The implication is probably that the monk made a monkey out of both husband and wife. The Host may also be playing upon another significance. In
adding 'in his wyves eek' he may be thinking of the lasciviousness popularly
attributed to the ape. Aelian claimed that he had heard of apes who had fallen
madly in love with girls and raped them (vii, 19, xv, 14) and an early proverb

states: 'A widdowe that ys wanton with a running head,/ Ys a dyvell in the kyttchine and a nape in her bedde.'[2]

For his essay on the art of writing a good letter Pandarus depends partly on Horace's *Ars Poetica*:

> 'Ne jompre ek no discordant thyng yfeere,
> As thus, to usen termes of phisik
> In loves termes; hold of thi matere
> The forme alwey, and do that it be lik;
> For if a peyntour wolde peynte a pyk
> With asses feet, and hede it as an ape,
> It cordeth naught, so nere it but a jape.'
>
> (ii, 1037–1043)

Horace's passage is more detailed. He imagines a horse's neck joined to a human head, bird feathers spread over limbs of a variety of animals, a comely woman terminating in a horrible-looking fish (1–5). Pandarus contracts the idea into one figure in which rhyme increases the comic effect.

Another allusion stemming from classical times occurs in the description of the temple in *The Parliament of Fowls*:

> The god Priapus saw I, as I wente,
> Withinne the temple in sovereyn place stonde,
> In swich aray as whan the asse hym shente
> With cri by nighte, and with hys sceptre in honde.
> Ful besyly men gonne assaye and fonde
> Upon his hed to sette, of sondry hewe,
> Garlondes ful of freshe floures newe.
>
> (253–259)

Chaucer's ass is the one which brayed when Priapus, during a festival of Bacchus, was about to seduce a nymph while she slept. Alluding only very briefly to this story from Ovid's *Fasti* (i, 415–440), Chaucer presents Priapus as the epitome of sexual frustration. The subsequent failure of the eagles to acquire a mate is reflected in the action of the men, garlanding Priapus with flowers.

The metaphorical use of *simia* is frequent in Latin and French writings of the twelfth and thirteenth centuries, being often applied to persons, abstractions and artifacts which have the appearance of being something which they are not. Peter of Blois calls beer *simia vini* (*PL*, CCVII, col. 1155) and it is possible that Chaucer has this definition in mind in addition to the tradition usually cited, when the Manciple says to the drunken Cook: 'I trowe that ye dronken han wyn ape' (*Prol MancT*, IX, 44). Peter of Blois may himself have been thinking of the same tradition whereby different stages of drunkenness are compared to different animals. It is a tradition which survived in certain French wine towns in the Middle Ages, where local wines were put at public entries for consumption by persons of rank and were designated as lion, ape, sheep and pig wines according to the phases of drunkenness which they were supposed to produce. In Hebrew literature the tradition is said to stem from Noah who went into partnership with the Devil to plant a vineyard. The Devil killed a lamb, a lion, a pig and an ape and as each was killed he made its blood flow under the vine. Thus he conveyed to Noah what the qualities of wine were: before a man drinks of it, he is as innocent as a lamb; when he drinks moderately he feels as strong as a lion; if he drinks more he resembles a pig and if he drinks to excess he behaves like an ape.[3] Here, then, the Manciple observes that the Cook has drunk too much beer and it has made a monkey out of him.

Even when he borrows Chaucer may add some dimension to the metaphor. In the *Roman de la rose* Jean de Meun laboriously describes how Art strives to emulate Nature. Art watches Nature work and then copies her, like an ape:

> Si garde coment Nature euvre,
> Car mout voudrait faire autel euvre,
> E la contrefait come singes.
> (16029–16031)

In *The House of Fame* Chaucer, in transferring the metaphor, gives it a richer significance. He pictures musicians of legendary fame playing on their instruments. Below them sit ordinary performers, gaping up at them and imitating them like apes — or as Art counterfeits Nature:

> Ther herde I pleyen on an harpe
> That sowned bothe wel and sharpe,
> Orpheus ful craftely,
> And on his syde, faste by,
> Sat the harper Orion,
> And Eacides Chiron,
> And other harpers many oon,
> And the Bret Glascurion;
> And smale harpers with her gleës
> Sate under hem in dyvers seës,
> And gunne on hem upward to gape,
> And countrefete hem as an ape,
> Or as craft countrefeteth kynde.
> (iii, 1201–1213)

While these musicians, whom Chaucer in his dream sees performing in the niches of the palace, are part of the allegory of those who minister to Fame, they have also another dimension. As with the bird choir in *The Book of the Duchess* (317) which, Chaucer was glad to note, included none who merely *pretended* to sing, we are again confronted with the actual world of entertainment. Chaucer has more to say elsewhere about harp-playing: in *Troilus and*

Criseyde (ii, 1030–1036), he stresses the tone of the instrument, the sharp pointed nails of the soloist, the necessity for variety in recital. Here, as Chaucer approaches Fame's palace, he notes that the less able musicians watch the masters in their prominent positions and endeavor to copy them. The music of the great 'sowned both wel and sharpe.' How the playing of their imitators sounded we are not told. But we know that the ape was regarded as an unintelligent imitator, and the alliteration of 'gunne on hem upward to gape' seems to convey disparagement of their efforts. The concluding line presents a further idea which, when added to the analogy, enables Chaucer to express very succinctly what may be his own views on the nature of artistic creations: practitioners of the Arts will always imitate the great who owe their genius to Nature.

I have already referred to the realism which Chaucer seems to display when, in *The Parson's Tale* (424), he compares the ape to the fashionably dressed man. In a further allusion to the ape Chaucer may again be using some personal knowledge of the animal.

In *The Prologue to The Monk's Tale* the Host, quoting his wife, states:
'Allas!' she seith, 'that evere I was shape
To wedden a milksop, or a coward ape,
That wol been overlad with every wight!'
(1909–1911)

Socrates seems to imply that the ape lacked courage: when Nicias contends that courage does not exist without a knowledge of the grounds of hope and fear, Socrates observes that in that case the lion, the stag, the bull and the ape have equally small pretensions to courage.[4] But cowardice is not a quality attributed to the ape, either by the early natural historians, the encyclopedists, fabulists or the bestiarists. The Host's wife, Goodelief, may merely be using a derogatory noun and applying an adjective appropriate to her husband. On the other hand, she may be using the adjective because it is an observable fact that each group of apes has its bullies and its underdogs.[5] An aggressive female dominates the troop, and there are various ranks of males who are all subservient to her. Such a situation is analogous to that existing between Goodelief and her husband and servants. Goodelief, a 'nagging shrewe' according to her husband, is apparently creating the situation which she deplores.

But despite the realism, the significance of both these illustrations is obviously symbolic inasmuch as the ape is the epitome of stupidity and folly. In a third allusion the meaning is wholly abstract and can only be understood in terms of specific symbolism. Chaucer may have been influenced by the many references to the ape in exegetical writings and also by the role which the ape played in art and sculpture.

In the *Nun's Priest's Tale*, Chaunticleer, in refuting Pertelote's contention that dreams are merely the outcome of physical disorders, cites several stories in which dreams come true. In the second *ensaumple* illustrating the prophetic nature of dreams he tells of two travellers one of whom dreams that he will be drowned if he sets sail the next day:

> Two men that wolde han passed over see,
> For certeyn cause, into a fer contrarie,
> If that the wynd ne hadde been contrarie,
> That made hem in a citee for to tarie
> That stood ful myrie upon an haven-syde;
> But on a day, agayn the even-tyde,
> The wynd gan chaunge, and blew right as hem leste.
> Jolif and glad they wente unto hir reste,
> And casten hem ful erly for to saille.
> But to that o man fil a greet mervaille:
> That oon of hem, in slepyng as he lay,
> Hym mette a wonder dreem agayn the day.
> Hym thoughte a man stood by his beddes syde,
> And hym comanded that he sholde abyde,
> And seyde hym thus: 'If thou tomorwe wende,
> Thow shalt be dreynt; my tale is at an ende.'
> He wook, and tolde his felawe what he mette,
> And preyde hym his viage for to lette;
> As for that day, he preyde hym to byde.
> His felawe, that lay by his beddes syde,
> Gan for to laughe, and scorned him ful faste.
> 'No dreem,' quod he, 'may so myn herte agaste
> That I wol lette for to do my thynges.
> I sette nat a straw by thy dremynges,
> For swevenes been but vanytees and japes.
> Men dreme alday of owles and of apes,
> And eek of many a maze therwithal;
> Men dreme of thyng that nevere was ne shal.'

(3067–3094)

The allusion to owls and apes is puzzling. Robinson, after justly observing that owls are commonly regarded as birds of ill-omen, refers to the suggestion that apes may be included simply for the sake of rhyme; another suggestion is that since owls and apes appear together in later works, *The Flyting of Dunbar and Kennedy*, *Campaspe* and *Tyll Owlglass*, the alliteration may have had something to do with their obtaining literary currency, and that the phrase means 'monstrous' or 'absurd.'[6] Skelton subsequently uses the phrase in *Magnyfycence*, when Fancy and Folly exchange a dog and a chicken (II, xvii, 1135). When the one says that he loves such japes, the other declares that his mind is all on 'owls and apes.' In the riddle in Lady Caroline Kerrison's *Commonplace Book*, already referred to in connection with the weasel, an owl and an ape and a woman are termed three 'lowrars'. In the Chester Play of Noah, Noah's wife conducts a procession of beasts into the ark, including 'apes, owles, marmoset,/weesells, squirrels and firret' (174–175).

As far as I know, no one has remarked that Chaucer's phrase is appropriate in that these two creatures do have a particular significance in dreams. The Talmud records that to dream of either creature is most unlucky, and according to Suetonius, Nero dreamed shortly before his death that the hindquarters of his favorite horse were changed into those of an ape. Even more specific is Artemidorus Daldianus, the celebrated soothsayer and interpreter of dreams in the second century of our era. In his enormous compendium on the meaning of dreams, *Onirocriticon*, he declares that to dream of either creature is ominous and signifies violent things to come. Particularly appropriate are his remarks on the owl. The owl belongs to the group of birds about which it is most unfortunate to dream. If a man dreams of one of these birds when travelling by land or sea he will either be involved in a great storm or meet with robbers: ὅ τι δ'ἂν τούτων τῶν ὀρνέων τις ἴδη πλέων ἤ ὁδέυων, χειμῶνι μεγάλῳ ἤ λῃσταῖς περιπεσεῖται.[7] Chaucer is, of course, well aware of the dire portent of the owl, and in *The Parliament of Fowls* refers to it as the bird 'that of deth the bode bryngeth' (343). Whether the owl which shrieked after Troilus is part of his dreams is not clear:

'For wele I fele, by my maladie,
And by my dremes now and yore ago,
Al certeynly that I mot nedes dye.
The owle ek, which that hette Escaphilo,
Hath after me shright al thise nyghtes two.'

(v, 316–320)

Certainly Troilus is correct in interpreting it as a foreboding of evil despite Pandarus' contention:

'Wel worthe of dremes ay thise olde wives,
And treweliche ek augurye of thise fowles,
For fere of which men wenen lese here lyves,
As revenes qualm, or shrichyng of thise owles.
To trowen on it bothe fals and foul is.'

(v, 379–383)

We cannot, however, infer that Chaucer was familiar with any specific piece of dream lore with regard to the owl and the ape, and a more obvious explanation may account for the reference. The owl and the ape were frequently juxtaposed in medieval paintings and carvings, and it seems reasonable to suppose that Chaucer was resorting to an allusion which was basically pejorative in terms of Christian theology.

One of the most striking representations of the owl and the ape occurs in an early thirteenth-century painted panel on the ceiling of the nave of Peter-borough Cathedral; a lively ape rides backwards on a goat and carries an owl. Millar shows a similar scene in his reproduction, an illustration on the top margin of the *Beatus* page of the late thirteenth-century Peterborough Psalter, except that the owl is perched in the center of the border and is regarded from the right by the goat and from the left by a fox with a cock in its mouth. In the early fourteenth-century East Anglian Ormesby Psalter the hunting ape rides a hound and swings a lure, while the owl is seated face to tail on a hare (fol. 147v). In the *Smithfield Decretals*, an ape with an owl on its fist watches a woman with a distaff chase a fox with a goose (fol. 175), and in the *Arundel Psalter* an ape on foot with a lure tries to attract the attention of an owl (fol. 40v). The ape, both mounted and unmounted, appears with the owl in the *Luttrell Psalter*: in one marginal illustration it has an owl on its gauntleted hand and rides a goat; at the top left of the Beatus page it crouches with the owl on its fist (fols. 13, 38). A carving on one of the early fourteenth-century choir stalls on the north side in Winchester Cathedral depicts an ape which holds out an owl in its paw and is apparently amused at the bird's blinking at the light. The same pair appear in the carving in the Cathedral at Wells, and a slightly earlier moulding at Bourges Cathedral has crockets formed entirely of owls and apes. An English homilist at the beginning of the fourteenth century refers to a symbolic design whereby human vanity is satirized in the figure of an ape riding an ass and holding an owl.[8]

The reason for the association of these two creatures is not far to seek. In pre-Christian times their ugliness caused them to be associated with all kinds of moral obliquity[9] and in the Christian era they came to represent *turpissima bestia* and *turpissima avis*. The ape in the bestiaries is a participant in the Fall and is likened to the Devil, and the she-ape of Aesopic fable becomes the devil-ape who carries sinners off to hell and leaves the good behind with God. The ape symbolizes all enemies of Christ, and in some illustrations of Christ's ill-treatment at the hands of the Jews and Romans, his persecutors have simian features with *camus* noses showing the entire nostril.[10]

That the ape as *figura diaboli* should give ground to the diversified comic figure of *le monde bestorne* may owe something to familiarity with the antics of the common performing monkey, but no similar amelioration occurs in the treatment of the indigenous owl, usefully engaged in destroying vermin. It is true that the *Physiologus* ascribed to Epiphanius of Cyprus states: 'Augustinus in enarratione Psalmi 101 Christum nycticoraci etiam comparat,' and that according to a thirteenth-century *Aviarum* the owl signifies Christ who loves the nocturnal darkness in that He does not wish us to die for our sins but be converted and live.[11] But the prevalent symbolism is that evinced in the numerous representations of the mobbed owl in medieval art and architecture and made explicit in bestiaries and homilies. The owl is the Jew and its preference for darkness signifies the Jews' rejection of Christ, when they said: 'We have no other king but Caesar.' Filthy habits are ascribed to it and it comes to be regarded as a representative of unclean sensuality. Like the ape, it is associated with the Fall and takes its place on the *arbor malorum*.[12]

The function in which these two creatures are engaged in medieval art and sculpture shows that they are playing their traditional roles. The ape is the Devil, the well-known fowler or trapper of souls. It is also the hunter in its own right, hating small birds — that is, those whose spirits are in harmony with God — and is indefatigable in its pursuit of them.[13]

The owl, used as the lure, does indeed reflect common hunting practise. Aelian alludes to it but attributes its efficacy to the bird's sinister magical powers (i, 29). In a spirited woodland scene on the *Beatus* page of an East Anglian psalter of the early fourteenth century an owl is being used by a furtive bird catcher at work under a limed twig. The crafty eyes of both man and owl are on the birds clustered on a tree above.[14] Batman, in his new edition of Bartholomew's encyclopedia in the sixteenth century, remarks on the practise, saying that since other birds attack the owl by day, fowlers catch other birds with the owl (fol. 180). In terms of Christian symbolism, however, the owl in the company of the ape represents once more the enemy of all true believers, seeking to ensnare the soul and to separate it from God.

The reverse riding positions, on the goat and the hare, the symbols of lechery, are a further reminder of the pejorative significance of the ape and the owl. Philip of Thaon in his bestiary remarks that the owl, like the Jew, flies backwards (2789–2802). In a painting of the thirteenth century, formerly on the lower part of the tower of the bridge across the Maine in Frankfurt, an elderly Jew was depicted as riding backwards on a sow, while a young Jew sucked at it, and another received the animal's excrements in his mouth.[15] This riding of head to tail is the typical position accorded in a popular primitive punishment. Criminals, particularly traitors, were thus ignominiously mounted and driven through the streets to torture and death. In the early medieval romance of Havelok, the villain Godard before he was flayed alive and hung, received such treatment — 'keste . . . on a scabbed mere, His nese went unto þe crice' (2449–2450). The same position is sometimes ascribed to the ape without the owl accompanying him. An illustration of the period shows an ape seated backwards on the rump of a white, two-humped camel, and brandishing a whip.[16]

The association of the owl and ape with the maze is also significant. The man scoffing at dreams says: 'Men dreme alday of owles and of apes, / And eek of many a maze therewithal' (*NPT*, 3092–3093).

Chaucer refers to a maze in the legend of Ariadne in connection with the Cretan Labyrinth, the House of Dedalus mentioned in *The House of Fame* (iii, 1920). He takes pains to describe it:

> . . . For the hous is krynkeled to and fro,
> And hath so queynte weyes for to go –
> For it is shapen as the mase is wrought –
> (*LGW*, vi, 2012–2014)

Chaucer, in using the word 'mase,' implies that it denotes some figure familiar to his audience, one which enables his listeners to appreciate the legendary structure which he is describing. It clearly means something more specific than the metaphor already in use to denote confusion. Nor can it be glossed as 'vain amusement' which seems to be its meaning in *The good wife taught her daughter*: 'Go þou noȝt to toune, as it were a gase /From house to house to seken þe mase.'[17] There were a number of turf mazes in medieval England, and treading the maze appears to have been a mid-summer ritual. A charter of Edward III, in 1353, commemorates the treading of a maze at Boughton Green, Northamptonshire, thirty-seven feet in diameter and called the Shepherds' Ring, at a three-day fair every June.[18] Early in this century country folk still used to kneel at the vestiges of a maze on Ripon Common, sunk in a hollow at the top of the Fairies' Hill, to hear the fairies sing.

But these mazes themselves, some of which still survive, adjoined ancient holy sites, and in Europe during the Middle Ages the vogue for depicting mazes in churches was at its height. Among the earliest examples are those at Orleansville, Algeria, said to date from the fourth century, Nevern in Pembrokeshire, Margam Abbey in Glamorganshire, Neuadd Siarman near Builth, and at the Church of St Patrick at Inchagoill, Ireland. By Chaucer's day mazes had been constructed in cathedrals at Pavia, Piacenza, Cremona, Rome, Ravenna, Chartres, Amiens, Rheims, Bayeux, Sens, Auxerre, Poitiers, Caen and Lyons, either on walls or on pavements. While there is no evidence that traversing the maze was a substitute for a journey to the Holy Land, it did represent a journey. The pavement labyrinth formerly on the floor of a guard chamber in the Abbey of St Stephens at Caen, for example, involved a journey of not less than one mile from one end to the other, through all its intricate meanderings. What such a journey meant the inscriptions to the mazes make clear. It constituted the pilgrimage of the soul through the wilderness of life to the after-life. Such symbolism is apparent in *Piers Plowman* where the dreamer believes that he is in a wilderness and the people whom he sees engaged in the journey of life are 'besy . . . aboute þe mase' (A, i, 6). The inscription of the labyrinth at Lyons added the warning: 'Hoc speculo speculare legens quod sis moriturus; Quod cinis immolutum quod vermibus esca futurus. . . .'[19]

Chaucer's maze, therefore, is likely to signify more than mere bewilderment: it is a reminder of life's journey and of its inevitable end. Its meaning supports the contention that Chaucer is also using owls and apes in terms of their significance in ecclesiastical architecture and art, a significance which has its basis in Christian symbolism. Thus interpreted, the allusion to owls and apes strikingly foreshadows the fate of the sceptic.

The dream consists in a death warning, given in strange circumstances. To one man 'fil a greet mervaille' (3076). He dreamed that a man stood by his bed and told him he would be drowned if he set sail on the following day. There was no reason to anticipate disaster because the wind 'blew right as hem leste' (3073). Yet the scoffer who disregards the dream is drowned under unusual circumstances:

> . . . Er that he hadde half his cour yseyled,
> Noot I nat why, ne what myschaunce it eyled,
> But casuelly the shippes botme rente,
> And ship and man under the water wente
> In sighte of othere shippes it bisyde . . . .
>
> (3099–3103)

Of the ships which sail at the same tide, his alone, apparently, meets with disaster. It is ironically appropriate that the man who dies should think that owls and apes in dreams are of no import, for supernatural evil, the quality with which these creatures are traditionally associated, accounts for his death.

Chaucer's use of specific details from the unnatural history of animals is small. Influential as the pseudo-scientific accounts were in fixing the natures of beasts and in causing many curious ideas to be commonly accepted, he appears to have taken very little interest in them. As in his use of proverbial lore, he seems to have been content to accept the popular attributes of animals which were already part of folk belief.

The mermaids to whom he refers in *The Nun's Priest's Tale* are more properly sirens. The first mermaids were Eurynome in Homer's *Iliad* (xviii, 398) and Ino of the Fair Ankles in the *Odyssey* (v, 346), who were both beautiful and benevolent. They seem to have been comparable to the Syrian fertility or 'fish-goddesses' for by the second century A.D. the Greek traveller Pausanias in his *Periegesis* (I, viii, 41, 4) describes Eurynome as having a tail. Sirens, on the other hand, who lured sailors to their death in the *Iliad* (xii, 41054) were bird women in Ovid's *Metamorphoses* (v, 552) and in Isidore's *Etymologies* (xi, 3, 30).

In medieval times the attributes of both mermaids and sirens became confused. Sirens *in delubris voluptatis* inhabited Babylon, according to Jerome (*PL*, xxviii, col. 842), and his use of it in the Vulgate caused it to be included in the bestiaries. Philippe de Thaon in his bestiary gave the siren a fish tail (1361–1374), and Pierre de Beauvais in his bestiary nearly a century later found three types of siren, two half woman and half fish and the other half bird (ii, 172). In temperament and appearance they seem to have some affinities with Virgil's Scylla who was a lovely maiden to the waist but a fearful dragon with wolfish belly and dolphin's tails below (*Aeneid*, iii, 426–428). But they were also musical, and their method of destroying men was to lull them to sleep with sweet sounds and then attack them like vultures. In the Latin-English vocabularies of the fifteenth century, the terms mermaid and siren, classified under 'nomina piscium marinorum,' are interchangeable.

Chaucer could have seen many illustrations of them in the art and architecture of the period, and some depict the transitional stage. A mermaid on a misericord in Carlisle Cathedral has feathers, claws and a fish tail; another in the little village church of Zennor on the Cornish coast has a fish tail with scales resembling bird's feathers; *Queen Mary's Psalter* shows one bird and one fish siren approaching four sailors sleeping in a boat; a somewhat earlier manuscript of the Canterbury School gives a mermaid a bird's head and a fish tail, and a thirteenth-century Latin bestiary depicts two sirens with birds' wings, tails, and taloned feet, and a third with a fish tail and taloned feet.[20]

Chaucer refers to mermaids after he has provided editorial comment on Chaunticleer's folly in listening to the advice of a woman. He depicts the cock, his fears allayed, disporting in the yard where the fox lurks:

> Faire in the soond, to bathe hire myrily,
> Lith Pertelote, and alle hire sustres by,
> Agayn the sonne, and Chauntecleer so free
> Soong murier than the mermayde in the see;
> For Phisiologus seith sikerly
> How that they syngen wel and myrily.
>
> (3267–3272)

Although the allusion to the mermaid may serve to remind the audience of another example of the destructive powers of 'woman divine,' its primary function is ironic. Chauntecleer bears some resemblance to the alluring song-stresses of the bestiaries with their birds' wings, tails and taloned feet. In the Smyrna *Physiologus*, the siren actually sports an abundant cock's tail.[21] His voice, too, is equally enchanting, being likened to that of 'any Aungel . . . that is in hevene' (3292). But instead of his voice overpowering all hearers it proves to be his downfall. Because of his pride in it he succumbs to flattery and is carried off by the fox.

The gay quality of the singing reminds us of the 'fruyt' of this *exemplum*. Merriness is not ascribed to the bestiary mermaids' song as Chaucer claims and its implications are not necessarily attractive. In the ballad of Clark Colven in Child's collection, the mermaid laughs merrily before wrapping a strip of her magic death-giving sark around her lover's head:

> 'Ohon, alas,' says Clark Colven
> 'And aye sae sair's I mean my head!'
> And merrily leugh the mermaiden
> 'O win on till you be dead!'
>
> (I, 388)

The homilist also finds the mermaid's song 'merry' when he likens it to the pleasures of the world.[22] The mermaid is indeed the symbol of earthly delights and is so depicted by both carvers and theologians. The fish, once a fertility symbol in the hand of the mermaid, comes to signify the soul in the grip of libidinous passion on a misericord in Exeter Cathedral, in Barfreston Church in Kent, and on the capitals of some of the columns of the ancient church of St Germain des Prés in Paris.[23] The mermaid herself represents corporal pleasures which, according to Honorius of Autun, Holcot and Berchorius and others, the Christian, like Ulysses, will resist.

The allusion to the mermaid suggests that Chaunticleer's sin is that of concupiscence. He is servant of Venus, 'goddesse of pleasaunce' (*NPT* VII, 3342), and his service is 'moore for delit than world to multiplye' (3345). A bestiary illustration shows a fox with a fowl in its mouth being pursued by a club-wielding peasant. Such a subject is popular in Gothic marginal illustrations. But the *significatio* applies to Chaunticleer: the fox, who is the devil, catches those who live by the flesh.[24]

With the exception of the monsters of classical mythology, Chaucer's references to fabulous creatures are few. He has no man-eating manticore or yale with mobile horns or two-headed amphisbaena. In addition to the mermaid, he has only two mythical oddities from the bestiary, the phoenix and the basilisk, and the nature of the allusions provide no evidence that he read this popular work. Through the sermons of Odo of Ceriton, John of Sheppey and others, such sensational beasts must have been enjoyed by many who had never read about them. Perhaps even the Shipman, when he says that his tale 'schal not ben of philosophie, /Ne phislyas, [*var.* phillyas, fisleas] ne termes queinte of law' (*Epil. MLT*, II, 1188–1189), is trying to show that he, a churl, has heard of the *Physiologus*, even though he has difficulty in pronouncing the word.

The phoenix occurs in *The Book of the Duchess* when the Knight is recalling the virtues of his lost love:

> Trewly she was, to myn yë,
> The soleyn fenix of Arabye;
> For ther livyth never but oon,
> Ne swich as she ne knowe I noon.

(981–984)

According to the *bestiaries* the phoenix is an Arabian bird which lives more than five hundred years. In old age it builds a funeral pyre, rolls itself in spices, sets fire to itself and on the next day emerges as a small, sweet-smelling worm which develops into a phoenix. Here it symbolizes Christ who had the power to come back to life.

The adjective *soleyn* suggests that Chaucer may have chosen the bird for its solitariness, a quality which, as Robinson points out, is emphasized in Ovid's *Metamorphoses* (xv, 392) and in the *Roman de la rose* (15977). But the bird has further qualities which are applicable to Blanche. The *Pearl* Poet regards the bird as unique, created immaculate by God, as was the Virgin:

> Now, for synglerty o hyr dousour,
> We calle hyr Fenyx of Arraby,
> Þat freles fleʒe of hyr fasor
> Lyk to þe Quen of cortaysye.

(429–432)

A similar idea is expressed by Albertus Magnus in a comparison between the Virgin and the phoenix in *De laudibus beatae Mariae Virginis* (vii, 3, 1). Uniqueness and perfection are the attributes of Blanche who, even among ten thousand, would be 'chef myrour of al the feste' (974).

The *Roman de la rose* (15977–16004) also stresses the immortality of the phoenix. When Death devours the phoenix, another phoenix remains alive and will remain though thousands were destroyed. In the Old English poem of the phoenix the death flight of the bird symbolizes the journey of the soul to the city of God, and to Odo of Ceriton the phoenix, *unica avis in terra*, is like the just man approaching death, ending his life in good deeds and embarking on eternal life.[25] The Old English poem likens the phoenix to the eagle, and it is possible that in selecting the phoenix Chaucer may have borne in mind that the eagle was the recognized emblem not only of St John but of John of Gaunt who received it from Edward III after the latter had used it as an extra crest. Through the phoenix Chaucer is thus able to offer consolation to the bereaved husband. The Patristic fathers declared that both birds were a sign of the resurrection.[26] Like the phoenix, the eagle had its renewal myth and was supposed to achieve complete regeneration by plunging into a fountain three times. Together, the birds are symbols of hope in the after-life.

Earlier in *The Book of the Duchess* Chaucer told the tragedy of Ceyx and Alcione, married lovers separated by death, but he omitted the well-known sequel whereby they became birds after death and were reunited. The reference to the phoenix transfers the metamorphosis to a Christian context. If Blanche was the phoenix she must always remain so and be ultimately reunited with the eagle.

King Alexander induced a basilisk to commit suicide by looking in a mirror, according to *The Wars of Alexander* (4837–4857). Romancers, homilists and natural historians all testify that the basilisk killed men by its glance and that the only creature which could kill it without difficulty was the weasel. The basilisk was the king of serpents and according to Pliny it could also kill by the fire of its mouth and by touch (viii, 21, 33). When a basilisk was killed by a spear by a man on horseback, its venom passed up the spear and killed both rider and horse. By mid-thirteenth century the basilisk was sometimes thought to hatch from a cock's egg and was given the body of a cock and the tail of a serpent. It was also called *basilicoc* and *cockatrice*, and was occasionally confused with the crocodile.

Chaucer's allusion is to the basilisk's most popular trait:

> This is that oother hand of the devel with fyve fyngres to cacche the peple to his vileynye. / The firste fynger is the fool lookynge of the fool womman and of the fool man, that sleeth, right as the basilicok sleeth folk by the venym of his sighte; for the coveitise of eyen folweth the coveitise of the herte. (*ParsT*, X, 852–853)

The use of the devil's five fingers for a lesson on lust is a homiletic commonplace; in Peraldus' work, which Chaucer is believed to have consulted, the fingers correspond to fornication, violation, adultery, incest and sins against nature, and in *la Somme le roy* they have the same correspondences as in *The Parson's Tale* — lecherous regard, lascivious speech, touching, kissing and the act itself. The basilisk represented the Devil who had caused Adam and Eve to sin, and it is not surprising that its lethal glance should be given sexual connotations. 'Why do we look at them?' exclaims the clerical misogynist Matheolus, referring to showily dressed women, 'I tell you because they slay us with a glance, like the basilisk' (I, 1955).

Whether Chaucer was also thinking of the basilisk in another passage which describes the strength of the weasel is uncertain. In *The Tale of Melibee* (1325) Chaucer quotes Ovid as saying that 'the litel wesele wol slee the grete bole and the wilde hert.' Chaucer's source, Renaud de Louens' *Le livre de Mellibee et Prudence* has 'la petite vivre occist le grant thorel.' There are three possible explanations for the alteration from viper to weasel: that Chaucer took *vivre* to represent the Latin *viverra*, a ferret, or that he was following a manuscript in which *meure/mure* (miniver) was written for *uiure*, or that he was influenced by the widely circulated belief that the weasel was a powerful little animal, capable of slaying the deadly basilisk. Weasel makes better sense here than viper because Prudence is using illustrations to support the contention that harm may come from seemingly innocuous sources. Chaucer's allusion to the hart, which is not in his source, makes one wonder whether there is some transference of ideas. In the bestiaries the weasel and the stag are the two animals credited with the ability to kill snakes.

In *The Knight's Tale* Chaucer describes Lygurge, King of Thrace:

> Blak was his berd, and manly was his face;
> The cercles of his eyen in his heed,
> They gloweden bitwixen yelow and reed,
> And like a grifphon looked he aboute,
> With kempe heeris on his browes stoute;
> His lymes grete, his brawnes harde and stronge,
> His shuldres brode, his armes rounde and longe;
> And as the gyse was in his contree,
> Ful hye upon a chaar of gold stood he,
> With four white boles in the trays.
> In stede of cote-armure over his harnays,
> With nayles yelewe and brighte as any gold,
> He hadde a beres skyn, col-blak for old.
> His longe heer was kembd bihynde his bak;
> As any ravenes fethere it shoon for blak;
> A wrethe of gold, arm-greet, of huge wighte,
> Upon his heed, set ful of stones brighte,
> Of fyne rubyes and of dyamauntz.
> Aboute his chaar ther wenten white alauntz,

Twenty and mo, as grete as any steer,
To hunten at the leoun or the deer,
And folwed hym with mosel faste ybounde,
Colered of gold, and tourettes fyled rounde.

(2130–2152)

The metaphor of the griffin requires explanation. Although an ancient folktale of the Flood states that the griffin was too obstreperous even to enter the ark and as a result became extinct, this mythical creature is frequently described and illustrated in medieval times and its existence does not seem to have been doubted. In *Mandeville's Travels* the griffin is said to swoop down and pick up oxen while they are at the plough, and misericords, such as that in Chester Wells Cathedral and in Tewkesbury, the bestiaries frequently illustrate the griffin seizing another animal.[27]

The griffin is, indeed, the subject of innumerable ecclesiastical carvings and sculptures. While its expression and actions vary, it is usually represented as having a lion's body and the face and wings of an eagle. These details are furnished by Aelian (iv, 27), Isidore (xii, 2, 17) and the bestiarists, and Chaucer appears to be thinking of such sources and to extend the simile of the griffin to apply to the Thracian king in general. The griffin's eyes, so Aelian records, are like fire, according to Ctesias; Lygurge's eyes glow between yellow and red. The eagle has feathers above its eyes 'so thick and projecting that they form a kind of roof or shade';[28] Lygurge's strong eyebrows have *kempe* hairs, an adjective deriving from the Old Norse *kampr*, meaning 'bristly, stout'. Both the griffin and Lygurge have lion-like physiques, and while Aelian refers to the black feathers on the back of the griffin, Chaucer says that Lygurge's hair behind his back shines as black as any raven's feather. Herodotus (iii, 116), Pliny (vii, i, 2) and others associate the griffin with gold and precious stones; Lygurge has a coronet set with rubies and diamonds.

Two further details suggest that Chaucer may also have been thinking of sculpture. Lygurge is accompanied by white alaunts, tall, heavy, hunting dogs praised by the Master of Game and commonly white in color. On a horn, believed to be a representation of the *Cornu Ulphi*, sculptured on a wall of York Minster, a griffin appears to be accompanied by white alaunts,[29] animals with which the griffin is frequently seen to be in combat.

Lygurge supports Palamon in his fight against Arcite for the hand of fair Emelye, while Emetreus, the great King of India, supports Arcite. The two Kings are Martian and Saturnalian men respectively, and Chaucer's descriptions of the two figures accord with those given by ancient and medieval astrologers for men born under the influence of Mars and Saturn. By means of the animal imagery Chaucer adumbrates the conflict. Whereas Lygurge's expression is that of a griffin, Emetreus's is that of a lion, and just as Lygurge has further characteristics of the griffin, so Emetreus is leonine with respect to his hair, the marks on his face and his voice:

47

His crispe heer lyk rynges was yronne,
And that was yelow, and glytered as the sonne.
His nose was heigh, his eyen bright citryn,
His lippes rounde, his colour was sangwyn;
A few frakenes in his face yspreynd,
Betwixen yelow and somdel blak ymeynd;
And as a leon he his lookyng caste.
Of fyve and twenty yeer his age I caste.
His berd was wel bigonne for to sprynge;
His voys was as a trompe thonderynge.

(2165–2174)

The similes emphasize the mortal nature of the conflict. While there are many representations of griffins without lions, particularly in connection with Alexander's hubristic flight to heaven, the lion is the animal with which the griffin is most commonly associated from earliest times. A jug now in the British Museum, which was found in Aegina and is dated 700–650 B.C., has a griffin's head for a spout and on its base is an illustration of a lion killing a stag. Lion and griffin are often in conflict, even though Aelian said the griffin would not fight either the lion or the elephant (iv, 27). They appear together in numerous sculptures such as the Romanesque façade of St Costanzo in Perugia, on the right jamb of the doorway of St Pietro in Spoleto, on the tympanum at Ridlington church in Rutland, on a capital in the choir of St Pierre, Chauvigny. Jointly, they are the subject of manuscript illustrations and of decorative motives on ecclesiastical garments, albs, chasubles and sandals.[30]

Usually the griffin represents an evil principle, gaining victory over animals and men whom he appears to tear to pieces. Dante's application of the griffin as a symbol of Christ in the *Purgatorio* (xxix, 107–108) probably derives from Isidore who, in his chapter on the griffin, also states: 'Christus est leo pro regno et fortitudine. . . . Aquila propter quod post resurrectionem ad astrea remeavit' (xii, 2, 17). I have not encountered such symbolism elsewhere.

Further allusions which may owe something to unnatural history concern the lioness, the tiger and the camel. The lioness occurs in the Wife of Bath's long preamble of a tale. Declaring that she persisted in her former habits after her marriage to the 'joly clerk,' Jankyn, she states: 'Stibourn I was as is a leonesse / And of my tonge a verray jangleresse, / And walke I wolde, as I had doon biforn . . .' (*WB Prol*, 111, 637–639). Her previous account of her extra-mural adventures and her admission that she 'evere folwede' her 'appetit / Al were he short, or long, or blak, or whit' (623–624) leave no doubt as to either the nature of these habits or the justification for Jankyn's wrath. But why the Wife should regard the lioness as 'stibourn' requires explanation. According to Pliny (viii, 16, 17), the species mates indiscriminately, and when the lion discovers the lioness's adultery with the leopard, he severely chastizes her. The bestiarists refer to the adulterous association of the lioness with both the pard and the hyena, and Pliny's account, converted into an *exemplum*, appears in the *Gesta Romanorum* (clxxxi). It is not a tale which seems to have much basis in fact. The lioness is usually monogamous, and crossbreeding of a male leopard and lioness in a Tokyo zoo which resulted in two litters in 1959 and 1963 appears to be regarded as something of a rarity.[31] Nevertheless the tale continued to be repeated by later natural historians and by the homilists, and it was used to furnish dramatic evidence of the lasciviousness of the female sex. Because of it, leonine features were assigned to women in some of the Gothic marginal illustrations, and the lioness came to signify the adulterous woman.[32] The Wife's comparison is therefore apt, and is one which would have been readily understood. She and the lioness are 'stibourn' in the same way, and their refractoriness evokes the same response from their spouses.

Chaucer may be using the word because it occurs in works of antifeminist writers. Le Fevre, translating and adapting Matheolus' *Lamentations* in 1370, expands on the remark that woman is worse than a tiger and includes a comparison to a lioness as well:

> Un vaillant auteur nous recite
> Que femme qui mari despite
> Vault pis et plus est felonesse
> Que n'est tigre ne leonesse.
>
> (i. 74)

Chaucer uses tiger in a similar way. In the ironic envoy to *The Clerk's Tale*, women are told to be 'egre as is a tygre yond in Ynde' (1199) towards their husbands. *Egre* appropriately means 'sharp', 'biting'. It also means 'fierce', 'enraged', and Chaucer may have been thinking of the Hyrcanian tiger described by Pliny (viii, 18, 25), and embellished in Ambrose's *Hexaemeron* (vi, iv, 21). This is the tiger which engages in furious pursuit of the hunter when its whelps are stolen. As I remarked earlier, the hunter throws down a glass sphere, and the tiger, seeing its reflection in the sphere, believes it has retrieved its cub and gives up the chase.

The same story may be alluded to in the description of Arcite in *The Knight's Tale*:

> Ther nas no tygre in the vale of Galgopheye,
> Whan that hir whelp is stole whan it is lite,
> So crueel on the hunte as is Arcite.
>
> (2626–2628)

If so, the image may point forward to Arcite's defeat, for in most accounts the tiger is unsuccessful. The relevant passages in the *Teseida* contain no reference to a tiger, but Chaucer appears to have been indebted to the *Thebaid* (iv, 315–316) and the *Metamorphoses* (iii, 217).

Chaucer's single allusion to the camel occurs in *The Envoy to The Clerk's Tale* to which I have just referred. The Clerk has told the tale of patient Griselda and has stressed its *exemplum*: just as Griselda showed fortitude in her trials, so everyone should show fortitude in whatever tribulation God chooses to send. With complete change of tone he then turns to the 'noble wyves' of his own day:

> Ye archewyves, stondeth at defense,
> Syn ye be strong as is a greet camaille;
> Ne suffreth nat that men yow doon offense.
> And sklendre wyves, fieble as in bataille,
> Beth egre as is a tygre yond in Ynde;
> Ay clappeth as a mille, I yow consaille.

(1195–1200)

Here the Clerk is urging wives to militant action, appropriately using the suffix which occurs in action nouns from the Old French *–aille, –ail*, from the Latin *–alia, –alium*.

It has been suggested that the main reason for the use of *camaille* is the pun: either the secondary armorial sense implies that woman's verbal thrusts are sharp enough 'to pierce right through a man's protective armor from front to back,' or, since *camaille* is both a piece of chain mail protecting head and throat and a kind of hood worn by ecclesiastics, the phrase may mean 'stand on the defensive . . . since you have good protective armor for a vulnerable part.'[33]

But Chaucer may mean the camel. Although the animal was subjected to many kinds of misrepresentation in art and sculpture, one feature regarding it seems to have been widely known: its habit of kneeling down to receive burdens. It is often depicted as kneeling, and in some instances a man grasping a scourge accompanies it. Such an action was emblematic of humility. In the cycle of virtues and vices used to decorate the plinths of the jambs of the central porch of the façade of Notre Dame early in the thirteenth century, the camel accompanies Obedience.[34] Isidore refers to *chamae* ($\chi\alpha\mu\alpha\iota$), an adverb meaning *humi*, 'on the earth,' to stress that the camel is a humble beast of burden (xii, 1, 35). Alanus adds that it ministers to the wants of men like a bought slave, 'quasi servos emptitius' (*PL*, ccx, col. 437); Bartholomew, as translated by Trevisa, gives similar characteristics and says that such beasts of burden 'ben meke to them that them charge' (xii).

Chaucer may be thinking of the camel's reputed humility and be applying the figure of the animal ironically to women or he may be thinking of other characteristics mentioned by etymologists, bestiarists and natural historians. The female camel is used for warfare, and it is probably for this reason that Farinator in his procession of the seven deadly sins mounts wrath on a camel (*titulus* 75). Sexually the camel is most receptive. This idea, possibly stemming from Aristotle who says that camels spend the whole day in copulation, is repeated by bestiarists, and appears to have a factual basis. Apart from the llama, of the group of animals which cannot be observed and experimented upon in the laboratory, only the camel is known to copulate outside *oestrus*. Chaucer's allusion may, therefore, be derived from observation as well as from a literary source.

There may be a further irony in the comparison of the husband to a cowering quail. A popular quarry for hawking, the quail is a courageous bird and the practice of making quails fight like game cocks, fashionable in ancient Athens during the time of Solon, is said to have continued into this century in some parts of Italy and China. Ovid contrasts the fate of a parrot, prematurely dead, though so peaceful a bird, with that of the quail who lives through his fights to reach old age (*Amore*, ii, 6, 27–28). Not a few of its desperate battles are occasioned by the fact that the quail unlike the partridge, a much maligned bird in the bestiaries, does not pair but takes many wives. In the *Roman de la rose* the young foolish quail is easily caught but the older bird is wily (21501). If Chaucer was making use of information available to him, the camel, ostensibly strong and enduring, and the apparently timid quail, the 'dazed quayle' as it is called in *Pearl* (1085) are fitting vehicles for the knowledgeable Clerk's rebuttal of the Wife of Bath, the camel because it is a humble beast of burden, martial and lascivious, the quail because it is a tenacious fighter and polygamous.

As far as animal fables are concerned, Chaucer's use is small. Apart from the full length presentation of a beast fable in *The Nun's Priest's Tale* he alludes to several fables only very briefly to provide illustrations for the human situation. The fables he uses are concerned with a conflict either between animals or between an animal and man. The allusion to the fable of the Wolf and the Mare in *The Reeve's Tale* (4054–4055) is discussed in a later chapter. It ironically emphasizes the miller's mistaken self-confidence and has subtle implications. In *The Knight's Tale* Arcite refers to the love triangle between himself, Palamon and Emelye in terms of the fable of the quarrelsome dogs and the thieving kite:

> We stryve as dide the houndes for the boon;
> They foughte al day, and yet hir part was noon.
> Ther cam a kyte, whil that they were so wrothe,
> And baar awey the boon betwixe hem bothe.
>
> (1177–1180)

The predatory habits of kites were more in evidence then than now. An Italian visitor to London in 1500 remarked that bread and butter given to young children by their mothers was snatched out of their hands by kites.[35] Until a law enacted in 1562 prevented butchers and poulterers from throwing their offal out into the streets, kites were regarded as useful scavengers and a penalty was attached to destroying them. Arcite's use of the fable calls his reasoning into question. The fable illustrates the futility of the quarrel but the moral which he illogically chooses to cite is that of 'ech man for hymself'

(1182). We see that Arcite has ceased to be reasonable because he is in the grip of libidinous passion, and it is not surprising that the wrathful fury who, according to Alanus' *Anticlaudianus* (viii, 147ff), punished such crimes, should destroy him.

A further reference to a fable occurs in *The Wife of Bath's Prologue* (692) 'who peyntede the leon, tel me who?' The Wife shows up the weaknesses of the hypothetical arguments of the schoolmen by drawing on experience from life, and the implications of her rhetorical allusion to the Aesopian fable of the lion and the man are consistent with her point of view. Just as a painting illustrating Samson's victory over a lion is invalid as an argument that the lion is inferior to man, so books written by clerks may be discounted. The lion in the fable demonstrated his superiority in a practical way. With equal empiricism, woman could demonstrate the perfidy of men, and her story would be quite different from that of the clerks.

In the instances so far cited there is no doubt concerning what fables Chaucer is using. The source of the allusion to the bear and its leader in *Troilus and Criseyde* is less certain. Troilus is the user:

> 'For trewely, myn owne lady deere,
> Tho sleghtes yet that I have herd yow stere
> Ful shaply ben to faylen alle yfeere.
> For thus men seyth, "that on thenketh the beere,
> But al another thenketh his ledere."
> Youre syre is wys; and seyd is, out of drede
> "Men may the wise atrenne, and naught atrede."'
>
> (iv, 1450–1456)

Criseyde has been trying to reassure Troilus now that the moment of parting is near. She will win Calchas over by appealing to his greed, by telling him of the property she has left behind, and she will soon return. Momentarily heartened, Troilus makes love and then again begins to express a lack of faith in the proposed strategy.

The phrase implies that the bear and his leader are of different opinions and seems to have a proverbial ring. It does not occur elsewhere in Middle English, however, and the comparison which is usually made to other proverbs — 'but nothing thinketh the fals as doth the trewe' (*Anel*, 105) and 'a trewe wight and a theef thenken nat oon' (*SqT*, v, 537) — is not very enlightening.

The phrase may refer to the performing bear. As I have already remarked, bear-baiting was popular in medieval England, and ancient amphitheatres used for similar purposes in earlier times were employed for such exhibitions. There were several rings for the baiting of beasts in London in Chaucer's day, and in the district of Saint Saviour's parish in Southwark, called Paris Garden, there were two bear-gardens. To advertise a bear-baiting, a bear-ward would parade the streets with his bear and in order to excite interest would demonstrate the ferocity of his charge. Illustrations of the bear and his leader which appear on misericords and in manuscripts testify to the friction between the warden and the bear, and the warden often holds a cudgel or whip.[36] Since the pair would go from village to village to give a performance they would be a most familiar sight, and Troilus' allusion may be to the recalcitrance of the bear towards its leader. If so, he is suggesting that although Criseyde may hope to manage Calchas as though he were a performing bear under her control, she will discover that he has ideas of his own. Such a comparison with reference to one whose cunning Troilus repeatedly stresses is indeed apt. Goldsmith, writing when bears and bear-wardens were still a common sight, declares that 'though this animal seems gentle and placid to its master, when tamed, yet it is still to be distrusted and managed with caution, as it is often treacherous and resentful without cause' and states that when it reaches maturity it can never be tamed.[37]

Support for the above interpretation of the cryptic allusion may be found in the reference to *performance* in the next stanza — 'it is ful hard to halten unespied/ Byfore a crepel, for he kan the craft' (1457–1458), and when Troilus declares: 'Ye shal not blende hym for youre wommanhede' (1462), we are reminded of the practice recorded by Bartholomew and others of blinding the bear on capture. The symbolism implied with regard to the sexes is likely to have been current in Chaucer's day for the bear was usually associated with male sexuality. In folklore there are innumerable tales of bear paramours,[38] and in exegetical writings the bear exemplifies masculine carnality. St Peter Damian, for example, states that Pope Benedict in after life was transformed partly into a bear and partly into an ass because in life 'iure igitur qui luxuriose et carnaliter vixit, in asini simul et ursi comparavit' (*PL*, CXLV, col. 429), and a work probably by Garner of Rochefort but usually attributed to Rabanus Maurus declares 'ursus est quilibet crudelis, ut in Isaia "Vitulus et ursus pascentur" . . . Ursus, immunditia, ut in libris Regum "Leonem et ursum interfeci ego servuus tuus", id est, superbiam et luxuriam ego exstinxi,' (*PL*, CXII, 1086). Chaucer may have been making a traditional equation and relating it to current practices.

On the other hand, he could be referring to the frequently cited story of the bear and the honey in the Renard cycle. The bear intends to bring the fox to court but the fox, by playing on the bear's weakness for honey, leads him to a great oak held open by wedges. When the bear reaches for the honey, which is in the tree-trunk, the fox removes the wedges and catches him. This story was so well-known that it was even cited as a method of catching bears, with the hunter taking the place of the fox. Bartholomew attributes the method to Theophrastus who, he says, learned it from hunters in Germany (lxii). If Troilus is alluding to this fable, he implies that Criseyde, as the bear, may think that she is as smart as the fox, Calchas, but she will be led into a trap. There seems to be a further extension of the figure in the stress that Troilus puts on Calchas' craftiness and in his statement:

> 'I not if pees shal evere mo bitide;
> But pees or no, for ernest ne for game,

I woot, syn Calkas on the Grekis syde
Hath ones ben, and lost so foule his name,
He dar nomore come here ayeyn for shame;
For which that wey, for aught I kan espie,
To trusten on, nys but a fantasie.'

(iv, 1464–1470)

His remark implies that just as the bear hoped to bring the fox to court, a place where the latter dared not come because of his crimes, so Criseyde may hope to lead Calchas back to Priam's court but she will not succeed.

The allusion thus adds to the large number of trapping, snaring and hunting images which appear in the poem. Criseyde, already ensnared by her uncle, is seen as the victim of another fox. The idea is implicit in Troilus' concluding saw, a saw also expressed in *The Knight's Tale*: 'In elde is bothe wysdom and usage;/ Men may the olde atrenne and noght atrede' (2448–2449). Criseyde is superior in youth, in physical strength, yet such qualities — her 'wommanhede' — will not give her the power to deceive her father.

Chaucer has only one full-length treatment of an animal fable, *The Nun's Priest's Tale*. The source of this fable has been widely debated. While the tale has affinities with both the French *Roman de Renart* and the German *Reinhart Fuchs*, discrepancies have led to the suggestion that Chaucer used some previous version now lost. But even if *The Nun's Priest's Tale* has essential elements of the earlier French work, Chaucer may well have been relying entirely on an oral tradition and on numerous illustrations of poultry-stealing foxes. The humorous mock-heroic treatment, the dialectics on favorite Chaucerian topics of dream-psychology, medicine, astrology and pre-destination all turned to comedy, the use of dramatic dialogue, vigorous description and of character-portrayal as vital as any in *The General Prologue* may point to artistic freedom and independence of models.

In many considerations of the meaning of the tale the cock has received more attention than the fox. In particular, Chauntecleer's colors have caused speculation because none of the earlier versions portray a cock in such splendor. As far as I know no one has remarked on the variety of rainbow colors of the cocks in the bestiary illuminations. The bestiary cock has indeed characteristics which are pertinent both to the teller of the tale, a celibate whose duty it is to attend the Prioress and her lady companions, and to Chauntecleer who 'hadde in his governaunce/ Severne hennes for to doon al his plesaunce' (*NPT*, 2865–2866). The cock is so called because it gets castrated; it also has a harem over which it holds sway: 'gallus non una sola gallina contentus est sed multas habet conjuges quibus omnibus dominatur.'[39] It is timekeeper, preacher and teacher, like the Nun's Priest and Chauntecleer, but it is ironically dissimilar to Chaucer's rooster in that it typifies vigilance and wisdom. When Chauntecleer beats his wings before singing he is performing an act which has a symbolical significance in the bestiary, and the difference between the motivation of Chaucer's rooster and that of the bestiary bird enhances the irony. Chauntecleer beats his wings because he is 'ravysshed' by the fox's flattery; the bestiary cock beats its wings because it is 'doctor aliis exemplum prebens.' It is the preacher who must awaken himself in order to awaken others.

One critic takes the rooster's colors to signify a particular breed, the golden spangled Hamburgs, but does not illuminate the tale for us; another, identifying the colors heraldically to denote Henry of Bolingbroke as the rooster and the fox as Mowbray's esquire and other personages, finds political implications; another, emphasizing that 'colors, red, black, azure, white and gold, are those associated with the priestly life,' and pointing out that the equation of cock with priest is most traditional in Christian literature, suggests that the tale is of a priest who is susceptible to the blandishments of a friar but saves himself just in time.[40] There is good evidence to support this last view, and in French vernacular literature of the previous century the fox often appears as a friar, and in two instances is called Russell, the name which Chaucer uses for his fox.

Chaucer may also have been influenced by the symbolism popular in other didactic literature and in art. So common is the idea of the fox preaching to poultry — to the deluded — that it is even expressed in the colloquial speech of the *Towneley Mysteries*. When Abel exhorts Cain to make his sacrifice to God, Cain replies: 'How, let furthe youre geyse, the fox will preche;/ How long wilt thou me appech/ With thi sermonyng?[41]

In the many representations in marginal illustrations of manuscripts, in wood carving and sculpture, the symbolism is more specific: the fox, in the garb of friar or monk, or with bishop's mitre or pastoral staff, either preaches to the cock and other birds or looks greedily at a singing cock. A goose or a duck may replace the cock, and sometimes, as in the early fourteenth-century *Gorleston Psalter*, the drama is made spiritedly domestic; the fox runs off with a frantic-looking bird while a woman brandishes a distaff (fols. 71v, 128). If Chaucer is identifying the fox with Daun Piers, the previous teller, two lines in *The General Prologue* 'he was nat pale as a forpyned goost./ A fat swan loved he best of any roost' (205–206), seemingly inconsequentially juxtaposed, take on a special significance. Chaucer appears to be glancing forward to the ultimate fate of the poultry-loving monk. At St George's Chapel, Windsor, which Chaucer was commissioned to repair in 1390, is a carving of three monks being conveyed in a wheelbarrow to hell's mouth, accompanied by a fox with a goose in his mouth.[42]

The Nun's Priest implies that the moral of his tale is to beware of flattery and deceit. He twice emphasizes the lesson:

> Allas! ye lordes, many a fals flatour
> Is in youre courtes, and many a losengeour
> ... Beth war, ye lordes, of hir trecherye.
>
> (3325–3330)

> Lo, swich it is for to be recchelees
> And necligent, and truste on flaterye.
> (3436–3437)

He clearly considers his tale to be homiletic and his warning is similar to that stated in an illustration of a fox running away with a large cock in his mouth — 'dum gallus canit viribus vulpis capit fraudibus.'[43] While he may be thinking of the more general symbolism of the fox as a 'falsus religiosus,' as it was to homilists such as John of Sheppey, his application certainly accords with the homiletic use of the tale of the wolf and the chickens to illustrate the sin of guile.

But there is also a lesson to be learned from the cock who has demonstrated the folly of being 'recchelees and necligent' (3436–3437), vices which the Parson associates with Sloth (*ParsT*, x, 710–711). Such a moral seems designed for the Monk, who neglects his spiritual duties and is contemptuous of criticism of the 'recchelees' monk (*Gen Prol*, 1, 179). The *exemplum* is most appropriate to the teller who is himself a priest, and it is made all the more effective by the implicit comparison to the bestiary cock.[44]

IV. *Animals Mainly from Nature*

SINCE Chaucer exhibits little interest in the world of nature for itself in his works, it is not surprising that over one hundred allusions consist of brief mention of beast or beasts as a generic term. Although the application may be graphic, as for example, when the deflowerer of a virgin is likened to a man who breaks a hedge and 'is cause of alle damage that beestes don in the feeld' (*ParsT*, x, 870), conventional phrases such as 'ne man ne beest' (*MerchT*, IV, 1539), 'no bryd ne beest' (*SqT*, v, 460), 'ne bryd ne beest' (*FranklT*, v, 874) are more common. When we examine the use of animals which are part of the English scene we find few details seemingly indicative of direct personal knowledge. Occasionally, however, Chaucer uses a word or phrase which suggests he has examined his subject almost with a naturalist's interest, and some claim might certainly be made for him as an ornithologist. Critics have found the ingenious suggestion that Chaunticleer and his wife can be identified as a particular breed of chicken very amusing. Nevertheless, some of Chaucer's descriptions of birds appear to have been based on personal observation.

The explanations offered for 'the throstil old' (*PF*, 364) are that the missel thrush was supposed to live to a great age and that it was believed to discard its old legs and acquire new ones when about ten years old.[1] But to turn to folklore to account for the adjective may be unnecessary. In 'The Darkling Thrush,' Thomas Hardy notes the same aspect: 'an aged thrush . . . .' The fact is, with its beard-like white chest beneath its brown face, the bird looks old. The yellowish buff edges to its greyish brown back and rump also give it a worn look. Similarly, in the case of the 'frosty feldefare' (*PF*, 364), another member of the *turdidae* family which Chaucer adds to Alanus' list, there may be an allusion to the appearance of the bird. With its slate grey head, nape and rump contrasting with its chestnut back and blackish tail, the fieldfare has a frosty appearance, particularly in flight, when the white axillaries and under-wings are conspicuous.

An equally simple explanation may be given for 'the fesaunt, skornere of the cok by nyghte' (*PF*, 357). Skeat suggests that Chaucer has transferred to the pheasant the qualities of Alanus' *gallus silvestris*, which is described as *domestici galli deridens desidiam* or he may be alluding to the fact that the pheasant will breed with the common hen. T. P. Harrison considers the proposal that 'just as the cock, Chanticleer, crows at dawn, so the pheasant crows at sunset before he climbs to roost,' to be equally feasible.[2] The phrase 'by nyghte' need not support the view that Chaucer is alluding to mating. It is possible that he is merely referring to the observable fact that although the wild pheasant will come and feed with domestic chickens around the barn during the day, at night, when the cock tries to herd it with the chickens into the barn to roost, it will refuse to obey. So, too, Chaucer may be considering what he has actually seen when he describes the swan as 'jelous' (*PF*, 342). The swan's death song referred to in the same line is a common legend repeated by Alanus and others. It has some basis in fact because, in the whooper swan, *cygnus cygnus*, a flute-like, wailing sound arises as the last breaths are exhaled through the long, twisted windpipe. But the swan with which Chaucer would be familiar is not the whooper swan, which is only a winter visitor in England, but the indigenous mute swan, *cygnus olor*, seen in the numerous swanneries, along the river banks and in the fenlands of medieval England. Swans pair for life, and one ornithologist, remarking on the nesting habits of the birds, states:

> A pair of swans are very jealous of their ownership [of the nest] and an intruder in the form of another swan is quickly driven away. On rare occasions a battle may be fought to the death.[3]

It seems, then, that 'jelous' may be an independent designation, based on fact.

The apprentice in *The Cook's Tale* is described as being 'gaillard he was as goldfynch in the shawe' (4367), and the subsequent description suggests that Chaucer is aware of an analogy between the apprentice and the bird with reference to appearance, behavior and song as well as to temperament:

Broun as a berye, a propre short felawe,
With lokkes blake, ykembd ful fetisly.
Dauncen he koude so wel and jolily
That he was cleped Perkyn Revelour.
He was as ful of love and paramour
As is the hyve ful of hony sweete:
Wel was the wenche with hym myghte meete.
At every bridale wolde he synge and hoppe;
He loved bet the taverne than the shoppe.
For whan ther any ridyng was in Chepe,
Out of the shoppe thider wolde he lepe —
Til that he hadde al the sighte yseyn,
And daunced wel, he wolde nat come ayeyn —
And gadered hym a meynee of his sort
To hoppe and synge and maken swich disport.
                    (4368–4382)

The goldfinch (*carduelis carduelis britannica*) has tawny brown feathers on its upper mantle, scapulars and back, and black on the back of its crown, the centre of the nape and hindneck. Its flight is described as a 'light, flitting and dancing action,'[4] and in courtship the male turns excitedly from side to side before the female, swaying the body. It flutters butterfly-like from plant to plant, and it hops. It is very gregarious, and has been described by one ornithologist as 'a sociable little bird, quick and engaging in its movements.' Chaucer may also be thinking of the bird when he stresses Perkyn's musical talents (4375, 4382, 4396). The goldfinch's song is described as 'a pleasing liquid twittering elaboration of the ordinary call-note' and is said to recall that of the canary.

An allusion to the bittern in a simple alliterative phrase which is apparently peculiar to Chaucer may be another instance of special ornithological knowledge. The Wife of Bath, making her point that women cannot keep a secret, gives her own version of how the world came to know that King Midas had ass's ears. In her account it is not the slave nor the barber nor the King himself who, unable to contain the monstrous secret, communicates it in such a way that the reeds pick up the tale, but Midas' wife who, finding herself bursting with a story which she has promised to disclose to no living soul, runs down to a nearby marsh:

And as a bitore bombleth in the myre,
She leyde hir mouth unto the water doun:
'Biwreye me nat, thou water, with thy soun,'
Quod she: 'to thee I telle it and namo;
Myn housbonde hath longe asses erys two!'
                    (972–976)

Critics usually point out that Chaucer is repeating folklore here. There were, indeed, two different accounts of the genesis of the bittern's cry, both equally fallacious. Even as late as the eighteenth century Goldsmith remarks: 'The common people are of opinion that it thrusts its bill into a reed, that serves as a pipe for swelling the note above its natural pitch; while others, and in this number we find Thomson the poet, imagine that the bittern puts its head under water, and then violently blowing produces its boomings.'[5] Chaucer seems to hold the latter view, but this fact has nothing to do with the artistic effectiveness of the simile. The bittern's cry is a booming echo of peculiar acoustic properties: the bellowing sound seems to be of the same volume whether the bird is close at hand or a mile distant. We do not know whether Chaucer ever saw one 'on rivere,' for Chaucer displays no enthusiasm for hunting. He may only have seen it at meals where it was sometimes served alongside swans, peacocks, cranes and herons. But its peculiar cry was commented on by both homilists and natural historians, and Chaucer must have heard it many times in the Essex marshes which, to this day, remain a favorite haunt.

One homilist, making use of a further fable that the bittern had two stomachs, likens the gluttonous man to the bittern, 'whiche wol sitte bi the watir and putte his bile in a rude (reed), and ther-with maket an huge soun; so that men may here him after cuntre.'[6] Chaucer's phrase suggests a more specific knowledge: the bittern's cry has been compared to 'the sucking of an old fashioned water pump when someone tries to raise the water' and 'bombleth' strikingly describes such a sound. Like Midas' wife, who steals alone to the marshes to disclose her secret, the bird performs its boomings only in solitude and it acts in a fiercely compulsive way. So appropriate is this brief simile that the Wife of Bath does not need to conclude the story. By telling her secret like the bittern, Midas' wife is, in effect, disclosing it to the world.

In a further reference to the swan, Chaucer may again be relying on what he has actually observed. The Summoner slightingly observes of gluttonous friars:

> Me thynketh they been lyk Jovinyan
> Fat as a whale, and walkynge as a swan
> Al vinolent as botel in the spence.
> (*SumT*, III, 1929–1931)

'Fat as a whale' is probably a very general reference to the large size and blubber of the whale and seems to have a proverbial ring. In the *Second Shepherds' Play* a wife is said to be '. . . as greatt as a whall' (105). Neither *whale* nor *swan* appears in the acknowledged source of the passage, *Jerome against Jovinian* (1, 40): 'Et tamen iste formosus monarchus, crassus, nitidus, dealbatus, et quasi sponsus semper incedens . . .' (*PL*, XXIII, col. 280), and *swain* has been suggested as an alternate reading for *swan*. *Swain*, in addition to meaning 'swain' in Middle English, can mean 'young man' or 'servant' as it does in *The Reeve's Tale* (4027). The word may be closer in meaning to the Latin *sponsus*, 'bridegroom', but the subsequent description is hardly applicable. The swan in traditionally associated with wine and was the emblem of the vintners. 'Walkynge as a swan' is a most apt description of the gait of a fat man. In its effort to move its feet the swan does indeed appear to sway from side to side like a drunken man. As one ornithologist observes, the swan 'though a most elegant and beautiful creature on the water, is an extremely awkward walker on account of its very short legs and large body.'[7]

Among the wild animals which haunt Chaucer's woodlands both in *The Book of the Duchess* and *The Parliament of Fowls* are 'the dredful ro, the buk, the hert and hynde,/ Squyreles, and bestes smale of gentil kynde' (*PF*, 195–196). The squirrels are depicted in *The Book of the Duchess* as they are on some of the misericords — sitting on a tree-branch, eating. Of the emblematic squirrel, which crosses a stream by sitting on a piece of wood and is therefore likened to the Christian grasping the Cross to pass over the troubled waters of life, there is no trace. For such animals as he uses in general description Chaucer is indebted to the *Roman de la rose* but he has less detail and appears anxious to abbreviate. In *The Book of the Duchess*, for example, the enumeration of beasts is terminated by means of a learned, if confused, allusion to Argus:

> And many an hert and many an hynde
> Was both before me and behynde.
> Of founes, sowres, bukkes, does
> Was ful the woode, and many roes,
> And many sqwirelles, that sete
> Ful high upon the trees and ete,
> And in hir maner made festes.
> Shortly, hyt was so ful of bestes,
> That thogh Argus, the noble countour,
> Sete to rekene in his countour,
> And rekened with his figures ten — . . .
> Yet shoulde he fayle to rekene even
> The wondres me mette in my sweven.
>
> (427–442)

In this passage Chaucer's reference to the deer shows some knowledge of sporting terminology. The male deer is called a fawn in its first year, a 'sore' in its fourth and a buck in its sixth, according to *The Book of St. Albans*. Elsewhere Chaucer uses other hunting terms. 'Slee the hert with strengthe,' occurs in Theseus' hunt, and in the dream hunt in *The Book of the Duchess* as the idiomatic equivalent of *chasser les cerfs à force*. 'Hertes with hir hornes hye . . . and hondred slayn with houndes,/ And somme with arwes blede of bittre woundes' are described in the *Franklin's Tale* (1191–1195); and the hunted stag which is *embosed* — meaning 'exhausted' or 'hidden in the woods' (*OF. embuschier, embuissier*) — appears in *The Book of the Duchess*.

Despite his five deer hunts (*BD*, 354–386; *LGW*, 1212–1213; *KnT*, I, 1673–1695; *FranklT*, V, 1189–1194; *MkT*, VII, 2257–2259) and his many allusions to hunting, Chaucer gives very little detail about the animals. When Aeneas hunts with Dido, the focus in on the excitement of the hunt and the impatience of the participants:

> The herde of hertes founden is anon,
> With 'Hay! go bet! pryke thow! lat gon, lat gon!
> Why nyl the leoun comen, or the bere,
> That I myghte ones mete hym with this spere?'
> Thus sey these yonge folk, and up they kylle
> These bestes wilde, and han hem at here wille.
>
> (*LGW*, 1212–1217)

In *The Knight's Tale* the occasion of the last hunt enhances the nobility of Theseus and the splendor of the royal riders. It is not the hunt of Venus; with Ypolita, his fair queen, and Emelye, 'clothed al in grene,' Theseus serves Diana:

> This mene I now by myghty Theseus,
> That for to hunten is so desirus,
> And namely at the grete hert in May,
> That in his bed ther daweth hym no day
> That he nys clad, and redy for to ryde
> With hunte and horn and houndes hym bisyde.
> For in his huntyng he swich delit
> That it is al his joye and appetit
> To been hymself the grete hertes bane,
> For after Mars he serveth now Dyane,
> Cleer was the day, as I have toold er this,
> And Theseus with alle joye and blis,
> With his Ypolita, the faire queene,
> And Emelye, clothed al in grene,
> On huntyng be they riden roially.
> And to the grove that stood ful faste by,
> In which ther was an hert, as men hym tolde,
> Duc Theseus the streighte wey hath holde.
> And to the launde he rideth hym ful right,
> For thider was the hert wont have his flight,
> And over a brook, and so forth on his waye.
> This duc wol han a cours at hym or tweye
> With houndes swiche as that hym list comaunde.
>
> (1673–1695)[8]

In *The Franklyn's Tale* the hunt is included for psychological reasons. The magician uses it to demonstrate his skill, and like the other examples which he gives of his art, it is calculated to appeal to the spectator, Aurelius, a young squire whose own interests are illustrated. The hunt is made even more attractive by being depicted as very successful, with tremendous slaughter. It is followed by scenes of hawking, with the quarry already in the bag, and of knights jousting. The demonstration culminates in a dance in which Aurelius has the tantalizing illusion of actually dancing with his lady:

> He shewed hym, er he wente to sopeer,
> Forestes, parkes ful of wilde deer;
> Ther saugh he hertes with hir hornes hye,
> The gretteste that evere were seyn with ye.
> He saugh of hem an hondred slayn with houndes,
> And somme with arwes blede of bittre woundes.
> He saugh, whan voyded were thise wilde deer,
> Thise fauconers upon a fair ryver,
> That with hir haukes han the heron slayn.
> Tho saugh he knyghtes justyng in a playn;
> And after this he dide hym swich plesaunce
> That he hym shewed his lady on a daunce,
> On which hymself he daunced, as hym thoughte.
>
> (1189–1201)

Such magical contrivances are the common stock of many medieval tales and the wonders described here parallel those in the great Khan's Court described in Mandeville's Travels:

> And þan comen Jongulours and Enchantoures, þat don many mervaylles . . . þei bryngen in daunces of the fairest damyselles of the world & richest arrayed . . . þei make knyghtes to jousten in armes full lustyly . . . þei make to come in huntyng for the hert & for the boor, with houndes rennynge with open mouth . . . .

It was also fashionable for 'tregetours' at court to produce by sleight of hand and machinery such scenic effects and make them seem like magic. When Queen Isabelle of France entered Paris in 1389, a master engineer from Geneva, having already fastened a cord from the highest tower of Notre Dame to the top of a house on the bridge of St Michael, left the tower and flew down singing, holding two lighted torches. At the palace itself the siege of Troy was staged and the heat and confusion became so great that a back door had to be broken down to give the Queen air.[9] Chaucer may himself have witnessed the magician's art many times at court.

The hunting scene is one of the means whereby the magician overrides the discretion of Aurelius. The squire, who has seen his own pastimes of the chase and of love so strikingly depicted, recklessly promises to buy magic for a sum which he later realizes will beggar him.

In addition to describing aspects of the hunt itself, Chaucer effectively applies hunting terms in metaphor. Criseyde is the unsuspecting deer being driven into the 'triste cloos,' the place at which the bowman stands to shoot the deer (*Tr*, ii, 1534–1535);[10] the husband, subjected to the physical or verbal assaults of his wife, is the weary hare on its form, worried by dogs (*ShipT*, VIII, 104–105), or the cowering quail; the Summoner in *The Friar's Tale* (1379) and Damyan in *The Merchant's Tale* (2014) apparently alike in their obsequiousness to superiors and in their lechery, are likened to the 'dogge for the bow,' the hound specially trained to be completely subservient to his master, making his attack only when so ordered, and only upon deer already wounded by the bowman's arrow.

Chaucer also refers to other current practises having to do with animals. Both the brawny Miller and the effeminate Sir Thopas are represented as winning the ram at wrestling matches (*Gen Prol*, 1, 548; *Thop*, VII, 740–741). The 'free bull' which the lord of the manor was privileged to provide to run with the common herd of the village supplies an apt smile for lecherous priests (*ParsT*, x, 898). But the allusions to hunting and other current practises are general and for the most part do not appear to have involved a close study in field or town of specific animals.

Other animals which are part of the English scene are the conies playing in the garden of *The Parliament of Fowls* (193), the polecat, the rat, the mouse and the cat. Chaucer's coney is a creature of convention, along with 'the dredful ro, the buk, the hert and hynde, / Squyrels, and bestes smale of gentil kynde' (*PF*, 195–196). Medieval sportsmen make a distinction between it and the hare. The hare is the king of venery, first beast of the chase, whereas the coney is not an animal to be hunted but is caught with ferrets, with large headed arrows from bows or with any weapon to hand. Manuscript illustrators often differentiate between the hare and the rabbit by showing the burrow of the latter.[11] Rabbits are usually well drawn whether in flight or at rest, and in some instances they look amicably out of their burrows as though from the windows of a house and seem to imply the zoological fact that they live in a social world not unlike our own.

Rabbits were not introduced into Britain before the early thirteenth century and there is no name for them in the Celtic or Teutonic languages. The earliest reference traced to rights in *warennis et cunigariis* appears in a charter granting land in Connaught to Hugh de Lacy in 1204, but the actual existence of a coney garth in England cannot be proved until 1241 when hay was to be carted from the King's *cunigera* at Guilford.[12] Because of the multiplicity of their natural enemies, rabbits were not plentiful even in the next century. Poaching conies was a popular sport and cases of trespass show they were valued both for their skins, which were exported as early as 1337, and as an item of food. In 1383 John Wengham, king's fishmonger, was appointed to provide rabbits and fish for the king's household, and in 1389 four hundred conies were served at a banquet given by the Bishop of Durham to Richard

II. Rabbits seem to have been restricted to certain areas. The fact that in 1395 twenty couples of conies at sixpence and eightpence per couple were procured at Bushey, Hertfordshire, from whence they were taken to Oxford at the transportation cost of one ha'penny apiece for a Determination Feast suggests that they must have been scarce around Oxford. Jean de Meun mentions conies as an item of food in the *Roman de la rose* (11750) but Chaucer depicts them merely as part of country life.

Jean de Meun also puts conies in his forest, a place full of dangers through which the lover will be led in quest of his love (15135ff), and these conies have a symbolic as well as a descriptive function. Such symbolism owes its popularity to word play on *con* and *conin*. The rabbit stands for a specific part of the female anatomy and for the woman as a whole. The male in pursuit becomes the hound. Jean de Meun makes this equivalence clear:

> En ce bois ci poez oir
> Les chiens glatir, s'ous m'entendez,
> Au conin prendre ou vous tendez,
> E le fuiret, qui, senz faillir,
> Le deit faire es reiseaus saillir.
>
> (15138–15142)

Not surprisingly, the same equivalence is represented in art and sculpture, a young man soliciting a woman while a hound pursues a rabbit. A marginal illustration in the 'Smithfield Decretals' suggests that the pursuit may sometimes be reversed. A lady has difficulty in urging her pet dog to action. Large rabbits look boldly out of their burrows with some amusement (fol. 160v). Chaucer uses comparable symbolism only with regard to the hare, and as we shall see later such symbolism is ambivalent.

Less attractive vermin are the polecat and the rat. These two creatures are mentioned in *The Pardoner's Tale*. The 'riotoures thre' have found gold under a tree and one of them goes into town to buy bread and wine while the other two guard it. He is the youngest, and when we hear the two older men conspiring to kill him on his return we feel pity for him. Both the words the Pardoner uses to describe the plot and his own commentary emphasize the villainy of the two men. One is to struggle with the man 'as in game' while the other pierces him 'thurgh the sydes tweye.' 'And thus acorded been thise shrewes tweye,' observes the narrator, 'To sleen the thridde, as ye han herd me seye' (829–836).

The pause between the lines completes the image of the two villains, having agreed on their plan, settling down to wait. The reader is then startled to discover that the same time is being used by the youngest man for an equally evil purpose:

> For this was outrely his fulle entente,
> To sleen hem bothe, and nevere to repente.

And forth he gooth, no lenger wolde he tarie,
Into the toun, unto a pothecarie,
And preyde hym that he hym wolde selle
Som poyson, that he myghte his rattes quelle;
And eek ther was a polcat in his hawe,
That, as he seyde, his capouns hadde yslawe,
And fayn he wolde wreke hym, if he myghte,
On vermyn that destroyed hym by nyghte.
(849–858)

This passage illustrates one of the ways in which Chaucer brings the story to life. The polecat does not appear in any of the known analogues. It is, however, an animal which occurs in other Middle English texts such as *Cleanness* (534) and *The Parliament of the Three Ages* (18) as *folmarde, filmarte* — 'foul marten.' Pole — is from *poule* and alludes to the polecat's fondness for chickens, for in winter it would often lodge near hen houses for purposes of plunder. But while it could constitute a nuisance it was also a beast of the chase and was valued as such. Dame Juliana Barnes, the reputed author of *The Book of St Albans*, included it as an animal of the 'stingand fute', along with the fox, the otter, the stoat, the badger, the weasel, and other animals. Its fur was highly prized, and it was from Flanders, the locale of *The Pardoner's Tale*, that it was exported in the closing years of Edward III's reign.[13] The specific reference gives credibility to the man's request. Chaucer's analogues did not tell him what to say to the apothecary. Chaucer shows the man getting poison in a way which does not arouse suspicion. The cunning exhibited is also a further illustration of the absolute evil of a man in the grip of *cupiditas*.

A plague of rats and mice occurred throughout Europe in the years immediately preceding the Black Death, and when the man in *The Pardoner's Tale* says that he needs poison for rats as well as for a polecat, he is making a probable request. Rats are not mentioned in the Epinal Glossary where the word *mus* is applied to shrews.[14] They first appear in Aelfric's works some three hundred years later but since *rata* was the word for house mouse among the Provençals it is possible that a similar significance may have been attached to the Old English word. Albertus Magnus refers to them in *De animalibus* (xxii, 123), but his description of them and of their arboreal habitat — 'Est autem magnum quod nos ratum vocamus, et est in arboribus habitans . . .' — is not necessarily proof that rats existed in Cologne where the work was written. The black rat was probably imported to Europe from the Levant by the Crusaders. It was certainly known in France from the early thirteenth century where it appears in the Renard cycle. Chaucer's Parson condemns those who believe that it is possible to divine the future 'by gnawynge of rattes' (*ParsT*, 604). Reginald Scot, in his *Discoverie of Witchcraft*, regards the superstition as an old one, viewed with scepticism even in Roman times: 'One told Cato, that a rat had carried awaie and eaten his hose, which the partie said was a wonderful signe. Naie (said Cato) I think not so: but if the hose had eaten the rat, that had beene a wonderfull token indeed.'[15]

The mouse was well-known to the ancients and must have arrived in Europe in remote times. As in the case of the rat, its association with the plague was not realized although, in antiquity, the priests of the plague-stricken Philistines certainly must have had a glimmering of the truth when they ordered them to make gold images of mice (I Sam. vi, 4). Like the rat, the mouse has a great propensity for following a definite track to and from its hole, and the proverbial expression that the mouse with only one hole is easily taken appears to have a commonsense basis. The saying is in many languages and Jean de Meun's Duenna in the *Roman de la rose* (13150-13153), uses it for an argument similar to that given by the Wife of Bath. Equally widespread is the proverbial expression 'as drunk as a mouse' already discussed (p. 23). It is, of course, easy to see why such an expression became popular. Mice, according to Brehms, are very fond of spirits,[16] and Skeat observes that since they are such small creatures they require very little alcohol to make them drunk. Widely disseminated is the fable of the mouse who fell into a pot of wine and was rescued by a cat. In return for being saved, the mouse promised to come when called. Later, in the safety of her hole, however, she refused to come out, saying that her promise was invalid because she was drunk when she gave it.

Chaucer's other references to the mouse suggest it was a common enough sight. The Prioress was so tender-hearted that she would weep if she saw a mouse caught in a trap (*Gen Prol*, 1, 144-145); Absalon would have caught the attractive young wife of the carpenter had he been a cat and she a mouse (*MillT*, 1, 3346-3347); the timidity of the mouse provides Pandarus with a picturesque expletive with which to condemn Troilus' bashfulness. 'Thow wrecched mouses herte, /Artow agast so that she wol the bite?' (*Tr*, iii, 736-737); in order to describe the most trifling sound, the Eagle compares it to the voice of a mouse — 'thogh hyt were piped of a mous' (*HF*, ii, 785).

Chaucer's allusions to cats are similarly partly derivative and partly based on a knowledge of the animal. The cat who wants to eat fish but fears to get his feet wet occurs in a rousing speech of unpredictable Lady Fame. She is castigating one group of suppliants who would like her favors without working for them:

> 'Fy on yow,' quod she, 'everychon!
> Ye masty swyn, ye ydel wrechches,
> Ful of roten, slowe techches!
> What? false theves! wher ye wolde
> Be famous good, and nothing nolde
> Deserve why, ne never ye roughte?
> Men rather yow to hangen oughte!
> For ye be lyke the sweynte cat
> That wolde have fissh; but wostow what?

He wolde nothing wete his clowes.
Yvel thrift come to your jowes,
And eke to myn, if I hit graunte,
Or do yow favour, yow to avaunte!'
(HF, iii, 1776–1788)

Gower uses a similar phrase in *Confessio Amantis* (iv, 1108–1109), 'as a cat wolde ete fisshes / without wetinge of his cles.' In Chaucer the proverbial expression is revitalized by the addition of the word *sweynt*, by the rough colloquial speech and by the scorn which the rhetorical question, the emphatic rhymes and the concluding imprecations convey.

A similar revitalization occurs in the description of the cat which Chaucer borrows from the *Roman de la rose*. The scene described by Jean de Meun is generalized:

Qui prendrait, beaus fiz, un chaton
Qui onques rate ne raton
Veu n'avrait, puis fust nourriz
Senz ja voeir rat ne souriz,
Lonc tens, par ententive cure
De delicieuse pasture,
Et puis veist souriz venir,
N'est riens qui le peust tenir,
Se l'en le laissait eschaper,
Qu'il ne l'alast tantost haper.
(14039–14048)

Chaucer's concrete references to milk, flesh, the couch of silk, and the mouse going by the wall not only humanize the scene but emphasize the irrational and powerful quality of the instinct which can prompt an animal to renounce the luxuries of domestic life for a mouse:

Lat take a cat, and fostre hym wel with milk
And tendre flessh, and make his couche of silk,
And lat hym seen a mous go by the wal,
Anon he weyveth milk and flessh and al,
And every deyntee that is in that hous,
Swich appetit hath he to ete a mous.
Lo, heere hath lust his dominacioun,
And appetit fleemeth discrecioun.
(*MancT*, IX, 175–182)

In *The Wife of Bath's Prologue* Chaucer refers to the practice of burning a cat's fur to make the cat stay home. The singed cat which is too ashamed to go out is, indeed, one of the commonplaces of the medieval pulpit. Jacques de Vitry tells the story of a handsome cat given to roaming until its master disfigured it by burning its tail and pulling out its hairs, and as we have already noted Odo of Ceriton briefly states the moral that erring wives must be treated in the same way.[17]

The comparison of the cat to a woman in her finery is understandable. Not only did the notion exist, stemming from Aristotle, that the female cat was peculiarly lecherous, but there was probably an even keener appreciation of the fine qualities of a cat's fur than now. A passage from Langland's *Piers Plowman* is illuminating in this last respect: 'I have as moche pitie of pore man · as pedlare hath of cattes / That wolde kille hem, yf he cacche hem myghte · for covetise of here skynnes' (B, v, 258–259). The vogue for wearing furs was such that every possible furbearing animal was used, and the skinner was just as likely to skin the cat sitting by the fireside as to buy expensive foreign skins. Cat was one of the furs which the common people, with the exception of carters and ploughmen, were allowed to wear by the Sumptuary Law of 1363. The corollary was: the higher the rank, the finer the fur, and carters and ploughmen were debarred from wearing any fur whatsoever. Apart from lamb, coney and fox, cat was the sole fur that might be worn by esquires and gentlemen under the rank of knight with land worth up to one hundred pounds a year, merchants, citizens, artizans and people of handicraft with goods and chattels up to five hundred pounds a year, and all yeomen, grooms and servants.

Not surprisingly, proverbial expressions reflect the current value. Langland cites one popular expression. Another phrase — 'I kep no more but the skin of a catt' — meant that the speaker kept everything of worth.

From Celtic times cats were tortured, burned alive, and skinned for purposes of divination and magic, and even in the eighteenth century were unwilling participants in such sports as the cat in the barrel and the cat in the bottle. The singeing of the cat's fur may imply that fire hazards were particularly acute with regard to this animal or may reflect yet another barbarity to which the cat was subjected. Bartholomew appears to suggest that it was common practice: '. . . and whan he hathe a fayre skynne, he is as it were prowde therof, and gooth fast abowte: and whan his skynne is brente, then he bydeth at home' (lxxvi). There may be a good reason for the efficacy of such a measure. Pepys in his *Diary* records seeing a singed cat emerging from a London chimney but the circumstances were extraordinary. A cat needs the hairs on its ears and whiskers to catch minute vibrations to tell it of movements which it has not seen.[18] When singed, it may be most unwilling to venture out of doors.

The Wife of Bath refers to the singed cat in a demonstration of the way she retained *maistrie* over her husbands by chiding them 'spitously,' and rebutting their criticisms. Accused of making herself too gay with her clothes, she says:

> Thou seydest this, that I was lyk a cat;
> For whoso wolde senge a cattes skyn,

> Thanne wolde the cat well dwellen in his in;
> And if the cattes skyn be slyk and gay,
> She wol nat dwelle in house half a day,
> But forth she wole, er any day be dawed,
> To shewe hir skyn, and goon a-caterwawed.
> This is to seye, if I be gay, sire shrewe,
> I wol renne out, my borel for to shewe.
>
> (*WB Prol*, III, 348–356)

Although the story is traditional, Chaucer contrives to apply the simile to the marital situation with a humor and sympathy not found in any of the analogues. The predominating image is not that of the singed cat but of an eager, attractive, restless creature. 'Slyk and gay' has a startling lilt: it suggests feline pride, zest for life, and also an approval of these qualities. The next two lines, which measure urgency in mundane terms of time, convey all the impatience to begin the 'olde daunce.' Then, abruptly, this animal vivacity is smeared because of the harsh-sounding name which the husband gives to such activity.

What of the cat-hole in *The Miller's Tale* through which the cat 'was wont in for to crepe' (3441) and the cat in *The Summoner's Tale* (1775) which the friar drove away from the bench? Certainly their mention serves the poet's immediate purpose. Old John's servant is able to peep through the hole into the room where Nicholas is pretending to see into the future. The Friar's gesture emphasizes his greed: 'Ful ofte /' he says, 'have I upon this bench faren ful weel;/Heere have I eten many a myrie meel,' (*SumT*, 1772–1774), and he removes the cat in anticipation of a hearty meal.

But it is a curious fact that, unlike any of the other works, both these tales hinge upon ritual with which the cat was associated. In his work on heresy, *Contra haereticos* (I, lxiii), Alanus de Insulis, in defining the heresies of the Catharists, glosses *Cathar* as derived from the obscene worship of a cat. Lucifer was said to appear in the form of this animal and the heretics kissed its *posteriora* (*tergum*) (*PL*, CCX, col. 366). Walter Map in his *De nugis curialium*, describes how the Devil descends as a black cat (*murilegus niger*) before his devotees. The worshippers put out the light and draw near to the place where they saw their master. They feel after him and when they have found him they kiss him under the tail: '. . . plurimi sub cauda, plerique pudenda, et quasi a loco fetoris accepta licencia pruriginis, quisque sibi proximum aut proximam arripit, commiscenturque quantum quisque ludibrium extendere preualet' (I, xxx).

In any orgies presided over by the Devil in the form of a cat or goat, kissing the Devil *a tergo* and copulation with him were regarded as activities inevitably attendant on the profanation of Christian ceremonies. Early in the fourteenth century even the Bishop of Coventry and Lichfield and Treasurer of the Realm, Walter de Langton, did not escape calumny, and in Ireland Dame Alice Kyteler of Kilkenny, said to be responsible for the deaths of her three previous husbands and for the wasting disease of her fourth husband, was accused of having carnal copulation with a devil who sometimes took the form of a cat — 'quandoque sibi apparet in specie cati.' *Osculum a tergo* was an accusation levelled against the wealthy Knights Templars in 1309. The indictment further stated 'Item, quod adorabant quemdam catum sibi in ipsa congregatione apparentem quandoque.' The Waldensians were charged with similar acts, according to a fourteenth-century tract, — '. . . in aliquibus aliis partibus apparet eis daemon sub specie et figura cati, quem sub cauda sigillatim osculantur,'[19] and in numerous accusations of heresy in the thirteenth and fourteenth centuries, such activities appear to be the epitome of blasphemy. As a result the cat was generally recognized as a demonic animal, and the homilist's evaluation 'murilegus est Diabolus' was widely accepted. Odo, expounding on the fable of the mice and its young, states that the cat which destroys the mice is the Devil: he tempts those who do not obey the Church, and seeks to devour them and throw them into Hell. 'If any beast hath the devil's spirit in him,' remarks the author of *The Master of Game*, momentarily ignoring Gaston de Foix, the sober authority of his hunting treatise, 'without doubt it is the cat.'[20]

When old John declares 'I crouche thee from elves and fro wightes' and proceeds to pronounce a spell to preserve the household from evil, he is acting more wisely than he knows. The Devil was indeed 'God's ape' and Nicholas, foretelling a second Deluge and instructing John how to survive it, is blasphemously playing God. Both he and the weasel-like Alison are associated in deeds of darkness even while merrily swearing 'by Jhesu' and 'by Goddes corpus,' and certainly Absolon who uses the *shot-wyndowe* for an altar and gets down on his knees to receive the unsavory kiss appears to recognize the heretical nature of the act: 'Allas!/My soule bitake I unto Sathanas . . .' (3749–3750).

As far as Friars are concerned, they appear to have been associated with witchcraft from the middle of the thirteenth century. One of them, on the authority of a demon whom he had conjured, informed Edmund, Earl of Kent that Edward II was still alive, although Edward III had already been proclaimed King; in 1402 the inclement weather which nearly destroyed the army of Henry IV in his campaign against 'that great magician, damn'd Glendower' was attributed by many to the diabolic activities of the Friars Minors.[21] A convent of Friars was of the same number as a coven of witches and its talents for divination and exorcism made it particularly liable to suspicion of witchcraft.

The sick man, Thomas, whom the Friar in *The Summoner's Tale* visits, is in the grip of wrath. It is true that he has no particular reason to favor the Friar's visit. As he reminds the Friar, he has not seen him for a fortnight. In the meantime he has lost a child. But the Friar's negligence is not the cause of Thomas's mood. His wife eloquently describes his anger and says that in bed he rejects with groans — 'lyk oure boor, lith in oure sty' — (1829) her attempts to make love. It was always assumed, of course, that the sin of wrath came from the Devil. Thomas is, indeed, said to be as one possessed, and mental unbalance was recognized at the time as being one of the qualities of *ira*.

The Friar attributes Thomas' disorder to the Devil. He tells him that the Devil has set his heart on fire (1982), warns him of the 'serpent that so slily crepeth / Under the gras, and styngeth subtilly' (1994–1995), and counsels him to 'hoold nat the develes knyf' always to his heart (2091). More disinterested assessors consider that 'his sike heed is ful of vanytee' (2208), that he is 'in a manere frenesye' (2209), and that his behavior has been inspired by the Devil (2221). The occasion which prompts these last comments is specific. It concerns the 'gift' which Thomas bestows on the Friar for the convent:

> 'A!' thoghte this frere, 'that shal go with me!'
> And doun his hand he launcheth to the clifte,
> In hope for to fynde there a yifte.
> And whan this sike man felte this frere
> Aboute his tuwel grope there and heere,
> Amydde his hand he leet the frere a fart,
> Ther nys no capul, drawynge in a cart,
> That myghte have lete a fart of swich a soun.
> The frere up stirte as dooth a wood leoun, —
> 'A! false cherl,' quod he, 'for Goddes bones!
> This hastow for despit doon for the nones.
> Thou shalt abye this fart, if that I may!'
> (2144–2155)

Thomas' peculiar action is full of meaning in folk tradition. It can denote one of two things. The Devil is said to flee in dismay from human flatulence.[22] A renowned remedy against him, claimed to be effective when all else failed, is to expose one's buttocks and expel *flatus* at him. Luther thought that the Devil feared anal affront most and when he could not get rid of him by jeering at him he would say: 'Teufel ich hab auch in die Hosen geschissen. Hastu es auch gerochen?' This homeopathic cure was one which Luther advocated all his life, and he relates the story of a young lady acquaintance who followed his advice with success — 'Sathanum crepitu ventris fugavit.' But if it could repulse the Devil, the same desperate method could also expel the imps of Satan. It is a curious fact that although Satan's abode was reputed to be a sulphurous dwelling, for centuries noxious fumes were believed to be efficacious in smoking the Devil out of the unhappy demoniac. *The Holkham Bible Picture Book* (fol. 30) shows Judas evacuating a devil *ex ano*, and a friar in the baberies of the north side choir stalls in St. George's Chapel, Windsor, stoops down with bare buttocks to make a similar ejection.[23]

Chaucer carefully prepares for the *flatus* in that he makes the Friar preach the virtues of abstinence and pun on the belching of more substantial clergy.

But he leaves the meaning of the solution tantalizingly ambiguous. Is the act inspired by contempt for the Devil in the form of a Friar or is Thomas expelling the cause of his disorder? Whatever the answer, the Friar's behavior, as expressed through the animal imagery, becomes similar to that already seen in Thomas. He acts as a man demented. Like Thomas he is compared to the swine, an animal recognized both as a receptacle for madness and as the emblem of wrath. But whereas Thomas was at least compared to the domesticated kind, the Friar 'looked, as it were a wilde boor; / He grynte with his teeth, so was he wrooth' (2160–2161).

In this tale, as in *The Miller's Tale*, the cat belongs to the cluster of images which hint at the significance of the roles of the protagonists. The cat's seat on the bench is a vantage point both for food and for commanding the attention of bedridden Thomas. By taking the cat's place, the Friar not only shows his greed and cunning but may suggest that he is a substitute for the demoniac powers with which the cat, by long tradition, is invested.

I believe that Chaucer's approach to the animal figure is sufficiently subtle to warrant this contention. We have already seen that even in regard to animals with which he was undoubtedly familiar, his allusions cannot often be called wholly realistic. The emblematic idea is rarely absent, and if he sometimes appears to be thinking of the genuine characteristics of animals, only infrequently does he seem to be content to use these alone. In some of his most successful figures he makes symbolism, folklore and realistic detail combine to vivify human character and action. The variety and complexity of his approach are even more apparent when we come to examine in detail his treatment of certain animals, both wild and domestic.

V The Boar

THE boar which was hunted in England was the *sus scrofa*, the Eurasian wild boar which had a coat of coarse black hair overlaying a thick, woolly, yellowish brown underfur. Fitzstephen describing London in 1174 says that wild boars frequented the forests surrounding London, and they were still numerous in the fifteenth century.[1] The term 'boar' was applied to the uncastrated male swine, both wild and domesticated. Chaucer usually makes the distinction clear by means of a qualifying adjective: the boars to which the knights in *The Knight's Tale* (1658) and the Friar in *The Summoner's Tale* (2160) are likened are 'wilde'; the boar which is used in describing Thomas' churlish responses to his wife's overtures in bed is clearly a domesticated one — 'he groneth lyk oure boor, lith in oure sty' (*SumT*, III, 1829). But in a further comparison in *The Knight's Tale* (1699) Chaucer omits any distinction, probably because he is translating directly from *Teseida* (v, 80).

Hunting the boar, as described in *Gawain and the Green Knight*, was an excellent if dangerous sport; the domestic animal appears to have been a hunter rather than quarry and constituted such a nuisance routing for food in the streets that even in the time of Edward I it might be killed on sight in the streets of London, the owner having the right to purchase a dead pig for fourpence.[2] Only the swine of St Anthony's hospital in Threadneedle Street, with little bells strung round their necks, were permitted to roam at will in search of garbage. A similar custom was observed in Venice and Florence where Tantony pigs were fattened at the cost of everyone except their owners, eating with impunity and sometimes attacking not only children but grown men.

Existing records provide justification for classifying all swine as wild rather than domesticated. In the second century A.D. Aelian observed that swine, from sheer gluttony, did not spare even their own young nor refrain from eating corpses (x, 16), and throughout the Middle Ages they continued to be dangerous animals. The spectacle of ravenous swine devouring infants is among the medieval phenomena of rapine pictured by Chaucer upon the walls on the temple of Mars in *The Knight's Tale*:

> Yet saugh I Woodnesse, laughynge in his rage,
> Armed Compleint, Outhees, and fiers Outrage;
> The careyne in the busk, with throte ycorve;
> A thousand slayn, and nat of qualm ystorve;
> The tiraunt, with the pray by force yraft;
> The toun destroyed, ther was no thyng laft.
> Yet saugh I brent the shippes hoppesteres;
> The hunte strangled with the wilde beres;
> The sowe freten the child right in the cradel.
>
> (2011–2019)

Dante in the *Inferno* (xxx, 22–34) compares Gianni Schicchi to a hog which attacks Capocchio, and like Dante Chaucer is depicting not the wild boar nor a demoniacal swine but the wild yet domestic hog which, once liberated from the sty, seizes upon anything which may stay its hunger. Chaucer vivifies the scene by referring to children *in the cradle*, and it is precisely to such incidents that contemporary records refer. Indeed, from the thirteenth to the seventeenth century, hogs were tried and condemned to be hung for killing and partially eating children, and even as late as 1820 a pig was discovered devouring a child aged a year and a half in its hedge trough at Newton St Cyres, Devon.[3]

According to John of Bridlington in 1370, Edward II was thought by some to be a carter's son who had been substituted by a nurse after the real son of Edward I was badly mauled by a sow. Typical of the records of the period is one regarding Agnes Perone, aged six months, of the Parish of St Giles, Oxford, May 7, 1392. 'Witnesses said that a sow ate off the head of the said Agnes, even to the nose, and so she died, and the sow was arrested.' Occasionally a victim who survived sought to establish legally that the loss of an ear was the result of such an accident and not a punishment for a misdemeanor.[4]

Chaucer's inclusion of the sow in the temple of Mars has also an iconographical significance. From an ancient fragment preserved in Plutarch's *Moralia* (IV, 'Amatorius' 13), it seems that Mars as the destroyer was represented by a boar among the Greeks and that the boar symbolized his antigenerative attributes. 'Blind is he, O women,' declares the poet, 'who does not perceive that Ares, in the form of a boar, sets all evils in commotion' — 'τυφλὸς γάρ, ὦ γυναῖκες οὐδ' ὁρῶν Ἄρης/συὸς προσώπῳ πάντα τυρβάζει κακά.'

Whether Chaucer was aware of this relationship we do not know, but he must certainly have known of the significance of the sow in apposition to Diana. Diana, in her role of Lucina, goddess of childbirth, was often depicted with a sow suckling her young. Martial records that in a representation of Diana in one of the great Roman festivals, a pregnant wild sow was killed which in its death gave birth in honor of Lucina (*de Spectac.* xv, 12–14). By assigning the sow to Mars, Chaucer stresses the emblematic contrasts of the two deities.

Chaucer also uses a proverbial expression, 'they walwe as doon two pigges in a poke' (4278), in *The Reeve's Tale*. Alayn approaches the Miller's bed in mistake for that of his fellow clerk and tells him he has seduced the Miller's daughter:

> . . . 'Thou John, thou swynes-heed, awak,
> For Cristes saule, and heer a noble game.
> For by that lord that called is seint Jame,
> As I have thries in this shorte nyght
> Swyved the milleres doghter bolt upright,
> Whil thow hast, as a coward, been agast.'
> (4262–4267)

Swynesheed means 'boor' or 'sluggard,' and probably owes its currency partly to *swineherd* which had already come to be used as a derogatory term. But the listener's reaction is anything but lethargic. The outraged Miller catches Alayn by the throat, and soon the two men are fighting on the floor, with broken noses and mouths.

> 'Ye, false harlot,' quod the millere, 'hast?
> A, false traitour! false clerk!' quod he,
> 'Thow shalt be deed, by Goddes dignitee!
> Who dorste be so boold to disparage
> My doghter, that is come of swich lynage?'
> And by the throte-bolle he caughte Alayn,
> And he hente hym despitously agayn,
> And on the nose he smoot hym with his fest.
> Doun ran the blody streem upon his brest;
> And in the floor, with nose and mouth tobroke,
> They walwe as doon two pigges in a poke.
> (4268–4278)

The proverbial expression 'a pig in a poke' is said to have arisen from the custom of purchasing a pig in a sack. Sometimes a dishonest trader slipped in a cat instead of a pig. 'Two pigs in a poke', however, seems to have the same meaning as 'thei faren ofte as don doggis in a poke,'[5] that is, they quarrel and fight. The term has an ironic appropriateness in that the fight is in a dark, confined area, and it is the kind of plebeian simile one might expect the Reeve to use.

The expressions 'his berd, as any sowe or fox, was reed' and 'reed as the brustles of a sowes erys' (Gen Prol, i, 552, 556) have also been regarded as proverbial but as far as the second phrase is concerned I have found no evidence supporting this claim. Seemingly proverbial are comparisons to the bristles of swine without reference to the color red — 'nought worth the brestel of a swin,' and 'bristled hij were as hogges'. Clearly the animal's bristles attracted much attention, one romancer claiming that 'a sowe /. . . hadde so grete bristells on her bakke that it trayled on the grounde,'[6] and Chaucer's similes appear to be based on factual description. Illustrations of pigs on misericords and in manuscripts show that they bear little resemblance to their smooth, sleek skinned descendants. They are usually represented with a ridge of bristles similar to those of a wild boar. As a chief source of meat, lard and tallow for candles, swine were important. Even the poor widow had three large ones (NPT, vii, 2830). Not surprisingly, they were a popular subject for illustration and were often vigorously depicted in Books of Hours and in marginal illustrations of country activities. The domestic variety was predominantly red. The swine eating acorns under a tree in the Bedford Book of Hours are red (fol. 11), and in the December illustration the frantic hog against which the farmer is spiritedly wielding his axe is covered with red bristles (fol. 12). The phantom pigs which Giraldus Cambrensis in Topographia Hibernica (ii, xix) describes as being produced by magic were red probably because that was the usual color of the animal, and certainly medieval illustrators thought that Biblical swine were red. In the Holkham Bible Picture Book children who mock the Christ child are turned into swine with red bristles and red noses (fol. 16), and the taloned and winged demons cast out by Christ enter the gaping mouths of brownish or reddish swine with decidedly red bristles and ears (fol. 24).

But if Chaucer's similes have a factual basis, their application to the Miller suggests that he may also be thinking of the symbolism attached to the boar. The boar, both wild and domesticated, was a symbol of lechery.[7] Clement of Alexandria, expounding on Moses' reasons for forbidding it as an item of diet, tells of its immoderate salacity (PG, ix, col. 81). The pseudo-Vincentian Speculum morale (iii, ii, 20) in the first half of the fourteenth century makes a similar equation, and the writer of Jacob's Well remarks that 'þe leccherous man or woman is lyche a swyn, þat louythe to be in a foul wose.'[8] In an illustration of la Pelerinage de la vie humaine lechery attacking the pilgrim is represented as Venus riding on a huge boar (fols. 83, 86v). Boethius also makes a similar equation which Chaucer translates: 'and if he be ploungid in fowle and unclene luxuris, he is witholden in the foule delices of the fowle sowe' (iv, pr. 3, 121–124). With regard to the Miller, the simile has symbolical implications which accord with other details in the portrait.

In *The Wife of Bath's Prologue* and *The Parson's Tale*, a Biblical proverb serves to make a direct analogy between the swine and lecherous humanity. Jankyn, haranguing his wife, declares: ' "A fair womman, but she be chaast also,/Is lyk a gold ryng in a sowes nose" ' (784–785). The Parson, quoting the same proverb of Solomon, 'a fair womman that is a fool of hire body lyk to a ryng of gold that were in the groyn of a soughe,' — adds a vigorous comparison: 'For right as a soughe wroteth in everich ordure, so wroteth she hire beautee in the stynkynge ordure of synne' (155–156). Nor can we be certain that Chaucer in *The Knight's Tale* is thinking only of the boar in the hunt when he likens Palamon and Arcite to boars on two occasions in the same fight:

> As wilde bores gonne they to smyte,
> That frothen whit as foom for ire wood.
> Up to the ancle foghte they in hir blood.
> (1658–1660)
> And whan this duc was come unto the launde,
> Under the sonne he looketh, and anon
> He was war of Arcite and Palamon,
> That foughten breme, as it were bores two.
> (1696–1699)

It is true that such a figure applied to two young men fighting over a girl is most appropriate in that boars at breeding time are said to fight with extreme ferocity. Aristotle claimed that they often fought with such fury that both combatants succumbed (*HA*, vi, 18, 2). But as a result of the Biblical incident of the evil spirits and the herd of swine, the swine's traditional reputation was often allied to mental disorders, and when Chaucer describes the fighters as being 'for ire wood' he is probably using 'wood' in the sense that he sometimes uses it elsewhere to denote the irrational quality attendant upon lust.

Theseus is to expose the absurdity of such passion, and the humorous exaggeration inherent in the description of the two knights fighting ankle-deep in their blood suggests that Chaucer is criticizing the excesses of courtly love. We have already noted that Theseus' hart hunt under the auspices of Diana is a virtuous hunt. If it is designed to stress the nobility and wisdom which he displays elsewhere, then the substitution of the boars instead of the hart as his quarry has a further significance. Early in English sculpture the hunter as priest is seen in pursuit of the boar. At St Mary's Parish church near Torquay he is wearing a chasuble, such as is seen in early representations of Saxon prelates, with a stole, and he winds the horn of salvation. Similar hunts appear on Norman doorways of churches at Brampton, Carston and

Little Langford in Wiltshire.[9] To exegetical writers Theseus exemplifies the epitome of wisdom, the great ruler of the city whose patron saint was Minerva. Chaucer establishes him as a merciful judge immediately after his encounter with the two young men:

> . . . 'Fy
> Upon a lord that wol have no mercy,
> But been a leon, bothe in word and dede,
> To hem that been in repentance and drede,
> As wel as to a proud despitous man
> That wol mayntene that he first bigan.
> That lord hath litel of discrecioun,
> That in swich cas kan no divisioun,
> But weyeth pride and humblesse after oon.'
>
> (*KnT*, 1, 1773–1781)

Just as the representation of the boar hunt described above denoted the forgiveness of repentant sinners, so Theseus is offering mercy to those that 'been in repentaunce and drede.'

The boar hunt also appears in decorative art in illustration of Meleager's chase of the Calydonian boar such as was anciently depicted on sarcophagus in the Conservatori in Rome and at Athens, and Chaucer has several allusions to this event. The most detailed presentation of this incident occurs as an interpretation of Troilus' dream in *Troilus and Criseyde*. Our concern, however, is not with Cassandra's account for which Chaucer is mainly indebted to Statius' *Thebaid* but with the boar in the dream itself which may throw light on one of the most puzzling aspects of the work.

In Boccaccio's version of the dream in *Filostrato* (vii, 23–24), Troilus sees his mistress beneath the feet of a great boar and it tears out her heart with its snout. Chaucer divides the elements of the one dream into two dreams. The first dream occurs after Criseyde has been debating with herself whether to yield to Troilus' love. A nightingale gladdens her heart by singing a love song from a tree outside her window. She then falls asleep and dreams that an eagle tears out her heart, replacing it with its own:

> And as she slep, anonright tho hire mette
> How that an egle, fethered whit as bon,
> Under hire brest his longe clawes sette,
> And out hire herte he rente, and that anon,
> And dide his herte into hire brest to gon,
> Of which she nought agroos, ne nothynge smerte;
> And forth he fleigh, with herte left for herte.
>
> (ii, 925–931)

Chaucer still assigns the dream of the boar to Troilus but alters some of the circumstances:

So on a day he leyde hym doun to slepe,
And so byfel that in his slep hym thoughte
That in a forest faste he welk to wepe
For love of here that hym these peynes wroughte;
And up and doun as he the forest soughte,
He mette he saugh a bor with tuskes grete,
That slepte ayeyn the bryghte sonnes hete.

And by this bor, fast in his armes folde,
Lay, kissyng ay, his lady bryght, Criseyde,
For sorwe of which, whan he it gan byholde,
And for despit, out of his slep he breyde.

(v, 1233–1243)

The reason for the introduction of a white eagle is obscure. Chaucer may simply use it to denote royalty, a perfect symbol in its whiteness, for the noble Troilus. A saint once appeared to the sinful St Mary of Oegines as an eagle — 'she sawe an egil vpon hir breste, þat as in a welle plonged the bile in hir breste' — but it was her sorrow that he carried away with him, not her heart.[10] A white eagle also appears in *The Knight's Tale* (2178) but, since white eagles are unknown, it is possible that here and also in *Troilus and Criseyde* Chaucer may be using eagle generically, as he does in *The Parliament of Fowls* (332–340) to cover goshawk, falcon, sparrowhawk or merlin. The falcon, emblematic of courage and nobility, would again be a fitting symbol for Troilus, and four stanzas later Pandarus may be referring to Troilus as a falcon if he uses 'don thy hood' figuratively to refer to the hood of a falcon (ii, 954). But although Troilus is likened to a bird of prey when he is about to consummate his love (iii, 1191) the figure is not sustained. Greeting him on his return from hunting trips, Criseyde is described as being 'as fressh as faukoun comen out of muwe' (iii, 1184).

The question also arises why Chaucer should transfer to the eagle the active qualities of the boar and make the boar passive, slumbering through the kisses of the faithless lady. The contrast emphasizes fundamental differences between the two suitors. The eagle exchanging hearts suggests the sincere wooer, a sleeping boar a gross, indifferent one. The boar was, as has already been noted, widely recognized as a symbol of lust. Chaucer's Diomede does, in fact, behave as the worldly minded, unabashed sinner to which the boar is equated in the tale of Trajan in the *Gesta Romanorum* (lxxxiii), and the boar is a more appropriate image for him than it is for Boccaccio's Greek warrior. Boccaccio's Diomede falls in love with the heroine; Chaucer's does not. As for Criseyde, her love affair with Troilus, reluctant though she was to embark upon it, seems to create in her a longing for a new experience. In the Greek camp her unhappy heart is set on fire 'thorugh remembraunce of that she gan desire' (v, 721), and the nature of the second dream implies that the new affair is differently motivated. Criseyde is no longer passive, no longer the 'sely larke' in the grip of the sparrowhawk (iii, 1191–1192). Confronted by the symbol of lust, she is active, 'kissing ay' the sleeping boar. Boccaccio's heroine is left heartless as a result of the boar's surgery. Not so Criseyde. The point is emphasized by the doubt which Chaucer implies:

> I fynde ek in the stories elleswhere,
> Whan thorugh the body hurt was Diomede
> Of Troilus, tho wepte she many a teere,
> Whan that she saugh his wyde wowndes blede;
> And that she took, to kepen hym, good hede;
> And for to helen hym of his sorwes smerte,
> Men seyn — I not — that she yaf hym hire herte.
>
> (v, 1044–1050)

As has often been remarked, Chaucer takes pains to make the heroine's capitulation understandable: she is by nature 'the ferfulleste wight' (ii, 450) and 'tendre-herted, slydynge of corage' (v, 825). Her sense of insecurity is all the more convincing because we are aware that she was precipitated into the arms of Troilus by Pandarus. Had the affair progressed naturally and, as would have been inevitable with a lover as diffident as Troilus, slowly, it might have seemed more solid to her, enabling her to face separation and loneliness with more assurance. More than one critic has remarked that Pandarus' pleasure in the affair seems to be too great. When he interprets the dream of the boar for Troilus, Pandarus is made to reveal unconsciously his motives. With a sure knowledge of psychology, Chaucer indirectly provides an explanation for his character's conduct, an explanation supported elsewhere in the text. At the same time he retains our sympathy for his creation because there is no reason to suppose that Pandarus understands what impelled him to accelerate the romance.

Pandarus is represented as an unhappy lover, 'bounden in a snare,' unsuccessful himself but able to help other lovers to success: 'I love oon best, and that me smerteth sore;/ And yet, peraunter, kan I reden the,/ And nat myself' (i, 667–669). He says that Troilus knows the identity of his lady but her name is never disclosed. Although his activities modify the character of the heroine who, in Boccaccio, makes the assignation herself, many scholars seem to feel that Chaucer has created in Pandarus something far more distasteful than the dashing intriguer Pandaro. It is possible that, in communicating human relationships, Chaucer has gone beyond his ostensible conception and that his creation has its own imaginative logic. The man who, in the middle of all his gay busyness of thrusting the love-letter in Criseyde's bosom, and japing, can be caught unawares, 'in a studye' (ii, 1180), seems to have incalculable, introverted qualities. As Criseyde rightly says: 'Whoso seeth yow, knoweth yow ful lite' (iii, 1568). Certain statements suggest that Pandarus would like to enjoy with his niece the relationship which Troilus is to have, and that the unnatural pleasure which he takes in furthering Troilus' romance may be inspired by the desire for vicarious gratification.

The second book, in which Pandarus is to set the affair in motion, opens with a reference to May 3, the Feast of Floralia, on which love was consummated. Pandarus is depicted as a frustrated lover:

> That Pandarus, for al his wise speche,
> Felt ek his part of loves shotes keene,
> That, koude he nevere so wel of lovyng preche,
> It made his hewe a-day ful ofte greene.
> So shop it that hym fil that day a teene
> In love, for which in wo to bedde he wente,
> And made, er it was day, ful many a wente.
>
> (ii, 57–63)

He is awakened by the swallow's song. It brings thoughts of an unlawful love which was not merely adulterous but involved the ravishing of a close relative, an *adfinis*, with whom such an association was forbidden on grounds of consanguinity, as indeed it was between uncle and niece under canon law.[11] Shortly afterwards he declares his love for his niece:

> 'Ye ben the womman in this world lyvynge,
> Withouten paramours, to my wyttynge,
> That I best love, and lothest am to greve,
> And that ye weten wel youreself, I leve.'
>
> (ii, 235–238)

Criseyde makes an equivalent protestation — 'ye ben he that I love moost and triste' (ii, 247), and she is astounded when she learns he has come to sue for a friend. Indeed, her shock is so great that she bursts into tears and feels that he has betrayed her:

> ... 'Allas, for wo! Why nere I deed?
> For of this world the feyth is al agoon.
> Allas! what sholden straunge to me doon,
> When he, that for my beste frend I wende,
> Ret me to love, and sholde it me defende?
>
> 'Allas! I wolde han trusted, douteles,
> That if that I, thorugh my disaventure,
> Hadde loved outher hym or Achilles,

Ector, or any mannes creature,
Ye nolde han had no mercy ne mesure
On me, but alwey had me in repreve.
This false world, allas! who may it leve?'
(ii, 409–420)

The relationship between them, accompanied by affectionate physical gestures and verbal intimacies, is exceptionally close. The completeness with
which Pandarus identifies his own wishes with those of Troilus and the intensity with which he presses his friend's claims are explicable if Pandarus
sees the young man as a projection of himself:

'But if ye late hym deyen, I wol sterve —
Have here my trouthe, nece, I nyl nat lyen —
Al sholde I with this knyf my throte kerve.'
With that the teris bruste out of his yën,
And seide, 'If that ye don us bothe dyen,
Thus gilteles, than have ye fisshed fayre!
What mende ye, though that we booth appaire?'
(ii, 323–329)

Pandarus' dramatic threat to cut his throat seems to suggest the intensity of
his involvement. Chaucer did not need to live in the twentieth century to perceive the sexual significance of the image of the knife. He uses it even more
emphatically elsewhere: the Wife of Bath in order to inform her lover that for
the pleasures of the bed he will be financially rewarded invents a dream in
which he slays her as she lay flat on her back in bed — 'and al my bed was ful
of verray blood/ . . . For blood bitokeneth gold, as me was taught' (WB Prol,
III, 579–581).

Even if Pandarus is only 'japing' he is at that moment pleading with her to
enter into a relationship which is ultimately sexual, and the image of the knife
appears again when thoughts of sexual consummation are uppermost in his
mind. Having succeeded in getting the couple to spend the night together, he
has apparently passed a wakeful night himself[12] and he loses no time in
seeking out Criseyde while she is still in bed. When she reproaches him for his
stratagem and blushingly hides her face under the sheet,

. . . Pandarus gan under for to prie
And seyde, 'Nece, if that I shal be ded,
Have here a swerd and smyteth of my hed!'
With that his arm al sodeynly he thriste
Under hire nekke, and at the laste hire kyste.
(iii, 1571–1575)

There is no parallel to this scene in the *Filostrato*, and the author's tone is,
in itself, obtuse at this point:

> I passe al that which chargeth nought to seye.
> What! God foryaf his deth, and she al so
> Foryaf. . . .
>
> (iii, 1576–1578)

Pandarus seems to be preying on two young people for the sake of an experience which he can only have through them. From the beginning it is not the spiritual affair which it is for Troilus, hence his immediate reaction to the news of Criseyde's departure is to give advice which he must know will be unacceptable but which seems to come from the heart:

> 'And over al this, as thow wel woost thiselve,
> This town is ful of ladys al aboute;
> And, to my doom, fairer than swiche twelve
> As evere she was, shal I fynde in som route,
> Yee, on or two, withouten any doute.
> Forthi be glad, myn owen deere brother!
> If she be lost, we shal recovere an other.'
>
> (iv, 400–406)

Criseyde has not yet left Troy but Pandarus can already speak of her in the past tense — 'fairer . . . / As evere she was' — because for him, now that consummation has been achieved, one woman is as good as another. It is true that his remarks are intended to comfort Troilus and that the narrator himself stresses, as Boccaccio did not, that Pandarus' proposal to abandon Criseyde is prompted by his desperate concern for his friend (iv, 428–431). But he appears to dismiss his own obligations towards his niece too readily, and to regard her not as someone for whom he has expressed great love, but as any woman. His alternative proposal that Troilus should fight for the possession of the lady (iv, 582–630) is, as he must be well aware, unacceptable because such an act would violate the principle of secrecy and destroy Criseyde's reputation. Nevertheless, he is prepared to make his proposal stand as a test of Criseyde's fidelity: 'And if she wilneth fro the for to passe,/ Thanne is she fals; so love hire wel the lasse' (iv, 615–616).

Pandarus is cynical, pragmatic, and, it seems, middle-aged. He is impatient with idealistic love, and his evaluation of Troilus' great love affair as 'casuel plesaunce' (iv, 419) suggests that the pleasure and importance of the affair to him lies solely in its physical gratification.

What would be a popular medieval interpretation of a dream about a boar and a woman embracing each other? In the romance of *Merlin*, the Emperor has a dream which may be regarded as comparable. He dreams of a huge sow, and of twelve 'lionsewes' (young lions) who lie with her. The sow signifies his own lascivious spouse.[13] In view of the symbolism of the animal, it would be difficult to avoid giving a sexual significance to such a dream. Pandarus, however, professes to see Criseyde and her father, youth and age, in an embrace. In order to make the image acceptable and to erase completely the sexual import of the dream, a factor which Troilus has already recognized, he claims to see Calchas dying and Criseyde embracing him in sorrow:

> 'Peraunter, ther thow dremest of this boor,
> It may so be that it may signifie,
> Hire fader, which that old is and ek hoor,
> Ayeyn the sonne lith, o poynt to dye,
> And she for sorwe gynneth wepe and crie,
> And kisseth hym, ther he lith on the grounde:
> Thus sholdestow thi drem aright expounde!'
> (v, 1282–1288)

Troilus has said nothing about Criseyde exhibiting grief. 'And she for sorwe gynneth wepe and crie' is Pandarus' own embellishment. Nor has Criseyde, at any point, exhibited any strong affection for her father. What seems to be produced here is a censored version of Pandarus' own fantasy. Impotent himself to achieve the desired relationship with his niece, he now sees himself passive, the very symbol of carnal desire, securing what has been denied him in life.

In further allusions to the boar, Chaucer makes the animal serve as a term of abuse. In *The House of Fame* (iii, 1777) those eager for fame are called 'masty swyn', a brief epithet which conveys the idea of greed and suggests that just as the animal has gorged himself on berries so those anxious for recognition are bloated with their own importance. In *The Prologue to the Manciple's Tale* (40) the Manciple, incensed by the smell coming from the mouth of the drunken cook, calls him a 'stynkyng swyn,' and at the conclusion of *The Pardoner's Tale*, the angry Host expresses his contempt for the Pardoner by saying that his 'coillons' should be enshrined in the excrement of a pig:

> 'But, by the croys which that Seint Eleyne fond,
> I wolde I hadde thy coillons in myn hond
> In stide of relikes or of seintuarie.
> Lat kutte hem of, I wol thee helpe hem carie;
> They shul be shryned in an hogges toord!'
> (951–955)

The enshrining is, of course, a reference back to the false relics which the Pardoner wished the pilgrims to kiss, and the Host uses *seintuarie* in the sense of a 'shrine for relics.' The juxtaposition of 'relics' and 'coillons,' particularly appropriate here, occurs also in the *Roman de la rose* (7108) where Reason accused of lewdness, asks whether 'relic' would be considered a filthy word had he called 'relics' 'coillons' and 'coillons' 'relics.' 'Coillon,' Reason declares, 'is a good word.' If Chaucer has this reference in mind he may be stressing that the Pardoner himself debases the meaning of sacred relics by his misuse of them.

The allusion to the pig emphasizes the savageness of the Host's insult and the intensity of his revulsion.[14]

These last three images are appropriately colloquial and have an earthiness which is made even more striking by the brevity and ease of expression. The latter qualities sometimes conceal the skill with which Chaucer makes the image of the boar serve his artistic purposes. Any apparent perfunctoriness is illusory. Recognizing that the boar's attributes, such as boorishness, ferocity, lechery and uncleanliness, are well-known, he is able to charge even a simple expression with sensation. Its effectiveness, however, also relies on the astonishing way in which he makes the animal allusion seem to emerge naturally from the situation, and to be so thoroughly appropriate to the occasion as to appear inevitable.

VI. *The Hare*

THE hare in medieval times was not only a favorite beast of the Chase but a creature endowed by folklore with various physical and psychological peculiarities. Chaucer alludes to it briefly either as part of the local scene or as an animal to which man can be compared, and he seems to be familiar with both hunting and popular lore. While he makes use of traditional ideas, he applies them subtly, and the full significance of his allusions is not always readily apparent in immediate context.

Even the direct reference to the hare as an animal of the chase underlines an important aspect of character. In *The General Prologue* the Monk is described as one who loves 'venerie':

> Grehoundes he hadde as swift as fowel in flight;
> Of prikyng and of huntyng for the hare
> Was al his lust, for no cost wolde he spare.
>
> (190–192)

The specific mention of the hare shows that the Monk is a hunting specialist. The hare is praised above all other animals in the hunting treatises.[1] Twiti, in

la Vénerie early in the fourteenth century, declares that 'she is the most mer-
veylous beste of the world.' Edward, second Duke of York, following *le Livre
de la chasse* by Gaston de Foix, Chaucer's contemporary, remarks in *The
Master of Game* that 'the hare is a good little beast, and much sport and liking
is the hunting of her, more than that of any other beast that *any man knoweth.
. . .*' Dame Juliana Barnes, in *The Book of St. Albans* first printed in 1486,
follows Twiti and says that the hare 'kyng shall be calde of all venery.'

The Monk is also a true huntsman in that he tracks and hunts the hare in
the proper fashion. All the hunting experts insist on the employment of dogs.[2]
Twiti remarks that the hare, in common with the hart, the boar and the wolf,
is *enchased*, hunted with greyhounds after having been tracked with the help
of the *limier*, whereas the buck, the doe, the fox and other vermin are *encoylid*,
pursued by dogs without prior assistance from the *limier*. Edward, second
Duke of York, strongly disapproves of the practice of snaring hares and is
careful to point out that it does not occur in England:

> Men slay hares with greyhounds and with running hounds by strength,
> *as in England, but elsewhere they slay them also* with small pockets and with
> purse nets, and with small nets, *with hare pipes*, and with long nets, and
> with small cords that men cast where they make their breaking of the
> small twigs when they go to their pastures. . . . But, *truly, I trow no good
> hunter would slay them so for any good.*

Sir Thomas Cockaine, whose work is based extensively on the earlier *Book of
Tristram*, a hunting bible referred to by Malory but now lost, also emphasizes
the use of dogs in the hunting of the hare.

Despite the text 'that hunters ben nat hooly men' (*Gen Prol*, 1, 178),
hunting prelates were common at the time and provoked strong criticism.
Langland would punish with death those prelates who hunted on Sunday, and
his parson Sloth confesses that he prefers hare hunting to construing psalms
for his parishioners; another writer of the period declares that 'thise abbotes
and priours don agein here rihtes;/ Hii riden wid hauk and hound and contre-
feten knihtes,'[3] and on a misericord in the church of Nantwich, Cheshire,
Renard appears as a hunting monk, with a hare suspended on a pole behind
him, and a bird in his hand.[4] The only appropriate ecclesiastical hunter of
hares is that cited in Knighton's *Chronicon* (11, 127) as William de Cloune,
Abbot of Leicester, 1345–1378, a friend of John of Gaunt, who stocked the
woods of Leicester Abbey and the surrounding forest with deer in order that
the King and his retinue might hunt there, but in order to know whether he
was Chaucer's Monk, we would need to have more information about hunting
Monks and about Chaucer than is now possible. We do know, however, that
hare-hunting was an aristocratic and social pastime and that Chaucer's
reference not only puts the Monk among the hunting élite but reveals his
disregard of two important principles of monastic discipline, labor and
claustration.

This reference to the hare also seems to suggest that the Monk is a keen lover of the flesh. The pursuit of small furry animals is associated with the hunt of Venus and the implications of 'deyntee hors,' 'venerie' and 'prikyng' are sustained both by the kind of animal which the Monk hunts and by possibility of a pun on 'hare.' I have already remarked that a similar pun existed in French where the rabbit, an animal renowned for its fertility, became a symbol for part of the female anatomy and hence for the whole woman: Latin *cunnus* developing into the old French *con* which, with the diminutive added, became *conin*, while *cuniculus* became *conil* or *connil*, and then *conin*.[5] Chaucer thus carefully vouches for the Monk's bland apostasy, and prepares us for the thrust in the final line: 'A fat swan loved he best of any roost' (*Gen Prol*, I, 206).

The line may indicate no more than that the Monk is an all-round *bon viveur*, and show why he is 'ful fat and in good poynt.' His evaluation of ecclesiastical opinion as a plucked hen and an oyster indicates that his mind is on food and that he disparages both a cheap fowl and the mollusc freely permitted in monastic diet. The proverbial expression concerning the wet hen is an intensification of 'nat worth an hen' (*WBT*, III, 1112). Its appearance as *mokraya kuritsa* in Russia and *mokra kura* in Poland suggests that the plucked hen may have been despised on aesthetic rather than gastronomic grounds, but Friar Thomas' lament in *The Summoner's Tale* (2099–2102) that he and his brethren have been forced to eat oysters in order to save for their Building Fund, shows that such shellfish was regarded as poor fare. The swan, on the other hand, was so popular that few medieval menus of feasts fail to include it. It was usually elaborately prepared to come first in the succession of dishes, and although its price was high — six shillings at Christmas compared with three-pence for a goose, twopence for a partridge and twopence halfpenny for a chicken — and it could only be kept on license from the Crown, gastronomically it held high place throughout the Middle Ages.

It is possible that in the Monk's house the swan is not allowed on meatless days. Odo, second abbot of Cluny, gives a horrifying *exemplum* of a monk who choked to death on a chicken bone after arguing that it was not flesh because birds and fish were one — 'volatile . . . non est caro, volatilia enim et pisces unam habent originem et aequalem creationem' (*PL*, CXXXIII, col. 78). Later there were certain dietary relaxations, but although the term 'meat' may not have included fowl, Knowles states that there is no definite evidence that fowl was allowed.[6] In specifying the swan as the Monk's preference, Chaucer may be demonstrating the way in which the worldly ecclesiastic 'leete olde thynges pace.' The Monk is no ascetic and he enjoys his favorite dish, regardless of rules.

The swan is also an ancient sign for both a tavern and a brothel and was one of the insignia of the early London stews.[7] Its wide use as an inn sign is accounted for by an old Dutch saying to the effect that the bird is fond of liquid, a joke current in many parts of Europe:

De Swann voert ieder kroeg, zoowel in dorp als stad,
Om dat hy altyd graeg is met de bek in't nat.

It is also referred to in 'Colin Blowbol's Testament,' where it is associated with Sloth, the sin which the Parson, in his condemnation of negligence in the service of God and 'reccheleesnesse' (*ParsT*, x, 679, 709, 710), would certainly ascribe to the Monk:

> Alas Sloth, that devoute woman
> Which hath the proprete of a swan
> Evyr to be in plenty of licour[8] . . .

Since Chaucer seems to be aware of this proverbial attribute of the swan in that he describes affluent friars as 'walkyng as a swan/ al vynolent as botel in the spence' (*SumT*, III, 1931), he may be implying that the Monk is fond of the bottle and the brothel. On September 14, 1372, John, the abbot of Wellowe and two of his canons were investigated for having similar interests. Their alleged offences were in connection with one, 'fetys Jonet,' whose chamber they had rebuilt with monastic timber instead of their own roofless refectory, and in whose company they had indulged in wine, best Grimesby ale, poultry, sucking pigs and other delicacies.[9]

The allusion to the hare in *The General Prologue* reveals that Daun Piers is no mild apostate from monastic rule. A further allusion in *The Tale of Sir Thopas* illustrates the nature of a knightly quest. The Flemish Knight 'priketh thurgh a fair forest,/ Therinne is many a wilde best,/ Ye, both bukke and hare' (754–756). The last line seems to have an ironic force, and the two animals a special significance. The 'bukke and hare' are usually regarded as beasts of the Chase, such as might have been hunted in Flemish as well as in English forests. They were certainly widely appreciated by huntsmen, and Chaucer himself displays a sporting knowledge of both animals: he has five deer hunts and he knows that the hare is coursed with hounds. Since Sir Thopas' hunting ability has already been stressed (736–737), the humor in the passage may simply be in the play on 'wilde', an adjective meaning 'undomesticated' as well as 'ferocious.'[10] The objection to such an interpretation is that both animals are hunted with dogs, and Sir Thopas has no dogs with him. The passage appears to have a subtler irony if 'bukke and hare' are considered not as game animals but as creatures possessing certain traditional attributes in common.

Chaucer may be thinking of the lack of courage traditionally ascribed to both the deer family and to the hare. Aristotle (*HA*, i, 1, 14) remarks on their timidity, and Isidore (xii, 1, 22–24) observes that the deer is 'timidum animal et inbelle,' and the hare 'satis timidum.' Chaucer himself in *The Parliament of Fowls* refers to 'the dredful ro' (195), and to the hare cowering in fear in *The Shipman's Tale* (104–105). But Chaucer's 'carpet knight' cannot seriously be considered as a follower of blood sports. He is in pursuit of different game, being inspired by violent romantic longings. Chaucer may have selected these two animals from the many listed in the chivalric accounts which he was parodying because of their conspicuous role in the Floralia. Chaucer was familiar with the description of the feast of Flora in Ovid's *Fasti* (v, 72), and he appears to give peculiar significance to May 3, the climactic day of the celebrations.[11] The two animals particularly associated with this licentious event are the roe and the hare, and Ovid describes how the 'imbelles capreae sollicitusque lepus' were hunted in the arena as a prelude to the orgies (v, 372). Since Sir Thopas 'fil in love-longynge' (772), Chaucer's selection of the two animals seems appropriate.

Such explanations assume that *bukke* means the male of the deer. But, with his liking for word-play, Chaucer may have kept in mind the alternative meaning and intended to suggest the he-goat also, thus juxtaposing the same two animals named in the description of the Pardoner in *The General Prologue* (684, 688). *Bukke* in this sense occurs extensively in Middle English, and Chaucer himself uses the phrase 'blowe the bukkes horn' in *The Miller's Tale* (3387) meaning literally 'to idle away time by sounding a goat's horn.' *Bukke* is also applied figuratively in the pejorative sense associated with *hircus*, and it shares with the hare a reputation for extreme lasciviousness. Probably stemming from the extraordinary fertility of the one and the libidinousness of the other, such a reputation has been so persistent as to require little illustration. The goat's nature is said to be so hot that a stone of adamant dissolves in its blood, and Isidore remarks, 'hircus lascivum animal et petulcum et fervens semper ad coitum. Cuius oculi ob libidinem in transversum aspiciunt, unde et nomen traxit' (xii, 1, 14).

The hare's sexual proclivities, which caused him to be associated with Dionysius and Venus, have become proverbial. Like the goat, it was an ancient symbol of generative power and, in the view of the medieval church, it represented unlicensed sexuality. An eleventh-century manuscript at Strasburg, concerned with the symbolism of the hunt depicted in ecclesiastical art and sculpture, states that the hare stands for incontinence, and even as late as the fifteenth century, in a bas-relief under a console on the façade of the cathedral church of St John in Lyons, it appears as a symbol of libidinousness behind Aristotle, the love-besotted philosopher of popular *lai*.[12] Among the scurrilous phrases given for the hare in a Middle English poem in a late thirteenth-century manuscript in *here-serd*, which the editor glosses as 'copulating hare,'[13] and the expression 'as mad as a March hare,' originally referring to the excitability of the hare in rut, indicates the persistence of the hare's reputation.

If the Knight's wild beasts are the goat and hare, they serve as appropriate symbols for a hero inspired by love-longing rather than by derring-do. His 'prikynge' then becomes associated with conduct which, while appropriate to John in *The Reeve's Tale* (4231), is most unseemly in one who 'was chaast and no lechour' (*Thop*, 745), especially since he displays similar abandon (774).

Thus, the phrase has a triple significance which underlines the ridiculousness of the hero's aspirations. As beasts renowned for their timidity, the deer and the hare illustrate the disparity between Sir Thopas' illusions and his immediate situation, and as animals hunted in the arena in the famous Roman celebration of spring and love, they serve to hint that the Knight is embarking on his own Floralia. When *bukke* is given the alternative meaning of 'goat' it is associated with the hare in a common symbolism which makes the nature of Sir Thopas's adventure unmistakeable.

Chaucer also uses the hare in simile for the purpose of illustrating human behaviour. An allusion to the proverbial expression already cited seems implicit in the Friar's remark in *The Friar's Tale*: 'For thogh this Somonour wood were as an hare, / To telle his harlotrye I wol nat spare' (1327-1328). Emerson, quoting Turberville that the hare 'is one of the most melancholike beastes that is,' suggests that the idea in the proverb is connected with that of melancholy attributed to the hare.[14] But melancholy is not the quality the Friar is attributing to the Summoner. *Harlotrye* implies that *wood* is used in the sense that it appears in Trevisa's translation of Higden's *Polychronicon*: 'In þat lond is a lake wonderful and wood (L. *furialis*) for who þat drynkeþ þer of he schal brenne in woodnesse of leccherie' (i, 197). The pun on *hare* and *harlotrye* reinforces the point. What the Friar is saying is that even if the Summoner fornicated as much as a hare, he would not spare the details.

In *The Shipman's Tale* occurs Chaucer's most striking image of the hare:

> 'Nece,' quod he, 'it oghte ynough suffise
> Fyve houres for to slepe upon a nyght,
> But it were for an old appalled wight,
> As been thise wedded men, that lye and dare
> As in a fourme sit a wery hare,
> Were al forstraught with houndes grete and smale.'
>
> (100-105)

The Speaker is Daun John, a bold and handsome monk of thirty (25-26), and he is addressing the 'compaignable and revelous' young wife of a rich merchant of Seint-Denys, in whose house he is 'as famulier . . . / As it is possible any freend to be' (31-32). He is subsequently to seduce her and cheat her in the matter of recompense. Like the Monk in *The General Prologue* (166), he is an 'outridere,' 'an officer, out for to ryde, / To seen hir graunges and hire bernes wyde' (65-66), and he too, to judge from his use of the hunting figure, appears to be familiar with the superior beast of the Chase.

The *form* is a slight depression in the ground in which the hare lies, and the animal, having no definite home and no burrow, is said to be strongly attached to it. Daun John is correct if he is implying that the hare is on its form in the morning, for the hare searches for its food in the evening. He is also correct in referring to 'houndes grete and smale,' for 'limiers', used for tracking the hare, were never any distinct breed of dogs, but were taken from various breeds and specially trained. Although dogs sometimes take the hare before it starts, 'wery' suggests that, in concrete terms, the situation is similar to that described by Turberville:

> I have also seen an Hare runne and stand up two hours before a kennell of houndes, and then she hath started and raysed an other freshe Hare out of her forme and set herselfe downe therein.[15]

But the Monk's thoughts are not on the chase; they are of a kind which make him 'wax al reed' (*ShipT*, VII, 111). He has the good wife on the psychoanalyst's couch and is trying to discover whether her husband satisfies her. Although the hare is a traditional symbol of generative power, the adjectives *appalled* and *wery* hint that, as far as married men are concerned, that power has now waned. Instead, the hare becomes associated with the other quality popularly attributed to it, with timidity, and the hounds may be equated with married women, whose insatiability was the subject of vehement clerical denunciations. In one of Nicholas Bozon's stories, the hare fleeing from dogs is explicitly likened to man fleeing from woman, and the stern advice is 'fugite fornicacionem.'[16] A similar symbolism is suggested by an illustration in an early fourteenth-century manuscript, the *Taymouth Horae* (fol. 69). A hare rears up from the grass as though it has been startled on its form. A lady sends a dog of the greyhound type in pursuit of it.

In his opening gambit, the Monk implies that whereas he is himself young and vigorous, requiring only five hours sleep, the husband, old and physically exhausted, behaves in the matrimonial bed like a frightened hare harried by dogs. After the oblique reference to conjugal relations, his enquiry becomes explicit:

> 'But deere nece, why be ye so pale?
> I trowe, certes, that oure goode man
> Hath yow laboured sith the nyght bigan,
> That yow were nede to resten hastily.'
>
> (106–109)

The suggestion that the wife looks pale as a result of her husband's ardor can only be ironical. Daun John has no grounds for ascribing uxoriousness to his host. Although the Merchant is rich, he is apparently very concerned about his financial affairs and he stresses the precariousness of trade — 'For everemoore we moote stonde in drede / Of hap and fortune in oure chapmanhede' (237–238). He is about to embark on a business deal involving twenty thousand shields (331), and the apparently parenthetical observation 'for he was riche and cleerly out of dette' (376) may imply that he makes love to his wife only after his transaction is successful and his worries are over. His wife clearly resents the time he devotes to his accounts:

> Up to hir housbonde is this wyf ygon,
> And knokketh at his countour boldely.

'Quy la?' quod he. 'Peter! it am I,'
Quod she; 'what, sire, how longe wol ye faste?
How longe tyme wol ye rekene and caste
Youre sommes, and youre bookes, and youre thynges?
The devel have part on all swiche rekenynges!
Ye have ynough, pardee, of Goddes sonde;
Com doun to-day, and lat youre bagges stonde.'

(212–220)

The astute Monk cannot have failed to notice his host's neglect of his wife, particularly when he and the wife take advantage of it to have a clandestine stroll in the garden accompanied only by a maid 'yet under the yerde' (97). According to the time-sequence given, the Merchant and the Monk have drunk and played for 'a day or tweye' (74), and on the third day the Merchant has shut himself up with his accounts 'til it was passed pryme' (88). The time that the Merchant has recently spent with his wife must have been brief, and Daun John knows it. By means of the expressive hunting image, conjuring up the picture of the timid husband, his ardour exhausted, quailing before his insatiable mate, he prepares the accommodating wife for the frank enquiry to follow and is able to elicit information most satisfactory to his purpose. It also adumbrates the conclusion in that the hare has a further characteristic which, metaphorically it seems, the Merchant shares. According to ancient and popular belief, frequently reiterated both in hunting treatises and in encyclopedias, the hare has poor eyesight. Bartholomew remarks on it (lxviii) and the modern Welsh for hare, *ygibddall*, means 'the purblind one.' The Merchant remains unaware of the nature of the transaction between his wife and his 'deere cosyn.' All he knows is that she has spent the money which Daun John gave her without realizing it was payment of a debt to himself. His final request is only that, in the future, she be less generous — 'na be namoore so large' (431).

Two proverbial expressions regarding the hare are applied to love in a bantering, ironic tone, and reflect the practical, commonsense attitude of those who use them. In *The Knight's Tale*, when the Duke discovers that Palamon and Arcite are fighting each other because they are in love with his niece, he suggests that 'the beste game of alle' is

'That she for whom they han this jolitee
Kan hem therfore as muche thank as me.
She woot namoore of al this hoote fare,
By God, that woot a cokkow or an hare!'

(1807–1810)

Neither the phrase, nor, indeed, most of Theseus' speech, is to be found in Boccaccio. There is also a variant reading *of an hare* instead of *or an hare*. Hinckley takes the former reading, saying that he suspects an allusion to some proverb, fable or bit of popular science with which he is unacquainted; Robinson takes the latter, but remarks that both reading and interpretation are doubtful and that there may have been a proverb to the effect that the cuckoo knows little of the hare.[17]

The meaning of the phrase seems clear when popular attributes of both the bird and the animal are taken into account. The cuckoo became associated with unfaithfulness as early as Roman times because of its practice of depositing its eggs in another bird's nest, and Pliny's account of the cuckoo's cannibalism (x, 9, 11) is substantially correct: the young cuckoo ejects its foster-brothers from the nest by dropping them over the side, and the adult cuckoo destroys nests containing other birds or eats the eggs. The cuckoo in *The Parliament of Fowls* is 'ever unkynde' (358) and is addressed by the merlin thus:

> 'Thow mortherere of the heysoge on the braunche
> That broughte the forth, thow [rewthelees] glotoun!
> Lyve thow soleyn, wormes corupcioun!
> For no fors is of lak of thy nature —
> Go, lewed be thow whil the world may dure!'
> (612–616)

The passage is no mere paraphrase of Alanus' statement: 'Illic curruca novercam exuens, materno pietatis ubere, alienam cuculi prolem adoptabat in filium; quae tamen capitali praemiata stipendio, privignum agnoscens filium ignorabat' (*PL*, ccx, col. 436). It suggests that Chaucer is familiar with the bird's habits and it makes a point similar to that implied in Theseus' remark, that the cuckoo is ignorant of the nature of true love.

The hare also has a reputation for being unnatural and lacking in normal affection. It is popularly believed to reproduce without mating and to eat its offspring on occasion, and in actual fact, the father takes no interest in its young.[18]

If Chaucer is referring to the quality which both creatures have in common in folklore, the reading *or* makes good sense and the implication must have been intelligible to his audience. Either reading is possible, however, if Chaucer is again punning on *hare*, as in *The General Prologue* (191) and *The Friar's Tale* (1327), and is using *cokkow* figuratively as in *The Manciple's Tale* (243) where the crow addresses his cuckolded master with the cry 'cokkow! cokkow! cokkow!' Emelye then knows as little of love as a cuckold or a whore, or as a cuckold knows of a whore, i.e., as the cheated husband knows of his wife. Whichever reading is taken, the phrase is presumably proverbial and applies to Emelye only so far as she too is unaware of the passions aroused by true love. Theseus is made to talk cynically about love in contrast to the two courtly lovers. The lapse from high style to homely colloquialism contributes a flippancy to his speech which is consistent with his down-to-earth character.

A similar common-sense attitude towards love is adopted by the Eagle in *The House of Fame*:

'For truste wel that thou shalt here,
When we be come there I seye,
Mo wonder thynges, dar I leye,
And of Loves folk moo tydynges,
Both sothe sawes and lesinges;
And moo loves newe begonne,
And longe yserved loves wonne,
And moo loves casuelly
That ben betyd, no man wot why,
But as a blynd man stert an hare.'

(ii, 672–681)

The last line contains a phrase which is usually taken as proverbial, comparable to the proverbs 'by chance a cripple may grip a hare,' and 'the hare starts when a man least expects it.' In the *Bury Bible* an illuminated initial shows a cripple starting a hare (fol. lv). The Eagle seems to imply that no one knows how casual love affairs begin, unless they begin in the same fortuitous way that a blind man can unintentionally start off a hare, a swift and unpredictable animal.

A further elliptical reference to the hare occurs in connection with Chaucer the pilgrim. In *The Prologue to Sir Thopas* the Host addresses Chaucer:

. . . 'What man artow?' quod he;
'Thou lookest as thou woldest fynde an hare,
For evere upon the ground I se thee stare.'

(695–697)

Fynde an hare is usually interpreted as a hunting figure, the implication being that Chaucer is looking on the ground in a searching manner. One critic, taking *for evere* to mean 'steadily, fixedly at this moment,' considers that 'the Host simply states that at this time Chaucer is staring at the ground as if in search of a rabbit.'[19] But when *fynde an hare* is used as a technical term in the hunting treatises, the understanding is that dogs are employed in the hunt. According to *The Master of Game*, 'the hare cannot be judged, either by the foot or by her fumes (excrements), for she always crotieth in one manner. . . .' Only across a muddy field or, as 'The Mourning of the Hare' shows, in heavy winter snow, is it possible to track a hare by its steps:

Att wyntter in þe depe snove
Men wyl me seche for to trace,
And by my steyppes I ame I-knowe
And followyȝt me fro place to place.

Even the humble, horseless hunter on the misericord at Ely Church has his dogs with him.[20] It seems, then, that if the Host is employing a hunting figure, he is either erroneously assuming that the hare is like the rabbit which has a burrow and can be tracked, or referring to Chaucer himself as a *limier* looking for a hare. It is perhaps worth remarking that among the Chinese a similar expression was proverbially used to denote stupidity. Its basis was a legend told by Han Fei-tsze concerning a husbandman in the state of Sung who was ploughing when he saw a hare dash itself against a tree stump and fall dead. The foolish peasant abandoned his plough, sat down beside the tree stump and waited for another hare to do the same.[21] The Host might well be using such a proverbial expression in his jocular and somewhat patronizing address to the small, plump pilgrim about whom he knows so little. I have, however, found no evidence to suggest that it existed in England.

Another interpretation is possible when the hare is considered in terms of popular superstition. The idea that it was a bad omen to encounter a hare pre-vailed until the end of the nineteenth century not only in England but in parts of Europe and Russia, as well as among Indians, Laplanders, Arabs and South African tribes. The first nine lines of the Middle English poem on the names of the hare states that a man who meets a hare 'shal him neuere be þe bet' unless he puts on the ground what he carries and:

> Blesce him wiþ his helbowe
> And mid wel goed devosioun
> He shall saien an oreisoun
> In þe worshipe of þe hare
> Þenne mai he wel fare. . . .

Then follow seventy-seven deprecatory terms, emphasizing that the hare is one who is 'euelei met' — bad luck to meet.[22] A similar idea is expressed in *Mandeville's Travels*, when the author, maintaining that 'summe bestes han gode meetynge, that is to seye for to meete with hem first at morwe, and summe bestes wykked meetynge,' places the hare in the second category.[23] If the Host is thinking of the popular lore regarding the hare, he may be implying that the expression on Chaucer's face is that of a man anticipating ill-luck. His further description of Chaucer as seeming 'elvyssh by his con-tenaunce' (*Thop Prol*, VII, 703) appears to support such an interpretation.

Elvyssh, in the passage cited, is usually given a favorable connotation. It has been taken to imply that Chaucer looks mischievous and hides a 'merry twinkle' in his eye or that he has an expression of pity, sympathy and religious feeling as a result of hearing the Prioress's tale.[24] Early and medieval opinions on elves hardly justify such an interpretation. In *Beowulf* 'eotenas ond ylfe and orcneas' (112) are among the brood of Cain and are punished for their struggle against God. In the *Anglo-Saxon Leechdoms* (II, 344, 352) so little distinction is made between an elf and a devil that the same herbs, lupin, fennel, bishopwort and wormwood, are recommended in a salve against elves and a 'liþe drenc' against a devil and dementia, with nine masses to be sung against an elf and twelve against a devil. In medieval times, the belief that

97

elves were cast out by God persists. According to the late thirteenth-century legend of St Michael contained in *The South English Legendary* 'ofte in forme of womman · in moni deorne weie/Me sicþ of hom gret companie · boþe hoppe & pleie/þat eleuene beoþ icluped · þat ofte comeþ to toune/And bi daie much in wode beoþ · & biniȝte upe heie doune' (11, 253–256), and even in the fifteenth century a medicine book contains a recipe against elves.[25]

Although the Wife of Bath and Sir Thopas appear to regard the female elf with favor, the one referring nostalgically to 'the elf-queene, with hir joly compaignye' (*WBT*, 111, 860), the other dreaming of an elf-queen wife (*Thop*, VII, 788), Chaucer uses *elf* in a pejorative sense in the spell: 'I crouche thee from elves and fro wightes' (*MillT*, 1, 3479), appears to equate it twice with the *incubus* (*WBT*, 111, 873–880; *MLT*, 11, 754–755), and applies the adjective *elvysshe* twice to alchemy (*CYT*, VIII, 751, 842), a craft which the Canon's Yeoman declares to be that of a fiend (984) and against God's will (1476–1478). Chaucer's references are, in fact, mythologically significant, for they show the transition from the old Teutonic belief in elves or trolls who made love to mortals to the theological conception which explains all such creatures as devils.

According to most of the examples cited in the *Middle English Dictionary* for their use in the period, the noun and the adjective, except when used non-committally, appear to have unpleasant connotations. *Elvyssh* in the pejorative sense is also a suitable term to apply to a man of whom the Host exclaims: 'This were a popet in an arm t'enbrace / For any womman, smal and fair of face' (*Thop Prol*, VII, 701–702), for such a description suggests the elf-*incubus*. The *incubus* became firmly established as an article of learned faith throughout western Europe as early as 1100. The first *incubi*, according to Higden's *Polychronicon* (ii, 231), lay with Cain's daughters and begat giants. In the early days of Christendom, according to Donegild, Custance is an *incuba*, 'an elf, by aventure, / Ycomen, by charmes, or by sorcerie' (*MLT*, 11, 754–755), but the Wife of Bath implies that *incubi* have become scarce since the advent of the mendicant friar (*WBT*, 111, 873–880). If the Host is comparing Chaucer to the *incubus*, he may even be making sly reference to the Prioress who has just been the center of attention; for women's religious orders were particularly harassed by visitations from *incubi*.[26]

The word *elvyssh*, then, appears to support the suggestion that in the words *fynde an hare*, the Host may be referring to a popular superstition. But even if he implies that Chaucer looks as though he expects to see the animal of ill-omen, he is only 'japing.' The subtitle to the prologue is 'Bihoold the Murye Wordes of the Hoost to Chaucer.' The tale just told has been of White Magic and has sobered the company. The Host jests with the whole group and then, professing to see in Chaucer's countenance an association with the Black Arts, demands a different kind of tale, a tale of mirth. Obligingly, Chaucer takes his hero to Elfland, a place with which, so the Host has implied, he should be familiar.

While allusions to the hare, both direct and in simile, serve to illustrate human character and may affect tone, their implications can be ambiguous, as we have seen. Chaucer's hare, as a creature both of the field and of folklore, has dimension and subtlety. The brief reference to the hare in *The General Prologue*: 'Swiche glarynge eyen hadde he as an hare' (684) also reveals the man, but here the image seems to have specific significance and throws light on the nature of the Pardoner's abnormality.

Chaucer is supposed to have revealed the Pardoner's 'secret' in one bleak line — 'I trowe he were a geldyng or a mare' (*Gen Prol*, 1, 691) — and although a gelding is sexless and impotent and a mare female and libidinous, scholars assume that the two animals have the same significance. Curry claims the support of ancient and medieval scientific opinion and interprets the line to mean that the Pardoner is a *eunuchus ex nativitate*. Sedgewick finds that a gelding and a mare amount to the same thing and accepts Curry's diagnosis of the Pardoner with the reservation that 'this is what everybody, medieval or modern, would "trowe" him to be from his appearance and voice alone.' Robert P. Miller, in a comparison between the Pardoner and the spiritual eunuch of Biblical texts and patristic commentaries, states that 'the images of the hare, goat and horse — all common symbols of lechery — do not prevent notice that this man is also described as a eunuch.'[27]

To regard the Pardoner as a true eunuch is to discount the references to his wenching, lechery, marital ambitions and association with the Summoner. To see him as a spiritual eunuch it is necessary to explain away as 'irony' the fact that whereas the Biblical eunuch is expressly forbidden entry *in ecclesiam Domini*, the Pardoner conducts most of his business 'in chirches.' Nor is there any evidence that Chaucer described the Pardoner with scientific or hermeneutical texts in mind. It seems more likely that he puts traits of some well-known person into the portrait, as Manly and others have suggested, and that he was describing an abnormality of which he was actually aware. If so, the abnormality may be identifiable from the standpoint of modern clinical medicine rather than from that of ancient and medieval writings. There are grounds for thinking that Chaucer may have made use of popular animal lore in order to disclose his diagnosis. When the two previous allusions to animals are taken into account, the analogy to the gelding and the mare appears to have an unequivocal significance, a significance which is obliquely supported by other details in the text.

Chaucer describes the Pardoner as having 'glarynge eyen . . . as an hare' (*Gen Prol*, 1, 684), and 'a voys . . . as smal as hath a goot' (*Gen Prol*, 1, 688). These brief comparisons are striking and specific. The eyes of the hare are large, prominent, placed on the sides of the head, and they have slightly elliptical pupils. They project beyond the surrounding surface and their protrusion appears to vary with the will of the animal.[28] They were popularly believed never to close, and an echo of this belief survives in the modern medical term for a complaint in which the patient is unable to shut his eyes, *lagophthalmia* from λαγώφθαλμος: hare-eyed. In describing the Pardoner's eyes, Chaucer seems to suggest that they have a bulging, watchful, unnatural appearance. As far as voice is concerned, the goat is commonly believed to have a high one. In fact, however, it produces sounds varying from a whistle to a snort, a broken splutter and a bleat.[29] The Pardoner's voice is evidently not that of a normal man.

But these two animals also have qualities in common. One of the most persistent beliefs about the hare is that it is a hermaphrodite or bi-sexual. This error appears in works of various periods and is said to have survived until the end of the eighteenth century. Aristotle does not record it, but the superstition appears in both Pliny (viii, 55, 81) and Aelian (xiii, 12), and in the Gwentian code of north-east Wales, supposed to be of the eleventh century, the hare is said to be incapable of legal evaluation because it is male one month and female another.[30] Twiti states that 'at on tyme he is male, at oþer female,' and in common with the writer of *The Master of Game* he applies masculine and feminine pronouns indiscriminately.[31] In the poem on the names of the hare in a late thirteenth-century manuscript, the word *ballart* occurs, which may be an allusion to the hare's reputed bisexuality, and in the fourteenth-century Welsh poem, 'Ysgyfarnog', the hare is termed *gwr-wreic*: a hermaphrodite.[32] Hermaphroditism may also be found in the goat. Some goats, says Aristotle in *De animalium generatione* (iv, iv, 770–771) have both male and female organs of generation. A similar statement is made by Albertus Magnus in his *De animalibus*: 'Et accidit haec monstruositas [hermaphroditus] aliquando etiam in capris quas Graeci virreagaryez vocant, eo quod membrum habent et maris et feminae' (xviii, 52).

Chaucer, in common, so it would seem from Curry's researches, with the medical authorities of his own age and earlier, knew little about sexual deviates. He recognized an abnormality but was unable to define it more exactly than by remarking 'I trowe he were a geldyng or a mare.' He sensed that the Pardoner could not function as a male and therefore called him a gelding. He felt that the man was lecherous and feminine, and he compared him to the mare, an animal traditionally regarded as being most lascivious and as symbolizing the lustful woman.[33] He was certainly not presenting a *eunuchus ex nativitate*, for, contrary to the opinions of the authorities cited by Curry, libido and potency are absent in the true eunuchoid.[34] Moreover, all true eunuchoids tend to be tall, often very tall, and it seems unlikely that such a conspicuous feature would pass unmentioned. In the composite picture, the references to the animals touch off implications which are reinforced by other details: the seemingly high-pitched voice, the smooth, hairless face, the long hair instead of the shaven crown required of a 'noble ecclesiaste,' and the concern with fashion evinced in 'hym thoughte he rood al of the newe jet' (*Gen Prol*, I, 682). The Pardoner, in fact, displays the peculiarities which are described as being characteristic of the testicular pseudohermaphrodite of the feminine type.[35]

If my interpretation is correct it reveals why he is addressed as 'thou beel amy' (*PardT Intro*, VI, 318), and why, instead of replying with cheerful, boasting repartee to be expected from the normal man, he receives the Host's indelicate threat to his 'coillons' in angry silence (*PardT*, VI, 952–957). It gives meaning to the pun on *burdoun* as both bass musical tone and as *phallus*. Indeed, it explains his whole relationship with the Summoner, a relationship hardly possible if he is regarded as a *eunuchus ex nativitate*, in view of the absence of *libido*. It explains why he should be contemplating matrimony (*WB Prol*, III, 166–168), and why he should boast of having 'a joly wenche in every toun' (*Pard Prol*, VI, 453). He is sexually abnormal, as the Host realizes, but at times he shows the typical desire of the deviate to conform to the sex in which he is reared, although physically he may be unable to do so.[36]

Certain remarks which the Pardoner makes may reflect fear and disgust arising from his knowledge that he is not like other men. Even some of his appurtenances, such as the round vernicle, the hymen-like fragments of veil and sail may suggest an obsession with his own abnormality. In his speech in *The Pardoner's Tale*, vaginal symbols recur: 'the shorte throte, the tendre mouth' (517), 'the golet softe and swoote' (543). He fiercely reviles both the womb and the 'stynkyng cod' (534), and when he dilates on the evils of drinking he presents a feminine viewpoint: 'O dronke man, disfigured is thy face, / Sour is thy breeth, foul artow to embrace' (551–552). The strange cry 'Sampsoun, Sampsoun,' which he assigns to the drunken man on two occasions (554, 572), has taxed the critics.[37] In view of the Pardoner's abnormality, it seems most significant. In Samson's hair is the secret of his virility; in the Pardoner's flowing locks is the secret of his own femininity. The former is betrayed through lechery; the latter may be betrayed through drunkenness.

The sexual deviate, while flaunting his abnormality, nevertheless dreads exposure. The emphasis on the indiscretion of the drunken man may stem from the Pardoner's terror that he may betray himself:

> Thy tonge is lost, and al thyn honeste cure;
> For dronkenesse is verray sepulture
> Of mannes wit and his discrecioun.
> In whom that drynke hath dominacioun
> He kan no conseil kepe, it is no drede.
> (557–561)

His treatment of the story of Lot (485–487) is also revealing. He castigates Lot for the drunkenness which led to his committing incest; he omits the fact that there were mitigating circumstances: that, according to Genesis 19:31–6, the daughters were largely to blame because they deliberately made their father drunk in order to seduce him and bear children. The intensity of the Pardoner's condemnation may arise partly from the fact that Lot committed a sin which he is unable to commit himself.

Simple as the phrase referring to the hare is, being a comparison based on factual description, it is, paradoxically, a most intricate image. It provides a visual picture, and, far more important, it carries an implication which, when applied to the portrait of the Pardoner as it emerges from *The General Prologue*, his remarks to the Wife of Bath, and his own prologue and tale, illuminates his personality. The Pardoner stands revealed as an unhappy, frustrated creature, haunted by his own sexual inadequacy, conscious of his separation from normal life. Through the Old Man, knocking with his staff at his mother's gate, longing to be let into his mother's womb, he seems to convey the anguished realization of his male impotency:

> 'Ne Deeth, allas! ne wol nat han my lyf
> Thus walke I, lyk a resteless kaityf,
> And on the ground, which is my moodres gate,
> I knokke with my staf, bothe early and late,
> And seye "Leeve mooder, leet me in!
> Lo how I vanysshe, flessh, and blood, and skyn!" '
>
> (727–732)

Chaucer's use of the shifting symbolism of the hare is an artistic triumph. Indicative of worldliness, timidity, lechery, physical exhaustion, ignorance of love, fortuitous love and sexual deviation, the animal provides striking illustrations of human frailty. But while the poet takes full advantage of the variety and ambiguity of ideas associated with the hare, he does not lose sight of values in presentation which are inherent in his approach to the animal figure in general. The oblique approach enables him to use irony; it also allows him to create an impression of objectivity. Paradoxically, when used in conversation, the image may tell us much about the speaker, but however it is used it tells us little about Chaucer. He remains uncommitted, his moral alignment uncertain. The image of the hare reveals human nature but conceals the point of view of the poet.

VII. *The Wolf*

WOLVES were numerous in medieval Europe and even in the first half of the fifteenth century they roamed in the woods in the environs of London and Paris.[1] Langland in *Piers Plowman* (C, x, 226) speaks of them worrying men, women and children, and the hunting treatises show that wolf hunting, which was part of a nobleman's training in ninth century England, continued throughout the Middle Ages. Sir Robert Plumpton of Mansfield, Nottinghamshire, still owned some land called 'Wolf-hunt land' in the early decades of the fifteenth century for his services in chasing wolves in Sherwood forest. Wolves were usually included in the first class of hunting beasts along with the hare, the hart and the boar, but from *The Master of Game* we learn that they were so numerous that they might legitimately be caught with various snares and poison as well as with hounds. Chaucer needed to go no further than Hampstead Heath to see them, and in the fifteenth-century illustrations in manuscripts such as *Le livre de la chasse* show dogs still wearing spiked collars for protection against wolves (fol. 13).

The concept of the wolf which appears to have exercised the imagination is not that of the hunted animal, a creature which, so modern zoologists tell us, has been much maligned. The wolf of ancient and medieval times is invariably regarded as a murderous beast of prey, particularly menacing at night and in winter. It not only became a natural symbol of death, the companion of the God of Battles, but, as the epitome of lust, opened the gates of bliss and was therefore both destroyer and begetter in Egyptian, Greek, Roman and Teutonic mythologies. In the Middle Ages, the Devil, according to bestiarists and homilists, was a wolf, and it is not surprising that Angela de Labarethe, said to be the first woman burned for having sexual relations with the Devil in 1275 at Toulouse, should have produced a monster with a wolf's head and the tail of a snake.[2] Bestiary illustrations show the animal approaching the sheepfold, the trees and grass curving to indicate that it is cunningly going against the wind to prevent the dogs from smelling its evil scent. Its more specific symbolism is that implied in Matthew 7:15, 'Beware of false prophets, which come to you in sheep's clothing, but inwardly they are ravening wolves,' and it occurs extensively.

Sometimes the figure is used for light irony, as in the fable by Marie de France, in which the wolf attempts to become a monk, being attracted to a pious vocation by cheerful thoughts of a fat living among the sheep. In the Renard cycle the wolf is an object of derisive laughter, greedy and credulous and thoroughly outwitted in all its schemes, and it also exemplifies the brutal force of the aristocrats against which the fox, as representative of the plebeian class, pits all his ingenuity; in didactic writings the wolf serves as a symbol of heretical priests, deficient orders or church abuses.[3] In a passage in the *Roman de la rose*, which Chaucer or one of his imitators translates, the wolf denotes false representatives of the Church and those in secular life, such as usurers, tax-collectors, coiners, bailiffs, officers, magistrates, accountants, who prey on the public:

> These lyven wel nygh by ravyne,
> The smale puple hem mote enclyne,
> And they as wolves wole hem eten.
> (6813–6815)

Chaucer's most common image is basically the same as Jean de Meun's, that of the rapacious wolf constituting a threat to the flock. But he treats it so briefly and allusively as to suggest that the figure is already proverbial. Whether he takes the image directly from a source, as in *The Legend of Good Women* (1798, 2318) in connection with Tarquin and Lucrece and Tereus and Philomena, or uses it independently, there appears to be no significant difference in treatment. The wolf stands for the secular or ecclesiastical taker of prey or possibly both (*ParsT*, x, 774, 792, *Gen Prol*, 1, 513). Its helpless victims are the sheep. The Physician includes the figure in a digression on the responsibilities of guardians and parents: those in charge of children must 'beth war, that by ensample of youre lyvynge, / Or by youre necligence in chastisynge, / That they ne perisse. . . . Under a shepherde softe and necligent / The wolf hath many a sheep and lamb torent' (97–102). Virginius is by no means neglectful of his fourteen-year-old daughter, but the false judge Appius, who plots to rape her, might appropriately be termed a wolf. Primarily, both here and in a further example in *The Parson's Tale*, where those engaged in ecclesiastical simony 'sellen soules that lambes sholde kepen to the wolf that strangleth hem' (792), the wolf serves a useful device to establish sympathy with the victim and to emphasize the extent and immediacy of the peril.

Although 'the pilours and destroyours of the godes of hooly church' who are worse than wolves (*ParsT*, x, 768) are not identified, the allusion to *new* shepherds who knowingly let their flock run to the wolf in the briars (721) has been taken to imply that Chaucer has some precise situation in mind. But the contention that Chaucer is referring to the government taken over by Gloucester in 1388 as 'newe sheepherdes' is hard to justify. The Parson implies that such shepherds are indolent; the Merciless Parliament, through which the five Lords Appellant, Gloucester, Derby, Arundel, Warwick and Nottingham, eliminated their enemies, was tenacious and ruthless during its one hundred and twenty-two days of office. Its military policy was successful in France and it cannot be blamed for the defeat at Otterburn where the Scots were the aggressors and outmanoeuvred the English.[4] The 'newe sheepherdes' may refer to new pastors who, through laxity or acquiescence, let their flocks fall into heresies. A contemporary homilist likens the wolf to a heretic, and sharp heresies are said to prick and rend men's consciences 'as thornes and breris pricken men, and torenden her clothes.'[5]

Two traditional allusions to the wolf have a learned source but may be based on popular lore or even on observation. In *The Parson's Tale* Chaucer uses the conventional image but adds a specific detail:

> And, as seith Seint Augustyn, 'they been the develes wolves that strang-
> len the sheep of Jhesu Crist'; and doon worse than wolves. / For soothly,
> whan the wolf hath ful his wombe, he stynteth to strangle sheep. But
> soothly, the pilours and destroyours of the godes of hooly chirche no
> do nat so, for they ne stynte nevere to pile.

$$(768-769)$$

Chaucer's contemporary, Bromyard, the great Dominican preacher, expresses a contrary view when he is castigating the oppressors of the poor. He says that the wolf kills more sheep than he needs for his personal sustenance because he has other people in mind. There is the dignity and pomp of his lady to be maintained, sons to be promoted, daughters for whom dowries must be found, a retinue to be kept.[6] Chaucer's observation is to be found in Aelian's *De natura animalium*, with a pseudoscientific explanation: περιτέινεται μὲν γὰρ ἡ γαστὴρ τῷδε, οἰδαίνει δὲ ἡ γλῶττα, καὶ τὸ στόμα ἐμφράγνυται (iv, 15). While there is no reason to suppose that the wolf's tongue does swell and block its mouth as Aelian claims, it is a fact of natural history that the wolf does not slaughter indiscriminately. Whether Chaucer was familiar with the habits of the wolf as a result of direct observation we cannot say.

In *The Manciple's Tale* he makes an allusion to the sexual life of the she-wolf. The teller, a 'lewede' man who in his practical transactions as steward to one of the Inns of Court is able to fool 'an heep of lerned men' (*Gen Prol*, 1, 575), is asserting that animal instincts cannot be suppressed. The bird, he says, will desert its golden cage for the forest, the cat, its silken couch, for a mouse:

> But God it woot, ther may no man embrace
> As to destreyne a thyng which that nature
> Hath natureelly set in a creature.
> Taak any bryd, and put it in a cage,
> And do al thyn entente and thy corage
> To fostre it tendrely with mete and drynke
> Of alle deyntees that thou kanst bithynke,
> And keep it al so clenly as thou may,
> Although his cage of gold be never so gay,
> Yet hath this brid, by twenty thousand foold
> Levere in a forest, that is rude and coold,
> Goon ete wormes and swich wrecchednesse.
> For evere this brid wol doon his bisynesse
> To escape out of his cage, yif he may.
> His libertee this brid desireth ay.
> Lat take a cat, and fostre hym wel with milk
> And tendre flessh, and make his couche of silk,
> And lat hym seen a mous go by the wal,
> Anon he weyveth milk and flessh and al,
> And every deyntee that is in that hous,
> Swich appetit hath he to ete a mous.
> Lo, heere hath lust his dominacioun,
> And appetit fleemeth discrecioun.
>   (160–182)

Superficially the Manciple's remarks bear some resemblance to the Franklyn's, and both men are to tell tales involving a husband, a wife and her admirer. But the Franklyn, while claiming that 'love wol nat been constreyned by maistrye. . . . Wommen, of kynde, desiren libertee' (*FranklT*, v, 764–768), finds that *gentilesse* ensures marital fidelity and love. The Manciple regards love only as an animal appetite. In his tale, the husband Phebus has *gentilesse* (123) but has to guard and pamper his wife for fear she will cuckold him. The bird and cat, ever ready to revert to their wild state, are analogous to the wife. Each prefers a crude diet to the dainties given in captivity.

Having moved from the bird to the cat, a common metaphor for woman, the Manciple is now prepared to use the example most fully illustrative of his attitude to women, an attitude already evinced in his cynicism regarding wives and in his failure to give Phebus' wife any individuality or even a name. His remark sounds so *knavyssh* that he subsequently denies the implication. Nevertheless, his point is that women have a natural taste for sexual depravity:

A she-wolf hath also a vileyns kynde.
The lewedeste wolf that she may fynde,
Or leest of reputacioun, wol she take,
In tyme whan hir lust to han a make.
(183–186)

The description of the she-wolf's mating habits occurs in Ovid's *Ars Amandi*,
the *Roman de la rose*, *The Master of Game* and other works, particularly in those
from the twelfth century onwards, and in all of them the comparison, either
implied or stated, is to Woman.[7] The writer of *The Master of Game*, however,
states with commendable insularity that the comparison is not applied in
Britain but overseas.

Although Chaucer may have acquired his information regarding the she-
wolf from a literary source, its appearance in hunting treatises suggests that
it had passed into popular lore. It may also have a basis in fact. The male wolf
has to win its mate in a fight against many rivals and may indeed be an un-
prepossessing sight. *The Master of Game* offers a similarly feasible explanation
that 'he haþ moost trauaylled most goo and fastest for hure þan oþere han,
and he moost poor, moost lene, and most wrecch.' But neither the Manciple
nor Chaucer, for that matter, is likely to be interested in zoological accuracy.
Consistent with the attitudes he displays, the Manciple is making the traditional analogy to the prostitute and her pimp. Despite his denial, he intends
his figure to apply to the action. Twice he describes the wife's lover as being
of 'litel reputacioun' (199, 253), and the wife is the activator, like the wolf
bitch in heat: 'Whan Phebus wyf had sent for her lemman, / Anon they
wroghten al hire lust volage'. Moreover, the 'fruyt' of the tale stems from
the point he has made with his 'ensaumples' of the bird, the cat and the wolf.
'Appetit fleemeth discrecioun' not only in the wife and in Phebus in his desire
for revenge but in the crow from whose inability to restrain his tongue
'comth muchel harm.' The figure of the wolf fits well into the discursive
moralizing of the piece and contains the kind of popular lore to be expected
from the crafty pretentious teller, with his 'lewed mannes' wit.

An allusion to the wolf in *Troilus and Criseyde* also appears to have a basis in
popular lore.

'Lo, Troilus, men seyn that hard it is
The wolf ful, and the wether hool to have;
This is to seyn, that men ful ofte, iwys,
Mote spenden part the remenant for to save,
For ay with gold men may the herte grave
Of hym that set is upon coveytise;
And how I mene, I shall it yow devyse.'
(iv, 1373–1379)

Criseyde is about to describe to Troilus how she will persuade her father to
allow her to return from Greece to Troy. She will bring goods from Troy
and tell her father that if she returns she can procure more for him.

Inasmuch as Calchas is a false prophet, the wolf is a fitting image to apply to him. But the meaning of the phrase is not clear. It is usually regarded as proverbial, implying 'you cannot have your cake and eat it too.' Its application would then be that Calchas, seeing he cannot have both property and daughter, would prefer to run the risk of losing her in order to satisfy his wolfish greed. I have been unable to find any other instances of such usage elsewhere, and Criseyde's explanation suggests a different meaning, dependent on the knowledge that 'whan the wolf hath ful his wombe, he stynteth to strangle sheep' (*ParsT*, x, 769). A sheep may glut a wolf with the result that the rest of the flock can be saved. Criseyde may save herself by sacrificing her goods.

Whatever interpretation we take, neither the figure nor its pedantic extension can be accurately applied to the situation. Criseyde is resorting to a proverb for the same purpose as such proverbs are still popularly used: to give an argument plausibility and the sanction of tradition. Chaucer adds that she was sincere. According to his authorities, 'al this thyng was seyd of good entente; / And that hire herte trewe was and kynde / Towardes hym, and spak right as she mente' (iv, 1415–1418). Nevertheless, the inappropriateness of the saw and the impression of diffuseness which it gives contribute to the lack of conviction in her argument and help to show why she is to fail in implementing her plan. She is self-deceived. She regards her father as the wolf, but thinks she can outwit him in dissimulation. Yet she has shown herself lamb-like from the beginning, passive, fearful of injury, already 'undere shames drede' (i, 180) even in the temple. Although Criseyde is a divided personality and as such is portrayed as both prey and taker of prey, in crucial situations she is imaged as the victim of the predator, viewed by Pandarus as a deer to be driven into the hunting station of the bowman (ii, 1534) and by Diomede as a fish to be hooked (v, 777). Falling in love, she dreams her heart is torn out by an eagle (ii, 925–931); at point of consummation, she is the 'sely lark' in the foot of the sparrow-hawk (iii, 1191–1192.) Even when she is compared to the singing nightingale, the stress is on its timorous nature (iii, 1233–1239), and the fear that is to finally prevent her from returning to Troy is that she may fall into 'the hondes of som wrecche' (v, 705). By her use of the figure of the wolf and the lamb, Criseyde unwittingly conjures up her own position in a wolf-like world. Her cynical evaluation of mankind, her reliance on the covetousness of human nature, also provide the explanation for her subsequent conduct; in a predatory world, one 'slydynge of corage' (v, 825) must grasp at the nearest shepherd's crook.

Two further images of the wolf, while they are also traditional, stem from sources different from those so far described. The one is from mythology, the other from the fables. In *The Knight's Tale*, at the feet of the statue of Mars, Chaucer places the traditional animal: 'A wolf ther stood biforn hym at his feet / With eyen rede, and of a man he eet' (2047–2048).

When Palamon and Arcite come to do battle for the King's sister Emelye, the King arranges to have oratories and altars of appropriate deities erected around the arena. Palamon is dedicated to Venus, Arcite to Mars and Emelye to Diana. In *Teseida* the temples are more distantly located and the prayers of suppliants have to travel far. Here Chaucer concentrates the action and substitutes mural paintings for the lavish backgrounds to the temples of Boccaccio. He may have been describing tapestries in sight of his audience, for the association between literature and such decorative arts was very close. If such was the case, his direct exhortation to his listeners has additional immediacy: 'First in the temple of Venus maystow se / Wroght on the wal, ful pitous to biholde. . . .' (1918–1919), as does his conclusion: 'Wel koude he peynten lifly that it wroghte;/With many a floryn he the hewes boghte' (2087–2088). The description of all three temples emphasize the pain and sorrow of the human condition. Venus' temple is illustrated with the distresses of lovers, that of Mars with images of destruction, that of Diana, the *diva triformis*, with her victims. The description of Venus herself denotes, in terms of medieval mythography, concupiscence of the flesh, and that of Mars death and rapine. Diana, in hunting attire, mounted on a hart, surrounded by dogs, is the virtuous huntress. In looking down to Hades, she is also Hecate, consort of Pluto who is to send the Fury to destroy Arcite. In illustration of her role as Lucina, goddess of childbirth, Chaucer depicts not her friendship and assistance but the agony of the woman in travail, which is so intense that the beholder believes he hears the cries. Diana herself is passive, like Emelye, her devotee.

Mars's wolf, who is devouring a man, carries a symbolic meaning which would have been readily understood by Chaucer's listeners. With Mars, both as a Death God and as the Father of Romulus and Remus, the wolf was a sacred animal, but from earliest times *lupa* meant prostitute as well as she-wolf, and the vocabulary of brothel-keeping in ancient Rome includes many related words, *lupanar, lupanarium, lupanus, lupariae, lupor*. We have already seen some instances of this figurative use but there are many others. Plautus, for example, in *Truculentus* (III, i, 656–657) refers to prostitutes as wolves and to young men who visit them as sheep; the bestiaries declare that prostitutes are wolves because they devastate the possessions of their lovers and a similar comparison is made by the homilists.[8]

The medieval mythographers condensed mythological material collected by etymologists and compilers of the last centuries of antiquity and emphasized meaningful attributes. Often the god was frozen in some one unchanging attitude which could be easily studied and reproduced. Chaucer's type of Mars in fury in armor mounted on a cart and accompanied by a wolf belongs to the repertory from which artists continued to draw until the end of the fifteenth century for paintings, sculpture, tapestries, enamels and miniatures. We see Mars as a Roman legion brandishing a sword in a battle chariot, as Lancelot in a peasant's wagon, and almost invariably the god is accompanied by a wolf.[9]

Chaucer's immediate source, according to Boyd Ashby Wise, is Statius' *Thebaid* (vii, 70) by way of Bocaccio's *Teseida* (vii, 37). Petrarch in *Africa* (iii, 186–189) has the same figure: '. . . Mavortis imago/ Curribus insistens aderat furibunda cruentis:/ Hinc lupus . . .,' and this furious image of Mars standing on a bloody chariot occurs also in Albricus' *Liber ymaginum deorum*, an important source book for artists and subsequent mythographers, possibly written by Alexander Neckam. This latter work appears with *De deorum imaginibus libellus*, written two centuries later, in a Latin manuscript in the Vatican library, Reginensis 1290. Both texts state that the wolf carries a sheep and the wolf is so portrayed in one of the pen drawings executed around 1420 in the same manuscript.[10] The etymology of Mars is given as *mares vorans*: 'consuming males.' Chaucer, as Skeat observes, appears to have transferred the epithet to the wolf. He may have felt that the wolf's significance as *lupa* made the action particularly appropriate.

He may also have been working out the contrast between the two deities: the one with a figure in front of him which is destroying life, the other with a woman in front of her creating life. His picture conforms to the trend of adapting mythology to the fashions of the day, of producing visual embodiments of pagan gods, with iconographical details borrowed not directly from classical literature but from the later mythographers.

His handling of the material is different from that of the mythographers. Albricus and also Berchorius in his *Ovide moralisé*, written around 1340, turned such figures into allegories of moral significance. Chaucer repeats the formula which these writers constantly used to describe the images: *pingebatur* appears as 'depeynted.' But, like Petrarch, he omits in his portraits of the gods what was meant to instruct. He retains essential details and characteristically gives a brief ironic conclusion. All the psychological and physical evils of war which he has already described so vividly are epitomized in the figures of the god and the wolf. But he adds: 'With soutil pencel depeynted was this storie/ In redoutynge of Mars and of his glorie' (*KnT*, I, 2049–2050).

In *The Reeve's Tale* we have a brief allusion by the Miller to a fable: ' "The gretteste clerkes been noght wisest men,"/ As whilom to the wolf thus spak the mare.' (4054–4405 5). In one of the Renard poems by Willem, Renard and Ysengrim meet a red mare with a black colt. At the bidding of Ysengrim, who is very hungry, Renard asks the mare if she will sell her daughter. She agrees, saying the price is written on her hind foot. Renard is suspicious and calls the Wolf, flattering him on his knowledge of languages. The Wolf tries to read the price and gets kicked for his pains.[11] Some versions have a mule instead of a mare, and in one of these the mule boasts of his genealogy which, he claims, is written on his foot. Chaucer may have been using some version in which the selling and boasting motifs are combined, for the Miller has an interest in genealogy and is very proud of his wife's superior breeding.

The Miller is congratulating himself on outsmarting the two young clerks, cheating them, despite their precautions, of their flour. Since he is a 'churl' and since he alludes so briefly to the fable, it seems that the story must have already passed into oral tradition. The Miller's identification with a mare is appropriate. The mare, as Aelian and others remark, is a most lecherous creature. The Miller with his simian features has all the attributes of lechery and, like the mare in the Renard poem, his coloring is red. Even more appropriate is the ironical foreshadowing of the sequel. Unlike Renard and Ysengrim, the two clerks do not ask for his womenfolk; they take. The kick is too late to repair the damage.

The Miller's brief use of fable offers further illustration of the way stories and ideas about the wolf had become popular knowledge. In all his allusions to the wolf, Chaucer draws his material wholly from these common traditions or from earlier writings. Knowing that the wolf has widely accepted connotations he is able to make even a brief and apparently commonplace allusion serve the function of a detailed image. Primarily, he regards the wolf as rapacious and dissimulating, as a menace to the gullible flock, but he is also familiar with the outwitted wolf of the fables and with some of the habits attributed to the wolf in popular lore. The figure is used sparingly and is introduced with appropriateness. The Parson's application of Biblical symbolism, the Manciple's dilation on the habits of the she-wolf, Criseyde's use of proverb, the wolf in the temple of Mars, the Miller's allusion to fable not only give point to the immediate situation but, in varying degrees, throw light on the characters concerned.

VIII. *The Horse*

WHEN the Romans invaded Britain they were met by chariots, drawn by little horses indigenous to the country. By Chaucer's day, a variety of imports, including the Great Horse of Chivalry, had been added to the native stock. The riding horse had become a prestige animal, a status symbol, and the British nobility vied with one another in importing choice, highly-priced animals from overseas. In the romances the hero was sometimes mounted on an Arab steed, a horse which might possess the added merit of having been won in battle from the Saracens, or he might ride breeds from Turkey, Greece, Italy, France, Gascony, Castile and Aquitaine. But of the kind of horses, hackneys, capuls, rouncies, palfreys, which an innkeeper such as Harry Bailey would keep to hire out to his guests, only some of the palfreys would be of imported stock. As far as ordinary folk were concerned, most of them rode country-bred animals, essentially of the same stock as in pre-Roman times.

Chaucer refers to the horse more than one hundred and fifty times, and he has one incomplete story involving a legendary magic horse. Some of his allusions, mainly brief, appear to be concrete with little or no figurative associations. Others employ proverbial expressions for the purpose of illustrative comparison or use images reflecting ideas about the horse which have exercised the imagination from earliest times.

The miniatures of the Ellesmere manuscript, drawn by three or possibly four different artists, show twenty-three of the pilgrims. Chaucer specifies the mounts of eight of them; the Monk rode a palfrey, the cook a capul, the Shipman a rouncy, the Wife of Bath an ambler, the Plowman a mare, the Reeve a stot, the Nun's Priest a jade, the Canon a hackney. Six of these are illustrated in the Ellesmere, and many of the other mounts can be identified.

The palfrey was *le cheval de parade*, very popular with knights and ladies, and it is referred to again in *The Knight's Tale* (2495), *The Reeve's Tale* (4075), and *The Legend of Good Women* (iii, 1116, 1198). The name palfrey derives from the *paraveredi*, the relay horses by which messengers travelled in the days of imperial Rome, and the horse is a pacer, taken from native breeds which have no propensity to trot. In order to alleviate the tedium of the journey, the medieval traveller might take a palfrey to fly a hawk at gamebirds or to course a hare, but the real hunting horse was the courser, and the Monk's 'deyntee hors' in his stable were probably coursers, expensive animals, for which Henry, Earl of Derby, in 1387 was prepared to pay four times as much as he would for a bay.[1]

The palfrey, both decorated and undecorated, was a great favorite with the ladies and seems to have ousted the mule which was regarded as steadier and of more certain pace. Contemporary illustrations stress the spirited quality of the palfrey and show ladies riding sidesaddle, sometimes accompanied by solicitous young men. Not surprisingly the palfrey is the mount of the worldly Prioress and her nun.

The bridle of the monk's palfrey jingles 'in a whistlynge wynd als cleere/ And eek as loude as doth the chapel belle' (*Gen Prol*, 1, 170–171). The jingling comes from the bells which hang on either side of the bridle, and it is only this sound which keeps the Host awake during the monk's gloomy recital of tragedies.[2]

The monk's worldliness is adumbrated by his jingling bells in two ways. Firstly, they connote the idle pleasures and egocentric showiness of the profane world. Their sound competes with the sound of the chapel bell. A story, for example, in the *Chronicon Novaliciense* tells of an old knight, Walther, who attaches bells to a staff and afterwards wanders the earth to test the concentration of monks in their religious duties. His custom is to enter a monastery courtyard at the hour of devotions and to strike the ground hard, two or three times, with his staff. Walther finds that all too few of the monks have sufficient discipline to ignore this sound from the secular world.[3] Secondly, the monk's bells have strong sexual overtones. Their sound is not merely a distraction from prayer but rather a direct summons to animal urges. Bells were associated with sexual love in medieval amulets. Sometimes the amulets represented a phallus, on which bridle and bells were hung and on which a female was riding. Moreover, the Belle was the name of a famous brothel near

Harry Bailly's Tabard Inn. Along with their chivalric pretensions then, the
Monk's bridle bells and expensive palfrey dramatically underline that cleric's
worldliness. He has, as Thomas Kirby says, 'a superabundant vitality that
reminds one of the fine horses he owns and the fine fat beasts he loves to
hunt.'[4]

The Parson has much to say about decorated horses when he is dealing
with the sin of pride, and to give force to his argument he even cites Zecha-
riah 10:5, which contains no reference to such elegant trappings as he describes:

> Also the synne of aornement or of apparaille is in thynges that apertenen
> to ridynge, as in to manye delicat horses that been hoolden for delit,
> that been so faire, fatte, and costlewe;/ and also in many a vicious knave
> that is sustened by cause of hem; and in to curious harneys, as in sadeles,
> in crouperes, peytrels, and bridles covered with precious clothyng, and
> riche barres and plates of gold and of silver./ For which God seith by
> Zakarie the prophete, 'I wol confounde the rideres of swiche horses.'
> (432–434)

He is not alone in his condemnation: Vincent de Beauvais condemns such
trappings with regard to the Knights Templars, and Wyclif censures worldly
priests 'with fatte horse and jolye and gaye sadeles, and bridelis ryngynge be
the weye.'[5] Alexander Neckam, on the other hand, maintains that the palfrey
himself enjoys the sound of little bells sweetly jingling on his breast —
'campanulis pectoralis dulce tinnientibus delectatur'[6] — and bells, like the palfreys themselves, seem to be associated with chivalry and romance. In *Richard
Coeur de Lion* (ii, 60) the messenger has five hundred bells suspended from his
horse and the whole harness of the Sultan of 'Damas' appears to be so decorated:

> 'Hys crouper heng al fulle of belles
> And hys peytrel, and hys arsoun;
> Three myle myghte men here the soun.'
> (ii, 223)

Isidore, who devotes more time to the horse than to any other animal,
looks for four things in a horse: *forma, pulchritudo, meritum, atque color* (xii, 1,
41–45). The Monk's horse, like his owner, is 'in greet estaat' (*Gen Prol*, 1,
203), and its color, like that of the rascally apprentice in *The Cook's Tale* (4368),
is 'as broun as is a berye' (207). When *Beowulf* was being written, the most
common color for a horse appears to have been dun, but brown or bay is
very popular in the Middle Ages, especially in the palfrey. Chaucer's phrase
is proverbial and might well apply to the rider as well as to the mount. For
the outdoor-loving Monk is 'nat pale as a forpyned goost' (205), and his
glistening bald head 'that shoon as any glas, And eek his face, as he hadde
been enoynt' (198–199) may bear some correspondence to the shiny appearance of the berry, particularly to the common *bai*, which also yields oil.

Unlike the Monk, Hogge of Ware is a 'sory palled goost' as a result of his indulgence in strong London wine or ale, and the little town of Bobbe-up-and-doun on the Canterbury Way seems to be an appropriate place to call attention to his erratic riding:

> Woot ye nat where ther stant a litel toun
> Which that ycleped is Bobbe-up-and-doun,
> Under the Blee, in Caunterbury Weye?
> Ther gan oure Hooste for to jape and pleye,
> And seyde, 'Sires, what! Dun is in the myre!
> Is ther no man, for preyere ne for hyre,
> That wole awake oure felawe al bihynde?
> A theef myghte hym ful lightly robbe and bynde.
> See how he nappeth! see how, for cokkes bones,
> That he wol falle fro his hors atones!'
>   (*MancT Prol*, IX, 1–10)

Dun is, of course, the word associated with British native ponies and in origin is probably Celtic (Welsh *dwn*, Gaelic *duinn*), referring to the horse color which the Germans call 'wolf-grey'. In medieval times it became the proper name for a horse, was used extensively in surnames, and was applied in the expression used by the Host to mean that the horse is mired — 'Dun is in the mire'. The phrase came to mean 'things are at a standstill' because of its association with a popular log-lifting game. In this country sport a large log was set in the middle of the players. With the cry 'Dun is in the mire' two men tried to move the log and if they failed the cry was repeated and a third joined them. It occurs figuratively later in Capgrave's *Life of St Katherine* (ii, 1046–1048) when the mother of the Saint expresses her helplessness over her daughter's refusal to marry: 'For as wyth me, dun is in the myre. She hath me stoyned and brought me to a bay. She wil not wedde, she wil be stylle a may.' The Host uses the phrase when there is a pause in the entertainment, as a prelude to demanding a tale from the Cook. He applies the expression jocularly, presumably finding it appropriate not only to the social situation but to the way the Cook is riding. The phrase is also apt in view of the Cook's weight — 'his hevy dronken cors' (*Manc Prol*, IX, 67), and when the Host's fears are realized, the company is forced to act very much like log-lifters in the game:

> This was a fair chyvachee of a cook!
> Allas! he nadde holde hym by his ladel!
> And er that he agayn were in his sadel,
> Ther was greet showvyng bothe to and fro
> To lifte hym up, and muchel care and wo,
> So unweeldy was this sory palled goost.'
>   (50–55)

The Host later refers twice to the Cook's horse as a *capul*. He is using a generic term which appears to be applied variously to riding-, war-, pack-, and carthorses. But while it is generic it has connotations very different from those of *stede* and *courser*, aristocratic terms which Chaucer sometimes uses interchangeably and always in knightly context. The word from Latin *caballus* is of Norse-Irish descent, and in the north, where the Irish palfrey-type of the kind later called 'Irish hobbies' was imported, it seems to denote palfrey. The young clerk John, born 'fer in the north,' calls his manciple's horse both a palfrey and a capul (*RvT*, I, 4075, 4088). But the most common capul in the fourteenth century appears to have been a carthorse or packhorse. Its price, according to those quoted in Rogers' *History of Agriculture and Prices*, for the period 1379–1391, ranges from thirteen shillings and fourpence to one pound and eight shillings. Palfreys for the same period average three pounds, one shilling and threepence, and hackneys one pound and four shillings. Later capul came to be applied contemptuously to a person, and it seems to be used in this sense in Skelton's *Magnyfycence*: 'thou girt kevil' (2217), the form in this instance deriving from the Old Norse.

The carter's recalcitrant horses in *The Friar's Tale* are called capuls and are in a team of three, customary at the time. The fact that the carter should call them Brock and Scot (*FrT*, III, 1543) does not tell us much about them. The *Middle English Dictionary* compares *brok* with Old Icelandic *brokkr*, trotting horse, and *brokkari*, cart horse, and Skeat cites a number of instances in which the word, influenced by Celtic *brok*, badger, was applied to gray horses. The *New English Dictionary* on the other hand, suggests 'an inferior horse, a jade' among the possible meanings for *Brok* and these meanings are also given in Wright's *English Dialect Dictionary* as having been current in Northumbria and Kent. Scot, from OE *scot, sceot*: tribute or payment, a word which survives in *scot-free*, became the name given to the best horse, the favorite who paid the rent, and is also the name of the Reeve's good horse (*Gen Prol*, I, 616).

Capuls are well illustrated in the fourteenth-century *Luttrell Psalter*, in the scenes of daily life taken from Sir Geoffrey's manorial estates at Ingham where we can see a team beginning to draw a haycart with an assisting push from side and behind (fol. 173v). Like the carter's horses which 'bigonne to drawen and to stoupe' (*FrT*, III, 1560), the capuls take the strain on the collar and bend the knee. Small and sturdy, the capul is the mount for humbler folk on journeys. The rebel John Ball is shown mounted on a capul in an illustration in Froissart's Chronicle (fol. 165). People in trade needing transport for their goods are likely to possess capuls, and it would not be surprising to find capuls serving as mounts for those engaged in the clothing trade, the Webbe, Dyer, Tapicer and Haberdasher, as well as for the Miller. The Miller's mount in the Ellesmere illustration even wears the hempen halter used in transport and is typically phlegmatic in its indifference to bagpipes. As in the Luttrell illustrations, the mount of the Cook has spiked shoes to prevent it from slipping. The Cook also appears to be flourishing a flesh-hook as a whip, a whip being an item usually assigned to carters. The customary practice was to urge the horse on with spurs, and in the Ellesmere illustrations, the Knight, the Squire, the Yeoman, the Monk, the Merchant, the Clerk, the Franklyn, the Shipman, the Doctor, the Wife of Bath, the Parson, the Manciple, the Reeve, the Summoner, the Pardoner, all have spurs. The Wife of Bath also has a whip — a highly significant item in view of her discussion on matrimonial relations — and it is interesting to note that while a whip seems to have been only an occasional item for a woman to carry except when driving a cart, Luxuria, in a finely illuminated manuscript of Prudentius' *Psychomachia*, is depicted as brandishing a three-thonged whip (fol. 15v).

We know that the horse which the Cook hired was a mare because the Manciple says: 'Yet hadde I levere payen for the mare / Which he rit on, than he sholde with me stryve' (*Manc Prol*, IX, 78–79). The mare was rarely the mount of a person of quality. Thomas à Becket, evangelizing in Flanders, incurred the distress of his hagiographer when he 'hurede him a mere for an Engliss peni wiþ an halter,'[7] and the romance *Havelok* has a scathing reference to a 'scabbed mare' (2440).

The rouncy (OF *roncin*) was *le cheval de service*. Most commentators have missed the point of the joke of it being assigned to the Shipman. It is not that the captain of the *Maudelayne* has been assigned the worst horse available for hire but that someone has maliciously given him a mount highly unsuited to the inexperienced rider. The rouncy was a very heavy, powerful animal, with prominent buttocks, which trotted. In romance, the Green Knight appears in King Arthur's hall on a rouncy. Sir Bevis hunts on it, squires do battle on it, carts and villains are drawn by it; in fact, it appears to have been excellent on the battlefield, and in Edward I's Falkirk campaign of 1298 four out of every five horses seem to have been rouncies and a good one fetched as much as or even a little more than an indifferent destrier; except for the front rank of knights, the mounts were rouncies, but knights, at least in Scotland, according to Froissart, might be mounted on 'bon gros roncins.'[8] It is most unlikely that the Seaman would accept anything but an impressive-looking mount. What he would not have been able to anticipate is its hard gait.

In contrast to the Seaman, the Wife of Bath, as might be expected in such a widely travelled pilgrim, selects a comfortable travelling mount, an *ambler*, a horse trained as a colt by means of ambling rings to go at an easy pace. 'Usage makithe custume . . .,' the writer of *The Book of the Knight of La Tour-Landry* exclaims pedantically, 'Sette a colte in aumblyng ringes, he will use it whiles thei aren on,'[9] and in case the ambler should forget its training, the Wife is equipped with spurs. Albertus Magnus says that the ambler is a very comfortable horse to ride and that it lifts the two feet on one side simultaneously. The Ellesmere illustration correctly shows it in motion, with fore and hind legs on the far side moving forward together. The pace of the ambler is usually slow and is therefore most suitable for this particular expedition for the pilgrims evidently travel leisurely. The Canon, who sent his yeoman to watch for any company of travellers that might halt at an inn on the road so that he could join them, is too late to start with them but manages to overtake them by hard riding (*Prol CYT*, VIII, 588–592). One reason for the delay would be that travellers of any consequence are well equipped with baggage. When the heroine of *Li roumans de Berte* wanders deserted in the forest, the author laments that she has neither packhorses laden with coffers, nor clothes in her bag — 'N'i ot sonmiers a cofres ne dras troussez en male' — and a lady traveller in the English romance of *Ipomydon* even carries her own tent.[10] Chaucer considers it worth remarking that the Canon has so little luggage that he carries only a *male*, on his horse's crupper:

> A male tweyfoold on his croper lay,
> It semed that he caried lite array
> Al light for somer rood this worthy man.
> (*CYT Prol*, VIII, 566–568)

The Ellesmere illustrations show the Wife riding astride and the Prioress and the nun riding sideways. It is true that the artist of *Psychomachia* of Prudentius depicts Superbia as riding astride as she dashes through the routed troops of her foes on an unbridled horse, but in Aelfric's translation of the *Pentateuch* a lady is precariously perched sideways on a horse and in the same manuscript in an illustration of Genesis 31:17, when Jacob moved his family to Canaan, the women are similarly perched on strange-looking camels.[11] Such riders have no stirrups but they may have a footboard on which to place both feet. They are seated, according to more modern practice, on the wrong side of the animal, with the left hand to the bridle. The two styles of riding seem to have persisted, with some modifications in the case of sidesaddle, into medieval times. A thirteenth-century calendar, sculptured in stone along the southern wall of the choir in the Cathedral of Tour-en-Bessin, illustrating the seasons, shows a woman riding sidesaddle accompanied by a bearded rider and a boy on foot with a stick in hand and horn at his belt; the thirteenth-century Trinity Apocalypse shows the woman on the Beast riding sideways, and a late fourteenth-century artist depicts the Duchess of Burgundy, ceremoniously entering Paris in 1369, as riding sidesaddle.[12] But the illustrator of *Queen Mary's Psalter*, who decorated his margins with subjects taken from contemporary life, shows a lady astride a palfrey blowing a mote on her horn while her companion on foot shoots unerringly at a stag, and two women riding astride while hawking (fol. 151). Gower in his Tale of Rosiphilee in the *Confessio Amantis* (IV, 1309–1311) says that a troop of ladies on beautiful horses all rode *on side*, and such a fashion may indeed have been considered more ladylike. However, in the psalter just mentioned, the Virgin is depicted rising astride when she impersonates the virtuous wife whom a knight sold to the devil in order to pay his debts (fols. 216v, 217). That Chaucer intended to present the Wife of Bath as riding astride may be inferred from his reference to her spurs. The implications of the Wife's horsemanship will be discussed later.

The lowly position of the mare has already been remarked upon. Although it is the mount of the Ploughman, its most common use was for draught in sled or double harness cart rather than for ploughing. It is true that the Bayeux tapestry depicts the horse at the plough but oxen appear to have been generally used, and the Knight in *The Knight's Tale* (886–887) provides a ploughing metaphor when he makes use of the rhetorical device of *occupatio*: 'I have, God woot, a large feeld to ere/ And wayke been the oxen in my plough.' The Miller also uses a ploughing image in the *Prologue* to his tale. The Reeve, a carpenter by trade, is enraged because the Miller intends to tell a tale of a carpenter and his wife and of how a clerk made a fool of the carpenter.

> . . . 'Stynt thy clappe!
> Lat be thy lewed dronken harlotrye.
> It is a synne and eek a greet folye
> To apeyren any man, or hym defame,
> And eek to bryngen wyves in swich fame.
> Thou mayst ynogh of othere thynges seyn.'
> (3144–3149)

In a speciously reasonable rejoinder, the Miller alludes to oxen at the plough. He means either that for all the oxen in his plough he would not take on trouble by deciding that he was a cuckold or — if we interpret *for* as 'because' and bear in mind that the ox, like the cuckold, has horns — that he would not, because there are oxen in his plough, imagine that he were one:

> 'Why artow angry with my tale now?
> I have a wyf, pardee, as wel as thow;
> Yet nolde I, for the oxen in my plogh,
> Take upon me moore than ynogh,
> As demen of myself that I were oon;
> I wol bileve wel that I am noon.'
> (3157–3162)

Even in the sixteenth century Fitzherbert favored ploughing with oxen, arguing that an old blind horse such as one might put to the plough might not ultimately be used, as oxen could, for meat.[13] In *Piers Plowman* oxen are used for the plough, and Piers says he uses 'a cart-mare/ To drawe a-feld my donge' (C, vii, 275). Chaucer's Plowman probably uses his mare for the same purpose. The first detail we learn of the Plowman is that he had hauled 'ful many a fother' of manure, and it seems that he has much in common with Piers:

> A trewe swynkere and a good was he,
> Lyvynge in pees and parfit charitee.
> God loved he best with al his hoole herte
> At alle tymes . . .
> (*Gen Prol*, I, 531–534)

The mare and the manure serve to illustrate his practical virtues. No task relevant to his calling is beneath him, and since he is not one to ape his betters, he uses the mount which he has at hand.

Another mare is that of the Reeve's, but this is 'a ful good stot,/ That was al pomely grey' (615–616) and since it is also called Scot it can be assumed that he has a good Norfolk cob. However, the market value of a stot in 1388, according to an evaluation in the *Calendar of Inquisitions Miscellaneous* (V, no. 45), was three shillings and fourpence compared with seven shillings for a horse. It was also a term of abuse for a woman. The Summoner, failing to extort either twelve pence or a new pan from a widow whom he has falsely accused of incontinence, calls her an 'olde stot' (*FrT*, III, 1630), and when used in this sense it appears to have a sexual connotation. The same appellation is used by the Scribes in the *Ludus Coventriae* (205) with reference to the Woman taken in adultery: 'Come forth þou stotte . . . How longe hast þou such harlotry hold?'

Similarly, *jade* is also applied to woman. According to the proverb:
> He that lets his horse drink at every lake
> And his wife go to every wake
> Shall never be without a whore and a jade.[14]

The *Middle English Dictionary*, however, gives the meaning 'a carthorse, hack,' and cites Chaucer as the sole user. The Host applies the term patronizingly to the Nun's Priest's horse:

> Telle us swich thyng as may oure hertes glade.
> Be blithe, though thou ryde upon a jade.
> What thogh thyn hors be bothe foul and lene?
> If he wol serve thee, rekke nat a bene.
> (*NP Prol*, VII, 2811–2814)

The derivation of the word is uncertain. The Old Norse *jalda* meant a mare too old to foal, and an Old Norse proverb, advising one not to be ashamed of poverty, states: 'Thou shalt not shame thee for shoes or breeks/ Nor yet for a sorry jade.' Later, Blundeville in *The Fower chiefyst Offices belongyng to Horsmanshippe* (1565) finds jades only suitable 'to brede horses for draught or burthen' and regards them as 'stubborne' (I, fols. 3, 12v).

The host calls the jade 'foul and lene' but the proverbial phrase seems to have been ignored by the artist of the Nun's Priest's horse in the Ellesmere manuscript. Whereas most of the illustrations are faithful to Chaucer's text, giving the Monk a plump horse decorated with bells and accompanied by hounds, and the Clerk a miserable grey beast with its ribs showing, the Nun's Priest's mount looks stocky and well-fed.

The young man in *The Romaunt of the rose* valued a good horse and 'wende to have reproved be/ Of theft or moordre, if that he/ Hadde in his stable on hakeney' (1135–1137). *Hackney*, possibly deriving from the Borough of Hackney, seems to be the equivalent of *nag* from O.E. *hnægan* 'to neigh.' Even in medieval times it could be equated with the hireling, for *hakenei-mon*, in the sense of horse-hirer, occurs in *Piers Plowman*, and even earlier.[15] The young man would despise it because in medieval France the *haquenée* was an ambling horse or mare, especially for ladies to ride on. In England, the hackney was an ordinary riding horse of a lower grade than a palfrey, and could be good or bad. According to the Household and Wardrobe Ordinances of Edward II, the King's thirty sergeants at arms were each allocated 'one horse for armes, one hackney and somter,' and the *Catholicon Anglicum* defines the hackney as *badius, equus meritorius*. Of the quality of the horse of the Canon Yeoman we know nothing. It seems to be a hired one; It is *pomely grys*, a word originally meaning 'spotted like an apple,' but by then 'dapple-grey'; and it sweats after the five mile pursuit. On bad roads such a horse was less comfortable than a palfrey because its next pace after a walk was a trot.

The Knight whose 'hors were goode' (*Gen Prol*, I, 74) and his Squire appear to be riding huge destrers in the illustration although such mounts would be unsuitable for a pilgrimage. The Destrer was a warhorse, capable of carrying the knight in heavy armor. When relaxing, the knight would probably use a palfrey while the squire on a hard-trotting cob or rouncy would lead the destrer on the right. The romance of *Kyng Alisaunder* describes knights hunting for deer 'on fote and on destrere' (801) and even puts maidens on destrers (4924). Chaucer, in his parody on such knightly tales, assigns a destrer to his comic knight Sir Thopas when he is hunting for adventure:

> And for he was a knyght auntrous,
> He nolde slepen in noon hous,
> But liggen in his hoode;
> His brighte helm was his wonger,
> And by hym baiteth his dextrer
> Of herbes fyne and goode.
> (*Thop*, VII, 909–914)

But the destrer was not likely to be seen in the hunting field, particularly in wooded country, except when there was no other way of exercising it.

The above details suggest that Chaucer knew as much about the various kinds of horses as most people today know about automobiles. He can vividly describe a nasty accident. In *The Knight's Tale* (2687) Arcite's horse stumbles: it starts because Pluto at the request of Saturn shakes the earth. Then, having leapt aside, it 'foundred as he leep.' *Founding*, lameness, was a common complaint in horses and a stock remedy was to 'take iiij egges and rost hem hard and all hote put in euery off the hors fete.'[16] Before the lameness of Arcite's mount can be rectified, however, the hero strikes his head and has his breast crushed by the saddlebows in his fatal fall. Chaucer also knows the steeplechase rider's trick of rolling like a ball under the horse's feet when un-horsed: 'There stomblen steedes strong, and doun gooth al;/ He rolleth under foot as dooth a bal' (*KnT*, 1, 2613–2614). He handles terms having to do with saddlery and stabling with ease — *bit, brydel, croper, harneys, lathe* (stable), *peytrel* (breastplate or 'false martingale'), *reynes, sadel, sadel-bow* (pommel), *spores, stall, trappures, trays* (harness), and *trave*. The last named term, used in connection with young Alison when she is resisting Nicholas' amorous advances can mean either the smith's shoeing shed or the actual framework for shoeing horses, and both might still be seen in southern France some fifty years ago. Chaucer's horses also *amble, daunce, go, lepe, praunce, skippe, springe, sterte, stomble, stoupe, trippe* and *trotte*.

Chaucer does not often specify colors of animals except for symbolic or decorative purposes or as they occur in proverbial phrase. The bulls decorating the room in which Venus and Mars make love are white because white is one of Venus' colors (*Mars* 86); red beasts, black bears, bulls and black devils occur in nightmares (*NPT*, VII, 2931, 2935, 2936); white bulls and white alaunts accompany Lygurge, King of Thrace, in ceremonial procession (*KnT*, 1, 2139, 2148); a col-fox 'ful of sly iniquitee' (*NPT*, VII, 3215) lies in wait for Chaunticleer; the Miller's beard 'as any sowe or fox was reed' (*Gen Prol*, 1, 552) and the 'toft of herys' on a wart at the tip of his nose are 'reed as the brustles of a sowes erys' (555–556). The kind of detail which occurs in the description of the fox in Chauntecleer's dream is rare:

> His colour was bitwixe yelow and reed,
> And tipped was his tayl and bothe his eeris
> With blak, unlyk the remenant of his heeris.
> (*NPT*, VII, 2902–2904)

Chaucer's horses, however, are given colors from snow or *paper-whit* to *blak*, ranging through bay, *broun*, dun, *lyard, pomely grys, pomely grey* and *dappul grey* and *salowe*. The last adjective occurring in the *Roman de la rose* (7390) means pale, and is the *equus pallidus* of Revelation 6:8. The word occurs in Fragment C and is therefore possibly not Chaucer's. In the Middle Ages white seems to have been prized most highly, and then dapple-grey and bay or chestnut. Griselda, the humble maiden whom the Marquis chooses as his bride, is set upon a horse 'snow-whit and wel amblyng' (*ClT*, IV, 388) after the impetuous nobleman has ordered the court ladies, 'who were nat right glad/ to handle hir clothes', to exchange her rags for rich apparel. Here Chaucer is following Petrarch's *Epistolae seniles*: 'niveoque equo impositam.' (XVII, 3, 74). When he comes to describe Dido's horse, in *The Legend of Good Women* (iii, 1198), however, he independently describes her 'thikke palfrey' as being *paper-whit* (1198). Paper, imported from Europe, was a not uncommon commodity in the fourteenth century, and its color was probably more cream than white. *Lyart*, as Tyrwhitt notes, occurs in Gawain Douglas' translation of the *Aeneid* for *albus, incanus* etc. and in Middle English means grey or dapple grey.

Does Chaucer know what qualities constitute a good horse? Appropriately, a young man furnishes the longest description. The young Squire, in his curled hair and embroidered coat, waxes as enthusiastic about a horse as the young man today would over a model car:

> Greet was the prees that swarmeth to and fro
> To gauren on this hors that stondeth so;
> For it so heigh was, and so brood and long,
> So wel proporcioned for to been strong,
> Right as it were a steede of Lumbardye;
> Therwith so horsly, and so quyk of ye,
> As it a gentil Poilleys courser were.
> For certes, fro his tayl unto his ere,
> Nature ne art ne koude hym nat amende
> In no degree, as al the peple wende.
> *(SqT,* v, 189–198)

This prestige horse drawn in terms of two Italian breeds has all the qualities praised by Isidore which were still repeated when Batman re-edited *De rerum proprietatibus. Gentil* is the term used in all the English editions of this work, and in the treatise by Blundeville to describe a well-bred horse,[17] and the requirements as stated by Trevisa are 'that he be stronge and sadde of body . . and that the syde be longe . . . that the loyns be grete and the thyes round and large, and brode brested . . . Fayrnesse is knowen by lyttyll heed . . . if the eares be lyttell and sharpe, if the eyen be grete.' Blundeville further remarks that the Apulian, later known as the Neapolitan, is a trim horse, 'being both comely and strongly made . . . his lymmes are so well proportioned in every point, and partly by his portlyness of his gate but chiefly by his long slender heade, the neather parte whereof, that is to say from the eyes downewarde . . . is also somewhat bending lyke a haukes beak which maketh hym to reyne with the better grace.'

The Lombardy horse, a great favorite with English kings, also confirms to the popular description of a good horse, being noted for its strength and its ability to wheel round in battle when travelling at a full gallop. The Squire in the Ellesmere illustration appears to be riding just such a horse, and it is demonstrating its skill by executing a high school air, the *corvetti* which, according to Blundeville, is 'a certaine continual prauncing and dauncing up and downe still on one place, lyke a beare at a stake.' It seems clear that the Squire believes the foreign commodity superior to the English. Such an attitude is not surprising, for horses of value possessed by English kings and nobles were, in almost all cases throughout the period, imported from the Continent.

Besides describing *forma* and *pulchritudo,* the Squire deals with a further quality to be looked for in a horse — *meritum.* He does not, of course, mention color because he is describing a magic steed made of brass. Stratman translates *hors-li* as 'like a [living] horse,' but the word as Chaucer uses it seems to convey the splendor, dignity and nobility of the horse, and 'quyk of ye' suggests vitality, intelligence, liveliness, the same sense of *quyk* which survives in the Yorkshire dialectal word *wick*.

While Chaucer is familiar with the breeds and habits of horses, his attitude is detached; he makes no allusion to the horse's loyalty and intelligence, the qualities repeatedly cited in the accounts of Pliny, Isidore, Neckam and others. In the brief, spirited sketch already alluded to, in which horses struggle with a cartload of hay in the slough, Chaucer's concern is not for the horses but for the reaction of their owner and the effect on the action. The scene provides an acute illustration of human inconsistency, with the carter first cursing his beasts for getting stuck in the mud and then praising them with obvious affection when they succeed in pulling out. Ironically enough, it is the Devil who makes allowances for such frailty, the Summoner who wishes to take advantage of it.

> Deep was the wey, for which the carte stood.
> The cartere smoot, and cryde as he were wood,
> 'Hayt, Brok! hayt, Scot! what spare ye for the stones?
> The feend,' quod he, 'yow fecche, body and bones,
> As ferforthly as evere were ye foled,
> So muche wo as I have with yow tholed!
> The devel have al, bothe hors and cart and hey!'
> This somonour seyde, 'Heere shal we have a pley.'
> And neer the feend he drough, as noght ne were,
> Ful prively, and rowned in his ere:
> 'Herkne, my brother, herkne, by thy feith!
> Herestow nat how that the cartere seith?
> Hent it anon, for he hath yeve it thee,
> Bothe hey and cart, and eek his caples thre.'
> 'Nay,' quod the devel, 'God woot, never a deel!
> It is nat his entente, trust me weel.
> Axe hym thyself, if thou nat trowest me;
> Or elles stynt a while, and thou shalt see.'
> This cartere thakketh his hors upon the croupe,
> And they bigonne to drawen and to stoupe.
> 'Heyt! now,' quod he, 'ther Jhesu Crist yow blesse,
> And al his handwerk, bothe moore and lesse!
> That was wel twight, myn owene lyard boy.
> I pray God save thee, and Seinte Loy!
> Now is my cart out of the slow, pardee!'
> 'Lo, brother,' quod the feend, 'what tolde I thee?
> Heere may ye se, myn owene deere brother,
> The carl spak oo thing, but he thoghte another.

Lat us go forth abouten oure viage;
Heere wynne I nothyng upon cariage.'
(FrT III, 1541–1570)

Particularly illuminating is the use of *thakketh*, from Old English *þaccian*, to pat, stroke. It is when the carter pats his horses that he encourages them to pull out of the slough.

This is the only scene which provides a psychological insight into the relationship between man and his horse. References to horses do, however, frequently illustrate character. The horses of the 'parfit gentil knyght' are of solid worth but are not ostentatious — 'his hors were goode, but he was nat gay' (*Gen Prol*, I, 74). The ascetic Clerk, who is not sufficiently worldly to eke out his income through secular employment, has a horse as lean as a rake (287). Similarly, the other mounts specified in *The General Prologue* tell us something of their riders, as we have already seen.

Horses are also used by Chaucer for the purpose of illustrative comparison. In *The Summoner's Tale*, Thomas' gift to the greedy Friar is made explicit by a down-to-earth analogy, which conveys the full force of the insult: 'Ther nys no capul, drawynge in a cart, That myghte have lete a fart of swich a soun.' (2150–2151).

But despite his apparent knowledge of horses, on one occasion Chaucer passes on traditional lore without comment. In *The Parson's Tale* Chaucer compares the man of 'fool-largesse' to 'an hors that seketh rather to drynken drovy or trouble water than for to drynken water of the clere welle' (816). In the *Bestiary* it is the camel which prefers muddy water and will stir up clear water with its feet before drinking, but Aristotle credits both the horse and the camel with the preference for muddy water (*HA*, viii, 8), and although the idea has no factual basis it is still repeated by Batman as late as the sixteenth century.[18]

Frequently repeated in medieval treatises and illustrations are Pliny's stories of horses' associations with famous men, of Bucephalus, the horse of Alexander the Great, which would never carry anyone but its master and brought him safely through most terrible battles; of King Nicomedes' horse which fasted to death when the king died; of Antiochus' horse which, on the death of its master, and being caught by the enemy, dashed itself and its rider to death over a precipice (viii, 42, 64–66). Chaucer, however, shows no awareness of such stories, and when he applies the horse figuratively the implications are unflattering to both man and beast. Usually he employs proverbial phrase. In *The Reeve's Tale* the Miller takes to his bed after dining handsomely on roast goose: 'This millere hath so wisely bibbed ale / That as an hors he fnorteth in his sleep' (4162–4163). A French analogue, *Le Meunier et les .II. Clers*, describes the Miller as snoring loudly — 'adont se couche et ronfle fort / Icel mouner et tost s'endort' — but contains no reference to the horse. The snorting of a horse is commonly regarded as indicating the animal's intention or desire to copulate. Darius won a kingdom by a strategy based on this assumption. According to the often repeated story in Herodotus (iii, 85–87), when the Persians decided to elect as king the one whose horse was the first to neigh at sunrise, Darius was successful either because he led his horse to the place where it had been coupled with a favorite mare on the previous day, or because his groom, having stroked the mare, touched the nostrils of the stallion at the crucial moment, whereat it immediately snorted. The implication of the analogy in *The Reeve's Tale* is thoroughly appropriate, for Symkyn's *camus* nose, a characteristic of primitive peasants, hot-blooded goats and lascivious simians, indicates a love of 'things venerian' according to ancient and medieval physionomists, and natural historians. Used here, the proverbial expression has ironical implications. Just as the Miller's initial action caused the clerks' horse to run off to the fen, to the breeding ground where 'wilde mares renne' (4065), so now his snores, by keeping Aleyn and John awake, prompt them to seduce the Miller's twenty-year-old daughter and his convent-educated wife.[19] The comparison, with its sexual undertones, is also apt in that the Miller by long tradition is associated with conjugal relations, *molere mulierem* being used to describe the sexual act, the husband being the miller who grinds and the wife the mill. Nor is it likely that Chaucer is unaware of such symbolism or of the *double-entendre* of the conclusion: 'Thus is the proude millere wel ybete, / And hath ylost the gryndynge of the whete' (4313–4314).

In the same tale occurs Chaucer's one allusion to an animal fable in which the horse is a protagonist, ' "The gretteste clerkes been noght wisest men," / As whilom to the wolf thus spak the mare' (4054–4055), which we discussed earlier.

Another proverbial expression, 'a colt's tooth,' is used somewhat wistfully by the ageing Reeve and by the Wife of Bath. In his *Prologue* the Reeve, infuriated by *The Miller's Tale*, nevertheless grows philosophical as he comments on the disparity between will and performance — 'for thogh oure myght be goon, / Oure wyl desireth folie evere in oon' (3879–3880). He observes:

> And yet ik have alwey a coltes tooth,
> As many a yeer as it is passed henne
> Syn that my tappe of lif bigan to renne.
> (3888–3890)

and he anticipates such imagery when he remarks: 'gras tyme is doon, my fodder is now forage' (3868). The Wife of Bath, talking of Jankyn, her last husband, declares:

> He was, I trowe, a twenty wynter oold,
> And I was fourty, if I shal seye sooth;
> But yet I hadde alwey a coltes tooth.
> (*WB Prol*, III, 600–602)

Blundeville refers to an operation whereby the *wange* teeth can be pulled out of a colt's mouth if it does not heed the bit (11, fol. 32), in which case to have 'a coltes tooth' might imply that one is incapable of restraint. But the phrase is usually interpreted to mean that, though no longer young, both the Reeve and the Wife still feel youthful impulses as far as sex is concerned, and it is considered to be proverbial. According to the examples given in the *Middle English Dictionary*, however, Chaucer is the sole user, and the phrase apparently does not occur again until 1588 when Greene uses it in *Perimedes*. Whereas the Reeve's own statement and the figurative implications of the rusty sword which he carried (*Gen Prol*, 1, 618) suggest that his prowess is no longer commensurate with his desires, the Wife, if she looks nostalgically on the past and flaunts her husbands' testimony of her sexual superiority to that of other women with somewhat pathetic credulity, nevertheless implies that she could cope vigorously with a sixth husband. What they appear to have in common at the time of the reference to a colt's tooth is a youthful marriage partner. It is usually assumed that the Miller takes his portrait of the 'riche gnof' from the Reeve, and he depicts him as married to a young wife. The Wife of Bath is Jankyn's senior by twenty years. 'To have a sweet tooth' is a proverbial expression meaning to have a liking for sweet things. In using the expression 'to have a colt's tooth,' Chaucer may be suggesting that both the Reeve and the Wife have a desire for youthful partners in love. The carpenter's young wife is, indeed, described as a 'joly colt' (*MillT*, 1, 3263), and as a 'colt . . . in the trave' (3282).

Another proverbial expression occurs in *The Prologue to the Wife of Bath's Tale* (655–658) and in *The Canon's Yeoman's Tale* (1413–1416) and may be implied in the reference to the proud, skipping cart-horse to which Troilus is compared in *Troilus and Criseyde* (i, 218–224). In two of these passages allusion is made to Bayard, a term which is also used as a proper or common name in *The Reeve's Tale*: 'thus pleyneth John as he gooth by the way / Toward the mille, and Bayard in his hond' (4114–4115). Originally Bayard was the horse of Renaud de Montaubon who was outlawed by Charlemagne for killing his nephew Bertolai in a game of chess. After a heroic stand, Bayard was abandoned to Charlemagne by its owner and thrown into the Meuse. From there it rose again and it still gallops over the hills of Ardennes on St John's Eve.[20]

Bayard was first used as a mock-heroic, allusive name for any horse, then as a proper name and to denote a reddish-brown horse. In popular usage it acquired qualities not to be found in Renaud de Montaubon's horse, and in proverbial expression it came to be associated with the blind, stumbling, foolish old horse, already derided in aphoristic phrase. As Skeat observes, Jankyn's comment in his harangue to his wife — 'whoso that buyldeth his hous al of salwes, / And priketh his blynde hors over the falwes / And suffreth his wyf to go seken halwes, / Is worthy to been hanged on the galwes' (*WB Prol*, iii, 655–658) — seems to be part of some old saying, and the same line appears in *Reliquiae Antiquae* (i, 233). A briefer proverbial comparison occurs with reference to Bayard, usually with some alliteration in an accompanying verb or adjective, as, for example, in *Cleanness* (886), 'þay blustered as blynde as Bayard watz ever' and in the *Reply of Friar Daw Topias* (53) 'but thou, as blynde Bayarde, berkest at the mone.' As can be seen even in the brief phrase 'as bold as Blind Bayard,' given in Skeat's *Early English Proverbs*, no. 288, the implication is of foolhardiness and presumption. Such an implication is made even more forceful in the Canon's Yeoman's elaboration of the figure when he dilates on the follies of those who seek to profit by alchemy:

> Though ye þrolle ay, ye shul it nevere fynde
> Ye been as boold as is Bayard the blynde,
> That blondreth forth, and peril casteth noon.
> He is as boold to renne agayn a stoon
> As for to goon bisides in the weye.
> So faren ye that multiplie, I seye.
> If that youre eyen kan nat seen aright,
> Looke that youre mynde lakke noght his sight.
>   (*CYT*, VIII, 1412–1419)

Gower uses the same figure in *Confessio Amantis* to condemn the practice of necromancy:

> 'Ther is no god, ther is no lawe
> Of whom that he takth eny hiede;
> Bot as Baiard the blinde stede,
> Til he falle in the dich amidde,
> He goth ther noman wole him bidde.'
>   (vi, 1280–1284)

The frequent inclusion of blind horses in the price lists of the period suggests the basis of the proverbial expression. Common inflammation, *gutta serena* or glass eye, *glaucoma* or green cataract are common eye diseases in the horse, and with inadequate treatment, complete blindness must have been the result. In the *Calendar of Inquisitions Miscellaneous*, v, in 1388, a blind horse is valued at two shillings, a stot at three shillings and fourpence and an ordinary horse at seven shillings. Horses for the nobility range between four and five pounds.

Besides using fable and proverbial lore relating to horses, Chaucer draws from the legends of the magic horse for the incomplete *Squire's Tale*. Here we are introduced to the world of chivalry and mystery, ostensibly set in the splendid pagan Tartary, such as was visited by Marco Polo a century earlier, with the twentieth anniversary of the King's reign serving as the occasion for feasting, yet with a setting and atmosphere reminiscent of Arthurian romance:

> Ful lusty was the weder and benigne,
> For which the foweles, agayn the sonne sheene,
> What for the sesoun and the yonge grene,

Ful loude songen hire affecciouns.
Hem semed han geten hem protecciouns
Agayn the swerd of wynter, keene and coold.

(52–57)

And the strange knight who rides into the hall on the steed of brass, with a magic mirror in his hand and a magic ring on his thumb, speaks with 'so heigh reverence and obeisaunce',

That Gawayn, with his olde curteisye,
Though he were comen ayeyn out of Fairye,
Ne koude hym nat amende with a word.

(95–97)

Indeed, the narrator's punning comment on the elegance of the knight's address — 'I kan nat sowne his stile, / Ne kan nat clymben over so heigh a style' (105–106) — might well be an ironic appraisal of the opening scene in *Gawain and the Green Knight* when an 'aiglich maister' on a green horse disturbs the New Year's feast of King Arthur and his knights.

Chaucer uses several of the motifs which occur both in tales of magic horses and independently in folk tales, and we do not know how Chaucer intended to develop the story. It is possible that further tales on the horse and on the mirror might have been developed in addition to the story of the Princess and the talking bird. On the other hand, Chaucer may have intended the falcon to play a part similar to that of the dove in the Moorish tale of Prince Ahmed where the bird tells the Prince how to find the magic steed and enables him finally to win the princess.[21]

That Chaucer was familiar with some of the themes occurring in the vast mythology of the horse is evident in *The Squire's Tale*. Nor is he likely to have remained unaffected by any of them if, as seems possible, they arise from sensations and images regarding the horse which are deeply rooted in the human psyche. Three, in particular, recur: the human transformed into the horse; the ride with death or happiness as possible sequels; and sexual violation by a supernatural being in equine guise. They are found not only in mythology but also in the anxiety dream where, according to some psychologists, their presence indicates that the glistening, swift-moving, potent animal serves as a vehicle for expressing infantile sexual conflicts often never adequately resolved, even in adulthood. Mainly through the influence of the Church but also through folk beliefs, it seems to me that these themes developed, coalesced and hardened in literary form, and acquired a symbolism so unvarying and so frequently reiterated as to have become eventually widely known. The symbolism is expressed in two principal figures, both of which appear in Chaucer's works at conscious and unconscious levels.

The first figure is that of the rider and the horse, which was used extensively from early times to illustrate the precarious hold of the soul over the body. Closely associated with it is the idea of the centaur, who serves as an awful example of what happens when the soul loses control. Plato applies the image in *Phaedrus* and it becomes a popular one with expository writers. Philo Judaeus, writing in Hellenic Alexandria in the first century of the Christian era, makes the image serve as a graphic commentary on Exodus 15:1 'I will sing to the Lord, for he has triumphed gloriously: the horse and his rider he has thrown into the sea.' Distinguishing between the horseman who controls his horse and the rider who is carried wherever his horse wishes, he remarks that whereas the former subdues his passions and is saved, the latter, having no control, is thrown into the sea.[22] The *Gesta Romanorum* (lxv) tells the story of a king on horseback who, having to choose from inscriptions on a cross which road to follow, wisely selects the road which promises to take care of him but not his horse. The *moralizacio* explicitly equates the horse with the body: 'Carissimi, iste imperator potest dici quilibet bonus christianus, qui habet circa salutem anime sue equitate. Equus, qui eum portat, est corpus ex quatuor elementis compositum, crux que stat in medio vie est consciencia tua.' Illustrative of the same idea are the figures of *Superbia* and *Luxuria* in Prudentius' *Psychomachia* who are mounted on headstrong steeds and are violently overthrown (fol. llv).

In England during the medieval period the image appears frequently. In some instances as in the *Ormulum*, the allusion is to the bridle which must curb man's sensual appetite — 'son se gluterrnesse iss daed, / Sone iss þe bodig bridledd' (11664). In others the equation is more specific: the unknown writer of 'A Tretyse of Gostly Batayle' states that 'like as one horse welle-taught beryth hys mastere over many peryllys and saueth hym fro perysshyng, so the body well-rewled bereth the soule ouer many peryllys off thys wrecched worlde,' and the fourteenth-century preacher Bromyard likens the sinner to the galloping horseman with the vices as his steeds.[23] Although the figure does not appear to have been transmitted through any of the versions of the *Apocalypse of St Paul*, a work which had a profound influence on treatments of the Body and Soul Legend, it is used most elaborately in *The Debate Between the Body and the Soul*,[24] a work extant in seven manuscripts of which at least five have been assigned to the fourteenth century. It is a horrifying dream-vision in which a worldly, pleasure-loving knight rides to hell, turning from hunter to quarry to be tortured by all the pains that Christian devils and the medieval imagination can devise. Driven on by hell-hounds, with fiends thrusting red-hot irons into his body, the victim is finally dragged to hell amid the obscene shouts of exultant demons. Set in a dream, with the poet awakening in terror, the work has close parallels with the *angstvolle Traumfahrt* of the nightmare, in which the helpless subject finds himself riding and ridden upon, hunter and hunted in a headlong chase ending in terrible punishment.

The same figure is even more clearly established in folk beliefs[25] than in the explanatory metaphors of hermeneutical writers. The nightly procession of ghostly huntsmen and their hounds is a recurring theme in many countries up to this century, and whether led by Odin, John Peel or Herodias, the wife of Herod who, in the Middle Ages replaced Diana as the female leader of the Furious Host, these riders had sinister powers and to meet them meant death. They are the equivalents of the hoofed demons in medieval sculpture and art who are depicted as waiting to pounce on the soul in its usual form of a miniature man emerging from the mouth of the recumbent dead, or as hauling away on their backs the souls of the unrepentant such as that of the robber on the Cross.[26] These nocturnal riders with their baying hounds are psycho-pomps, carrying souls away to the infernal regions.

Our second figure is an ambivalent one which again expresses itself in erotic dreams, the woman in this instance being equated with the horse or, as in the nightmare, with the rider. The less alarming analogy whereby the woman is the horse to be bridled and controlled by man is so commonplace as to become proverbial — 'seinem Gaule und seinem Weibe soll man nie den Zügel schieszen lassen,' 'Freien ist wie Pferdekauf: Freier, tu' die Augen auf!' and 'it is yuel to kepe a wast hors in stable . . . but it is worse to have a woman at racke and at manger.'[27] Medieval didactic writers make frequent use of the analogy of a woman to a horse. Wyclif, who applied the English proverb just cited, in The lanterne of liȝt declares: 'þere ben þoo þat steerchen or poppen her facis, þat bridilen here heedis wiþ gigge haltiris' (132, 10); and the writer of Peter Idley's Instructions to his son declares that women will not go to church 'till they be entired, ibrideled and peytrelled, to shewe hir arraye' (11, 1042). One of the earliest farming treatises to be published, Fitzherbert's Book of Husbandry, gives the properties of various animals including women. The sixth property is that they should be 'easye to lepe vppon,' the eighth that they be 'well sturrynge under a man,' and the tenth 'ever to be chowynge on the brydell,'[28] and these metaphors were already traditional. So fundamental is the analogy in our thinking that token symbols such as the bridle, harness, collar or saddle-girth are often substituted. The symbolism persists even to-day in the marriage ceremony in which the ring is the halter used by the groom to harness his bride. The brank or scold's bridle, an iron noose believed to date from medieval times, which was placed over a woman's head to hold down her tongue, might even have a chain and ring attached so that the victim could be led like a horse, and in cases of wife-selling the unfortunate woman always wore a halter.[29]

The alternative equation, in which the woman is the rider, is also commonplace, being inspired by dreams of the incubus, the niht-genga of the Anglo-Saxon Leechdoms, the dread mara who turns her victim into a horse and rides him in the most exhausting way. The figure is often used to denote the woman who tries to reverse the positions of the sexes. The widely current medieval story described by Gower in the Confessio Amantis (viii, 207) of Aristotle 'whom that the queene of Grece so hath bridled, . . . that he foryat al his logique' applies the image and it is the subject of illustrations in wood, stone and ivory. The figure sometimes splits: in the numerous stories of the Rosiphilee type, such as the Lai du Trot and the early thirteenth-century Conseil *d'amour*, in which sexual love is praised, the free-hearted beauties are gorge-ously arrayed on white palfreys, the hard-hearted on broken-down nags; in the second type of hunt described by Helinand, a thirteenth-century monk of Froidmont and repeated by a work formerly attributed to Vincent de Beauvais, in which sexual love is illicit, devils become black horses and pursue the guilty woman. Helinand further states that on account of the lustful nature of horses 'daemones igitur in equos transformati significant sessores suos se hujus modi sceleribus oblectasse.'[30] The association with the night-mare ride becomes explicit in the version in *Jacob's Well* in which a Knight meets a dead woman, an adulteress fleeing from the Furious Host, and hears in the distance 'þe voys of feendys, lyche þe voys of hunters and of here houndys, wyth orryble hornys and cryes' (1, 166–167). But the most persistent application of the figure occurs in the witch who rides through the air on an abbreviated form of a horse during her vile excursions and, not unexpectedly, when caught was sometimes bridled and tethered to the stake by a collar. She surely derives from the *mara* of the nightmare, from the anxiety dream of night flight. This same dream gave rise to Epona, the goddess of horses, the woman who looms up large and sexual on artefacts as various as a potter's lid in the New Forest two thousand years ago or the felt appliqué on a Scythian saddlecloth some five hundred years earlier.[31]

If, as is contended, the symbolism of the horse and the rider is deeply implanted in the imagination, it is not surprising that it occurs in Chaucer's works, nor that the second analogy, being concerned with the most funda-mental of human relationships and being part of colloquial tradition, should appear more frequently than the first. Chaucer's brief riding images to express sexual relations — 'he priketh harde and depe as he were mad' (*RvT*, 1, 4231) 'al be it that I may nat on yow ryde' (*NPT*, VII, 3168) — are too well known to require further comment. The 'pryking' of the Monk (*Gen Prol*, 1, 191), like that of Sir Thopas (*Thop*, VII, 774), may, as Tatlock suggested in 1916, have a similar meaning, and certainly the three allusions to the Monk's fine horse or horses and the illustrations of his worldliness emphasize that the prelate's body and not his soul is in control. Peraldus, from whom the Parson appears to derive his denunciation of richly decorated horses, refers to the fourfold commission of the sin of pride which is involved in such ostenta-tion: 'Primo in multiplicatione equorum . . . secundo in non necessario usu equorum . . . tertio in nimia exquisitione equorum, sicut accidit illis qui equos volunt habere impinguatos ad pascendum oculos hominum. Quarto in superbo ornatu equorum,' and Wyclif insists that 'prestis wasting in oþere þingis, as ben horsis, haukis & houndes . . . ben ful dampnable bifore god,' contending that such men are going to hell.[32] We have already remarked, when we were considering *The Nun's Priest's Tale*, that two lines in *The General Prologue*, 'he was nat pale as a forpyned goost. / A fat swan loved he best of any roost' (205–206), seem to imply that the poultry-loving Monk is hell-bound. The Monk's fondness for riding confirms his destination, and the image, which Chaucer uses to emphasize that the prelate's appearance is certainly *not* that of a cloistered ascetic, may point forward to the tortured spirit in the hell hunt which the Monk must ultimately become.

Traces of a hunt analogous to the nightmare ride are to be found in *The Book of the Duchess*. It is a dream hunt and earlier in the poem the narrator suggests that 'a sicknesse' which he has suffered 'this eight yeer' (37) may account for his inability to sleep.[33] Such a statement, irrespective of whether it was inspired by convention or by genuine experience, provides a psychologically sound reason for the introduction of the nightmare ride:

> And as I lay thus, wonder lowde
> Me thoght I herde an hunte blowe
> T'assay hys horn, and for to knowe
> Whether hyt were clere or hors of soun.
> And I herde goynge, bothe up and doun,
> Men, hors, houndes, and other thyng;
> And al men speken of huntyng,
> How they wolde slee the hert with strengthe,
> And how the hert had, upon lengthe,
> So moche embosed, y not now what.
>
> (344-353)

As in the account of John Peel, the sound of the horn arouses the narrator from his bed and he immediately becomes a compulsive participant in a swift ride from bedroom to field where he overtakes the hunters, and thence to 'the forest syde' (372) in time for the uncoupling of the hounds. Details given are consonant with those characteristic of the Wild Hunt and the nightmare ride. The nightly procession of riding souls was always presided over by some legendary figure and might represent an army as well as a hunt.[34] Chaucer selects as leader a hero usually associated with military deeds and he gives to the hunt a strange dream-like duration apparently extending from early morning until midnight, the crucial hour of supernatural occurrences. He also suggests the illogicality of dream fantasy: the horse is present in the room, is ridden to the hunt, yet is absent after the sounding of the *forloyn*; at the beginning of the dream the hart is 'moche embosed' (353), yet the hunt appears to begin later, and after being 'yhalowed, and rechased faste / Longe tyme' (379-380) the hart is still able to escape; the *forloyn* is merely the signal which the hunter blows when he has become separated from the hounds or from the rest of the hunt, yet the Dreamer appears to be omniscient and interprets the signal as denoting that 'this hert rused, and staal away' (381).

Although convention, which overrode realism at the beginning of the dream, takes control at the point where the stag escapes, and the elegiac theme precludes the pursuit to the death of a terrified quarry, the hunt has a meaning highly relevant to the subsequent action. Chaucer is well aware that we dream in symbols (278-283), and despite the artificialities of the dream convention he is able to offer a symbolism appropriate to the genuine dream. We have already remarked that in the nightmare ride the pursuit of the soul is closely associated with the figure of the horse and rider, and that the roles of hunter and quarry are often interchangeable. The Man in Black is both the quarry whom the Dreamer 'stalked even unto hys bak' (458) and the hunter in sombre pursuit of death itself:

> 'The pure deth ys so ful my foo
> That I wolde deye, hyt wolde not soo;
> For whan I folwe hyt, hit wol flee.'
>
> (583–585)

The Dreamer's role is emphasized through word-play. Puns and word-play, often of the feeblest kind, are a conspicuous feature of dreams. 'When a dream wishes to imply that the dreamer is hiding something, it may depict him as going into Hyde Park; . . . when it wants to refer to the "soul", it visualizes the "sole" of the foot,' and Freud remarks that 'besonders ausgiebigen Gebrauch vom Redensart — und Wordwitztraum macht (nach Henzen) die altnordische Sagaliteratur, in der sich kaum ein Traumbeispiel ohne Doppelsinn oder Wortspiel findet.'[35] In *The Book of the Duchess* the pun is not made obvious until the conclusion of the hunt '. . . al was doon, / For that tyme, the hert-huntyng' (1312–1313) but the frequent repetition of the word *hert*(e) points up its special significance. At the beginning of the hunt, the quarry is 'the hert . . . moche embosed' (352–353). The Man in Black is so pale that 'hit was gret wonder that Nature / Myght suffre any creature / To have such sorwe, and be not ded' (467–469). From lines 488 to 1313 *hert*(e) is reiterated twenty-five times, and although the Dreamer deems that 'this hert be goon' (540), the emphasis is on the lamentations and physical condition of the heart. When the Knight fell in love he relied on his lady's glance and on his heart because her eyes so gladly saw his heart (840–842); his heart is now so unhappy that he cannot describe his lady's face (896–897); because of his inexperience, with his heart yearning for love, the task of wooing was difficult (1090–1093); the lady was so much in his heart that he could not forget her (1108–1111); she had the heart (1153), and he made songs of his feelings to gladden his heart (1171–1172); when he debated whether to declare his love, he was so unhappy that it seemed to him that his heart would burst in two (1192–1193); his declaration of love was made with sorrowful heart (1211) but:

> Whan that myn hert was come ageyn,
> To telle shortly al my speche,
> With hool herte I gan hir beseche
> That she wolde be my lady swete;
> And swor, and hertely gan hir hete,
> Ever to be stedfast and trewe.
>
> (1222–1227)

The lady became his 'herte swete' (1233), and when she showed her mercy and gave him a ring, his heart grew glad (1275–1276). Finally, as in *Le Jugement dou Roy de Behaingne*, their hearts were a pair (1289). The final pun — 'al was doon, / For that tyme, the hert-huntyng' (1312–1313) — makes the meaning unmistakeable. The pursuit of the hart is the pursuit of the heart,[36] of the Man in Black. 'The hert . . . moche embosed' (352–353) becomes the suffering human heart, and the Dreamer retains the function traditionally assigned to the rider in the dream hunt — that of a psycho-pomp.

In *Troilus and Criseyde* the horse and rider figure illustrates the principle underlying the poem — the instability of the human condition. Smitten by love, Troilus is the prancing carthorse. He is subject to the dictates of passion just as the horse is subject to the carter's whip:

> As proude Bayard gynneth for to skippe
> Out of the weye, so pryketh hym his corn,
> Til he a lasshe have of the longe whippe;
> Than thynketh he, 'Though I praunce al byforn
> First in the trays, ful fat and newe shorn,
> Yet am I but an hors, and horses lawe
> I moot endure, and with my feres drawe.'
> (i, 218–224)[37]

Although the use of the proper name, proverbially associated with blindness, hints at the nature of Troilus' affliction, the analogy is not the usual one. Chaucer depicts the horse not as unruly but as well-behaved in submitting to the bridle of love. The conventional figure soon occurs, however. Pandarus, in order to stress the necessity for control of the passions, implies that Troilus is the rider — 'Now loke that atempre be thi bridel' (i, 953). As the rider Troilus makes two appearances in the street before Criseyde's window during the courtship. When body and spirit are strained by love, he appears as a war hero on a wounded horse. His battle-scarred helmet 'by a tyssew heng his bak byhynde' (ii, 639) and his shield 'todasshed . . . with swerdes and maces,' is full of arrows (ii, 640). Although he seems magnificent to the onlookers, especially to Criseyde, he blushes and lowers his eyes. He makes his second appearance after some progress has been made in the love affair, and this time he rides past his 'beste gere' (ii, 1012), still humble, yet bold enough to salute his lady for the first time:

> With that he gan hire humbly to saluwe,
> With dredful chere, and oft his hewes muwe;
> And up his look debonairly he caste.
> (ii, 1257–1259)

He does not permit himself any 'unbridled cheere' (iii, 429) during courtship, and although Pandarus warns him after consummation: 'Bridle alwey wel thi speche and thi desir' (iii, 1635), Criseyde, when the parting comes, is able to say that Troilus' delight was always bridled by his 'resoun' (iv, 1678).

But at the final separation, 'resoun' is not in control: Troilus can hardly sit on his horse for pain (v, 35). Once Criseyde congratulated herself that she stood 'unteyd in lusty leese' (ii, 752); now Diomede's hand is on her bridle (v, 92). Longing for death in his misery, Troilus assigns his steed to Mars (v. 306), and thereafter he rides solely on Criseyde's account. Restless in the house of Sarpedon and restrained there only by Pandarus (v, 495–497), he rides home hoping to find Criseyde has returned, and on the next morning 'as soone as day bygan to clere' he insists on riding to her house (v, 519). His riding is governed by his emotion — 'and, as God wolde, he gan so faste ride / That no wight of his contenance espide' (v, 538–539). He rides incessantly, obsessed by memories of his love:

> Fro thennesforth he rideth up and down,
> And every thyng com hym in remembraunce
> As he rood forby places of the town
> In which he whilom hadde al his plesaunce.
> 'Lo, yonder saugh ich last my lady daunce;
> And in that temple, with hire eyen cleere,
> Me kaughte firste my righte lady dere.'
>   (v, 561–567)

As he stands at the gates of Troy he thinks of Phaëthon, the rider who lost control of his horse in the heavens — a rider so often associated with incontinence or pride by medieval artists — and he fears that the celestial disaster will recur (v, 663–665). As his hopes diminish, 'he walketh by potente' (v, 1222), and after his fear that Criseyde is unfaithful to him is realized in his symbolic dream, no further mention is made of his horse. He makes immense slaughter of the Greeks (v, 1802), but never again is he presented as the rider who can be compared to Mars — 'It was an heven upon hym for to see' (ii, 637). Indeed, his bay steed has already been surrendered by Criseyde to her new lover, as a token that she rejects Troilus' physical passion, and at death Troilus' 'lighte goost,' sailing up 'ful blisfully' to the eighth sphere, is able to appreciate the vanity of life and love.[38]

The second analogy of the horse and rider is used to describe Venus' behaviour to her humble lover in 'The Complaint of Mars' — 'And thus she brydeleth him in her manere, / With nothing but with scourging of her chere' (41–42). The figure in *Anelida* (1, 183) is more brutal and presents an image of the rider tightly holding in the animal by the bridle and keeping him at the stick's end, that is, beating him with the end of a stick. The equine imagery is extended in the following lines: 'Her daunger made him both bowe and bende, / And as her liste, made him turn or wende' (186–187). That the figure should occur more extensively, however, in the account of the Wife of Bath, is not surprising. Alison's portrait is acknowledged to show the influence of a whole series of satires against woman, and clerical anti-feminine diatribes frequently apply the horse and rider analogy — 'Femme fu chevalier, et l'omme / Fu le cheval portant la somme.'[39] The Wife is concerned with the most basic relationship between the sexes and it is in this connection that such imagery is popularly employed.

The Wife's equitation is thus as significant as that of the Monk, and the horse and rider figure serves to emphasize her unfortunate ambivalence. She appears to be an experienced horsewoman and, since she wears spurs, she apparently rides astride. The assigning to her alone, of all the pilgrims, 'a paire of spores sharpe' (*Gen Prol*, I, 473) seems significant. Antifeminist writers such as Le Fevre picture woman as riding her husband and using spurs on him, 'Son cheval en fist la barnesse / Et le poignait comme une asnesse' (1091). The sexual significance of the spur is, of course, obvious, and indeed, etymologically *cauchemar* derives from *calcar*, a spur, and *mara*, an incubus. The line immediately following the reference to the spurs — 'In felaweshipe wel koude she laughe and carpe' — contains a *double-entendre* which explains the reason for the allusion. *Felaweshipe*, besides denoting casual or temporary companionship, can signify sexual intercourse, and according to *The Middle English Dictionary*, *carp*, in addition to meaning to joke, can mean to complain or even to attack. Chaucer appears to indicate here the possible attitudes which the Wife adopts in her marital relations, foreshadowing the fuller description in the prologue to her tale, and his conclusion underlines the significance of *felaweshipe*: 'Of remedies of love she knew per chaunce, / For she koude of that art the olde daunce' (*Gen Prol*, I, 475–476).

In contrast to the spurs, the Wife's large, roundish hat (*Gen Prol* I, 470) gives an impression of generous feminity and suggests that she can adopt a more accommodating position. It is therefore not surprising to find an ambivalence in the horse and rider figure when it recurs in her Prologue. Even the Wife's own lines in her tale later — 'For trewely ther is noon of us alle, / If any wight wol clawe us on the galle, / That we nel kike' (939–941) — suggest the equivalence of the woman to the horse, for *gall* (OE *gealla*) is a well-known term for a horse pustule. A similar analogy is made in a poem 'Schole-house of women': 'Rub a scald horse upon the gall, And he wil bite, wins and went' (1014). The reason for the ambivalence lies in the Wife's horoscope. Her horoscope is in Taurus and her dominant planet is Venus, but the combined good effects of both are vitiated by the presence of the evil planet Mars. Curry, in his *Chaucer and the Medieval Sciences*, explains the psychological result:

> It is Mars who impels her to gain at all costs the dominating power over her husbands ... Truly, whatever one may say of Venus' influence it is turned into a baser order when Mars is discovered in conjunction. So the Wife of Bath appears in the Prologue to her tale: a fair Venerean figure and character imposed upon and oppressed, distorted in some measure and warped, by the power of Mars.[40]

Mars is a horsegod, and etymologically the word is connected with *grind*, *crush*, and *mara*, the night fiend. It is unlikely that Chaucer was consciously comparing the Wife with the dread visitant of the nightmare or *cauchemar* but by endowing the Wife with secret marks he may have invited comparison.

The seal of Venus and the mark of Mars were commonplace to medieval astrophysiognomists, as Curry states. But the secret mark came to be relied upon as the most certain method of detecting a witch, and among the various forms that a *mara* might take the most common was that of a witch who plagued men with her solicitations, riding on them and using her spurs. Reginald Scot, in writing of the traditional belief in the *Discoverie of Witchcraft*, published in 1584, states: 'If she has any privy mark under her armpit, under her hair, under her lip, or in the private parts, it is presumption sufficient for the judge to proceed and give sentence of Death upon her.'[41] Mars gives the Wife her 'sturdy hardynesse' (*WB Prol*, 111, 612), and under his influence she sees herself as the rider, exacting tribute from the man who is her 'dettour' and her 'thral' (155). When Venus is dominant, she is the horse, and the use of equine imagery makes the duality apparent. Her early remarks constitute a defense of her promiscuity, and her use of 'harneys' (136) shows that she is thinking of herself, the harness being traditionally associated with the *vulva*. In the matter of marital relationships she regards herself as the rider and says: 'this is to seyn, myself have been the whippe' (175). But she is also the horse which 'koude byte and whyne' (386), a treacherous animal which can show aggression or can whinny, as Skeat observes, 'as if wanting a caress,' and the proverb immediately following confirms her ambivalence: 'Whoso that first to mille comth, first grynt' (389). This phrase is explained by the wife herself. In order to forestall her husband's just complaints, she attacked first:

> I pleyned first, so was oure werre ystynt.
> They were ful glade to excuse hem blyve
> Of thyng of which they nevere agilte hir lyve.
>
> (390–392)

But, traditionally, as I have already stated, the miller and the mill are popularly associated with conjugal relations. Etymologically the mill ($\mu\acute{\upsilon}\lambda\eta$) is linked to *pudenda muliebra* ($\mu\acute{\upsilon}\lambda\lambda$os) and to *molere*: to grind, and *mola salsa*: coarsely ground meal, and Chaucer himself seems to be aware of the excessive virility which is attached to the Miller as a type. In view of the subject of the contention, the proverb has a further significance. Alison has already anticipated her later image in associating female sexuality with 'barly-breed' (*WB Prol*, 111, 144). Now, by means of the traditional equation of the mill with the woman, she indicates her prompt acceptance of the most precipitous wooer.

The horse and rider figure is obliquely continued in the Wife's account of Jankyn. In describing only 'his crispe heer, shynynge as gold so fyn' (304) and his 'paire / Of legges and of feet so clene and faire' (597–598), she unconsciously seizes upon those attributes which acquired paramount importance in the lore of the horse because of their associations with generative power. The horse's mane was identified with the potent rays of the sun, and its leg and foot not only caused streams or vegetation to appear but becomes the property of the medieval devil,[42] whose temptations are predominantly libidinous in character. It is Jankyn's virility which impresses the Wife. She praises his performance in bed (508), and when she considers his extreme youth she feels compelled to describe herself as a siren of forty whose physical attractions, according to the testimony of her husband, were unsurpassed (600–608). Not surprisingly, she loses her dominance over the male to such an extent that she can be equated in proverb with the blind horse which the criminally foolish man rides over fallow ground (656). Finally, however, Jankyn capitulates and the Wife triumphantly recalls:

> He yaf me al the bridel in myn hond
> To han the governance of hous and lond,
> And of his tonge, and of his hond also.
> (813–815)[43]

The horse and rider figure was readily accepted by the imagination from early times, and in terms of medieval theology the first analogy even arises out of the second, for Eve is synonymous with the sins of the flesh. Chaucer's oblique and incidental handling of the figure suggests that he may have been influenced more by popular than by literary usage. But, as in the case of the Christian apologists, he may have been attracted to it because of the opportunities it afforded to illustrate aspects of control. Smitten by love, both Troilus and the Wife of Bath are compared to the blind, blundering horse to be restrained by the rider; the widow congratulating herself on her single state yet contemplating taking a lover is an unharnessed animal in fine pasture but the young, mismated wife with an importunate lover is like a colt in a farrier's frame (*MillT*, 1, 3282).

Even when the horse is regarded primarily as an animal serviceable to man, symbolism may be suggested. The mount often reflects the disposition of the rider. Sometimes the inference is obvious; on other occasions the correspondence is oblique. A clumsy or unmanageable horse belongs to churls such as the Shipman or carter; a horse that chases wild mares to lecherous clerks. The pilgrims' horses may tell us about their riders, and the omission of a mount for the Parson, who, Chaucer stresses, traversed his parish *on foot*, seems significant.

The horse out of control is not only represented as stupid, blind and recalcitrant but, either directly or by implication, as lustful, and the colt is associated with lust and wildness. A hero, whether he be Troilus, Theseus or Aeneas can, at the height of his powers, control his horse; the weak or grief-stricken, such as Criseyde, Phaëthon or the later Troilus, do not have control of their horses and disintegrate either morally or physically. The Pardoner, insecure in his ambivalent role, is, ironically, the one who offers insurance against a fall from a horse and a broken neck:

> Paraventure ther may fallen oon or two
> Doun of his hors, and breke his nekke atwo.
> Looke what a seuretee is it to yow alle
> That I am in youre felaweshipe yfalle,
> That may assoille yow . . . .
> (*PardT*, vi, 935–939)

While Chaucer must have been familiar with the laudatory accounts of the natural historians and encyclopedists, he makes no use of them. He shows no affection for the animal and pays no tribute to its widely extolled loyalty and intelligence. He rarely enlarges upon references to horses in his sources and he selects proverbial expressions of pejorative connotation. The one tale in which a horse might have played a heroic role is unfinished. In hunting or daily life, although he shows an awareness of the various kinds of horses, he exhibits none of the Gawain's Poet's sensuous feeling for their elegant appearance or trappings but is usually content to let clichés or generalized attributes serve as description.

Particularly striking are the ways in which Chaucer deals with the tension inherent in the figure of the horse and rider. In *The Book of the Duchess* he moves unexpectedly yet easily from its psychologically sound manifestation in the dream-hunt to a substitute-release in the elegy; in his portrayal of the Wife of Bath he makes it a subject for humorous analysis; but in *Troilus and Criseyde* he allows the tension to remain unresolved because the answer to the question 'what nedeth feynede loves for to seke?' (v, 1848) lies in the painful, ephemeral beauty of the world already described.

IX. *The Sheep*

AMONG the Hebrew writers of the sacred books, living in pastoral communities, the sheep appears to arouse contempt for its need of leadership and its stupidity rather than any deeply felt affection. The lamb, however, with its whiteness and inoffensiveness, becomes a symbol of peace and innocence, and in the New Testament, while the stupid sheep represent erring humanity, Christ is symbolized not only as the Good Shepherd but as the sacrificial lamb, the *Agnus Dei*. The symbolism has prevailed in literature, art, sculpture and religious thought up to the present day.

Chaucer was Controller of Customs and Subsidy of Wools, Skins and Hides in the Port of London at a time when the prosperity of the wool industry and the shortage of agricultural labor had caused more and more arable land to be turned over to sheep-rearing. It was not until the second quarter of the fifteenth century that a depression in the wool market occurred and sheep-rearing became curtailed. The sheep, whether the small, short-wool kind of the mountains or the larger, long-wool kind of the grassy lowlands, were bred primarily for their wool and not for their meat, and belonged not only to the secular and ecclesiastical landowners but to the villeins, some of whom had long established rights to free pasture. One of the main problems was to keep

the sheep free from sheep rot and scabs. In the *Shepherds' Plays*, one shepherd
claims to have lost all his sheep through rot, another hopes to cure his of
scabs and rot by applying henbane, horehound, ribble, radish, egremont,
finter, fanter, fetter-foe and pennywort, and their remarks reflect a plight
prevalent all over England in the last half of the fourteenth century.[1]

Chaucer was primarily a city man and there is nothing to suggest that the
post he held from 1374–1386 aroused his interest in the animal as such. He
makes more use of stereotyped ideas contained in proverbial phrase and religious symbolism than he does of the practical details indicative of personal
knowledge. His concern is not with the animal but with the way in which it
throws light on humanity.

Nevertheless, his allusions to sheep in daily life have concreteness and a
sense of actuality, and in demonstrating the Pardoner's skill in salesmanship,
he shows he is well aware of the problem of sheep disease. The cure is to dip
the Pardoner's sacred relic in the well:

> ... and forthermoore,
> Of pokkes and of scabbe, and every soore
> Shal every sheep be hool that of this welle
> Drynketh a draughte.
>
> *(Pard Prol, VI, 357–360)*

Sheep are included among the lord's property that the cheating Reeve controls (*Gen Prol*, I, 597), and one sheep is among the effects of the 'povre
wydwe, somdeel stape in age' in *The Nun's Priest's Tale*: 'Thre large sowes
hadde she, and namo,/ Three keen, and eek a sheep that highte Malle,'
(2830–2831). The Reeve is engaged in both agriculture and husbandry in an
area where, so it might seem from his successes, both activities may prosper.
The fact that the widow has only one sheep has been taken to indicate that she
is living in a grain-growing area; in good pasture country she would have had
more.[2] Such an observation does not take into account her poverty, however,
nor the fact that she is less likely to have learned her profession of dairy-
keeping in a grain-growing area 'For she was, as it were, a maner deye' (2846).
The one sheep, it seems, serves to emphasize the poverty and simplicity of
existence in the sooty parlor and homestead, compared to the gracious living
of Chauntecleer who is 'roial, as a prince is in his halle' (3184). The widow is
too poor to have more than one sheep, but such is the unsophisticated good-
ness of her peasant life that even that sheep has identity. While the name
Malle is useful for the purposes of rhyme, it is also appropriately plebeian and,
as the derisive remark of the third shepherd in the Towneley *First Shepherds'
Play* suggests, is associated with stupidity and misfortune:

> Ye brayde of Mowll that went by the way.
> Many shepe can she poll bot oone had she ay
> Bot she happynyd fulle fowll; hyr pycher, I say
> Was broken;

'Ho, God!' she sayde,
Bot oone shepe yit she hade,
The mylk pycher was layde,
The skarthis was the tokyn.
(Stanza 18)

The plain name has none of the pretentiousness suggested in the Gallic elegance of 'Pertelote.'

But the name also suggests why the widow keeps the sheep. Pollard in his edition of *The Nun's Priest's Tale* conjectures that the word 'deye' is used in its intermediate sense of a woman engaged in farm work and keeping poultry. The allusion to Malle as well as to the three sows makes the nature of her activities much more specific. In a marginal illustration of the fourteenth-century Luttrell Psalter is a wattled sheep pen with the hurdles kept in position by four rings at the corners. Inside the pen is a woman milking a ewe, the milk being caught in a green bowl (fol. 163v). In Anglo-Saxon times, according to Alfric's colloquies,[3] ewes were often kept for their milk, and the practice continued in medieval times, particularly in grain-growing areas where the milk was either sold as such or was made into cheese. It does not seem to have been a practice common in rich pasture areas or among the wealthy, but in Sussex, records show that in the fourteenth century a considerable number of ewes were kept by villeins.[4] Bartholomew, as translated by Trevisa, maintained that 'shepys milke is more hote and drier than cowe mylke with lesse butter and more chese; and nourisshyth therfore the lesse' (lxvii), but to the widow and her two daughters ewe's milk made into cheese would be a good source of protein, calcium and fat, even if it was something forced on them by their circumstances. The sheep's name has a three-fold function: it tells of the widow's lack of sophistication, of her poverty, and of one of the ways in which she was 'a maner deye' (2846).

When Chaucer uses the sheep and lamb in metaphor and simile, he expresses conventional views. Among the proverbial expressions he employs for the purpose of illustrative comparison are the meekness of the lamb, the stupidity or helplessness of the sheep, and the lamb longing for the teat.

He applies a proverbial phrase in *The Second Nun's* Tale: 'As meke as evere was any lomb . . .' (*SecNT*, VIII, 199). It is one of three proverbial expressions occurring within the space of five lines and has a perfunctory ring. The references to the bee, the lion and the lamb are also in Chaucer's source, the *Legenda aurea*, and Chaucer appears to have been content to reproduce the triteness of his original.

In the allusion to the sheep cowering in the fold, which occurs in Palamon's arraignment of Fortune, Chaucer gives concreteness to a proverbial concept by using a specific image: 'What is mankynde moore unto you holde/ Than is the sheep that rouketh in the folde?' (*KnT*, I, 1307-1308). While Palamon's speech expresses ideas found in Boethius' *De consolatione philosophiae* and

Ecclesiastes, the reference to the sheep appears to be Chaucer's own. But the image does not arise out of an apparent familiarity with pastoral life and is not particularly suited to the teller. The allusion to the sheep's proverbial meekness is more effective when used by the Wife of Bath in demonstrating the way she deals with a complaining husband:

> Thanne wolde I seye, 'Goode lief, taak keep
> How mekely looketh Wilkyn, oure sheep!
> Come neer, my spouse, lat me ba thy cheke!
> Ye sholde been al pacient and meke,
> And han a sweete spiced conscience,
> Sith ye so preche of Jobes pacience.'
> (*WB Prol*, III, 431–436)

The brief phrase aptly conveys her contempt and gives ironic point to the next line where the use of the word *ba* serves as a reminder of the sheep's bleat and turns her proffered affection into mockery. Also effective, in that it is strikingly suited to the character of the speaker, is the remark of the besotted Absolon outside Alison's window: 'I moorne as dooth a lamb after the tete' (*MillT*, I, 3704). While the phrase may be termed proverbial, it is also self-revealing: it emphasizes Absolon's obsession with oral satisfactions and prepares for the *dénouement*.

The traditional religious symbolism of the sheep and the lamb, as used by Chaucer, requires comment only in a few instances. The most extended figure of the shepherd and his sheep occurs in the description of the Parson in *The General Prologue*:

> This noble ensample to his sheep he yaf,
> That first he wroghte, and afterward he taughte.
> Out of the gospel he tho wordes caughte,
> And this figure he added eek therto.
> That if gold ruste, what shal iren do?
> For if a preest be foul, on whom we truste,
> No wonder is a lewed man to ruste;
> And shame it is, if a prest take keep,
> A shiten shepherde and a clene sheep.
> Wel oghte a preest ensample for to yive,
> By his clennesse, how that his sheep sholde lyve.
> He sette nat his benefice to hyre
> And leet his sheep encombred in the myre
> And ran to Londoun unto Seinte Poules
> To seken hym a chaunterie for soules,
> Or with a bretherhed to been withholde;
> But dwelte at hoom, and kepte wel his folde,

So that the wolf ne made it nat myscarie;
He was a shepherde and noght a mercenarie.

(496-514)

Basically the concept of the shepherd and sheep, which appears in the description of the Parson and in *The Parson's Tale* itself (721, 768, 792), is that of John 10:11-14. The imagery is used with simplicity and directness. It not only suggests that the good Parson himself possesses similar qualities but gives an impression of sincerity to the tribute. When the imagery is replaced by direct description of how the Parson might have behaved in London, a strikingly different quality is apparent. The cynicism subtly enhances the value of the tribute: it implies that the tribute comes from one well qualified to make an appraisal and from one who, for all his sophistication, has been moved to give unequivocal praise.

Traditional symbolism contributes significantly to tone in *The Clerk's Tale*. The sheep and lamb are among the objects of religious connotation which Chaucer seems to use in order to give the tale a hagiographic element. The first allusion to sheep in the tale — 'a fewe sheepe, spynnynge, on feeld she kepte' (223) — occurs in Petrarch's Latin letter, *Epistolae seniles* (xvii, ii), and the anonymous French prose translation, *Le livre Griseldis* (18), the two works which Chaucer is said to have consulted regularly throughout the composing process.[5] But two allusions to an ox's stall (291, 398), which are not in Chaucer's sources, suggest associations with the Nativity, and prepare for the presentation of Griselda as the meek, suffering lamb whose child is to die:

Grisildis moot al suffre and al consente;
And as a lamb she sitteth meke and stille,
And leet this crueel sergeant doon his wille.

(537-539)

The comparison of Griselda to a lamb is not in Chaucer's sources, and its religious connotations are subsequently reinforced by Griselda's own lyrical address to her child:

And thus she seyde in hire benigne voys,
'Fareweel my child! I shal thee nevere see.
But sith I thee have marked with the croys
Of thilke Fader — blessed moote he be! —
That for us deyde upon a croys of tree,
Thy soule, litel child, I hym betake,
For this nyght shaltow dyen for my sake.'

(554-560)

Compared with Petrarch's letter and *Le livre Griseldis*, in which Griselda does not address her child but merely makes the sign of the cross with serene brow, there is pathos and simple manner of utterance reminiscent of the medieval lyrics in which the Virgin speaks to her infant. The image of the lamb, the ox's stall, and later Griselda's comparison of herself to a worm (880) and her fears regarding the cruel hounds (1094–1096) are all illustrations from the animal world which do not appear in Chaucer's sources, and they emphasize Griselda's peasant simplicity and saint-like humility. Sparingly used in the work, they also provide striking contrast to the ironic envoy where the contemptuous epithets, *Chichevache, camaille, tygre* and *quaille* appear within the space of a few lines (1188–1206).

There are also two references to sheep which present problems of interpretation. The first occurs in *The Miller's Tale*. Nicholas, a young Oxford clerk, persuading John, an elderly carpenter, to prepare for the Flood, says:

> 'Hastou nat herd,' quod Nicholas, 'also
> The sorwe of Noe with his felaweshipe,
> Er that he myghte gete his wyf to shipe?
> Hym hadde be levere, I dar wel undertake
> At thilke tyme, than alle his wetheres blake
> That she hadde had a ship hirself allone.'
>
> (3538–3543)

He is alluding to incidents in the lost apocrypha, *The Book of Noria*, in which Noah's shrewish wife tries to thwart her husband, and to a legend which appears in its most complete form in Russian but is widely current in Europe and other Slavic countries. An illustration in the tenth-century manuscript containing the Caedmonian poems shows Noah's wife at the foot of the gangway, refusing to enter the Ark. Equally recalcitrant, she appears on one of the bosses of the nave of Norwich Cathedral, and in windows at Malvern Priory and York Minster. Sometimes Noah is with her — fingering his beard with obvious mortification at Malvern, praying resignedly in the bows of the ship at York — sometimes it is her son who seeks to placate her. A more detailed representation of the legend occurs in the Newcastle *Play of the Flood* and in the fourteenth-century *Queen Mary's Psalter*. Noah, enjoined to secrecy by God, reveals to his wife what he is building and the wife tells the Devil the secret. She later enables the Devil to enter the ark because she herself demurs until Noah says: 'Come in, you devil!'[6]

That John, 'gnof' or bumpkin though he is, would know of this drama is carefully vouched for by the fact that he is living in a city where the Mystery Plays are enacted. Absolon, the other admirer of John's young wife, enjoys playing the part of Herod in such productions (3384). Nicholas' plan which he now discloses to John is designed, of course, to enable him to seduce the wife. When he says that Noah would have given all his black wethers to have his wife sail by herself, he is reminding the carpenter of how the devil got into the Ark. Had Noah's wife sailed by herself, Noah would not have had the trouble of trying to get her aboard and the Devil would not have entered. John is to avoid such problems by providing separate tubs, for himself, for his wife and for Nicholas.

The allusion to Noah is ironically appropriate in that whereas the first deluge was a punishment for lechery — 'by the synne of lecherie God dreynte al the world at the diluge' (*ParsT*, x, 839) — this second deluge is invented as a means to lechery. The Devil was in collusion with Noah's wife, unknown to her husband; Nicholas, who is blasphemously playing God, is secretly plotting with John's wife. The allusion also sharply emphasizes the contrast in the behaviour of the wives. Whereas Noah's wife was reluctant, Alison is eager — 'Allas! go forth thy way anon./ Help us to scape, or we been dede echon!' (3607–3608).

As far as I know, no other explanation has been offered for the color other than that Chaucer may have used the word solely for purpose of rhyme. Tyrwhitt remarks that it would be in vain to look for the anecdote in Genesis. Neither Skeat nor Robinson gives any comment on the lines beyond a reference to the drama, and none of the Mystery Plays extant mention black sheep. Nor can we be certain whether 'wether' means *vervex* or *aries*. Bosworth and Toller give Old English 'weþer' as both; Skeet gives 'wether' as a castrated ram, stating that the original sense was doubtless 'yearling'; the Middle English Vocabularies gloss 'wedir' as both.[7] Trevisa refers to a 'wether wiþ gildene flees' (ii, 355) in translating from Higden's *Polychronicon*, which has *aries*. Chaucer, on the other hand, refers to 'a ram . . . that hadde a fles of gold' (*LGW*, 1427–1428). The Dublin Abraham and Isaac Play refers to Abraham's sacrificial ram as a 'wedyr' but the Brome version calls it a 'rame.'[8]

The connection between sheep and Noah's wife may have some proverbial basis. 'It is better to marry a shrew than a sheep' and 'Be she lambe or be she eaw, Give me the sheepe, take thou the shreaw' are cited as sixteenth-century proverbial expressions. Here the sheep appears to stand for a woman without a will of her own, and Tusser, one of the authors quoted, implies in his *Five hundred pointes of husbandry* that shrewishness in a woman is to be expected and is no deterrent to marriage. In *Bastard's Chrestoleros* the writer, complaining that English sheep-farming is taking up too much land, concludes 'Till now I thought the proverbe did but jest/ Which said a black sheepe was a biting beast,' but no explanation or earlier instance of the proverb is apparent.[9] In France a black sheep is *une brebis galeuse*: an itchy, scabby sheep, and it is possible that Chaucer is using some proverbial expression which implies that Noah does not care what his wife does.

On the other hand, Nicholas may be implying that the black sheep are valuable to Noah — that Noah would give much to have his wife sail by herself.

If Chaucer's wethers were rams, they might be regarded as valuable because of their importance to the rest of the flock. He might also term them black because of an ancient custom, still sometimes observed today, of smearing the ram's breast with colored pigment, usually black, at breeding time. The pigment shows up on the sheep and tells the shepherd which ewe has received the ram.[10]

If Chaucer was using wethers simply as a synonym for sheep, there are three reasons why he might have called them black. He might have been referring to the tar with which they were smeared before winter in order to combat murrain and various cutaneous infections or he might have been thinking of a belief expressed by Albertus Magnus that the milk of black sheep was better than that of white — 'lac nigrarum ovium melius est, et in capris est a contra' (xxii, 129). Alternatively, he might have been alluding correctly to the color of primitive sheep. Although even professional archaeologists construct neolithic sheep as being white, the primitive type was probably very dark. The ancient centre of sheep domestication lay in the north, as far north as Bokhara or the Arab Caspian Steppe. From the primitive type came the glossy karakul lambskins, the raw material for trade in Persia and astrakhan furs, still regarded as highly desirable, even today. From the same breed also came the black Colchian long-tailed sheep with the valuable fleece which gave rise to the legend of the Golden Fleece, when anciently imported to Greece.[11] But if black was the usual color of Biblical sheep, whiteness is stressed as a desirable quality. David likens sheep to snow, Solomon speaks of the teeth of his mistress resembling a flock of sheep just come up from washing, and the Lamb is the unvarying symbol of purity. In consequence, in the medieval period Biblical sheep are commonly thought of as being mostly white, and there seems to be no means by which Chaucer might have derived correct information. Flocks of black sheep still existed and travellers wrote about them but they had no way of knowing that they were primitive. The brilliant illustrations of the Noah episode in the *Bedford Book of Hours* show both white and black sheep (fols. 15v, 16v) but in many psalters, bestiaries and books of hours, sheep are usually either left uncolored or are colored white or buff.[12]

The term *wether* is also meaningful if Chaucer was thinking of wool. Wether sheep, as a result of castration, lose all sexual power and develop in form and size to something intermediate between the two sexes. They are much hardier animals than breeding ewes, being more resistant to disease and to inclement weather, and at times, particularly in mountainous areas, they have been maintained in large numbers for their wool.[13] The thirteenth-century *Li livres de santes* by Aldebrand of Sienna states that the meat is beneficial from the wether, but a fourteenth-century manuscript of the same work says that wethers produce particularly good wool. Certainly in some areas in England wethers were bred for their wool until they reached old age.[14] It is tempting to suppose that Chaucer was thinking about the animal in his professional capacity as Controller of Customs and Subsidy of Wools, Skins and Hides in the Port of London, and that what he means is that Noah's wife was so obstreperous that Noah would be prepared to give his finest wool-bearing sheep to get rid of her company.

Further problems of interpretation occur in connection with the sheepbone in *The Pardoner's Prologue* (350–371) and *The Parson's Tale* (603). The Pardoner's sheepbone, which cures cattle of a variety of diseases, multiplies the livestock of the owner under certain conditions, and removes jealousy, belonged to a Holy Jew whose identity is unspecified. All we are told is that the shoulder-bone was 'of an hooly Jewes sheep' (351), and that the ritual to be followed for enlarging resources is 'as thilke hooly Jew oure eldres taughte' (364). Both Jacob and Gideon have been put forward as the Hebraic patriarch whom the Pardoner had in mind,[15] but neither have convincing claims to the title. In Genesis 30:37–43, Jacob's sheep multiply when they drink at the water-troughs, as a result of wizardry brought about by wooden rods, not by a sheepbone. Gideon's fleece which is used to divine God's will is not a 'miracle-working fleece,' as it has been called. In Judges 6:37–49, God performs the miracle on the fleece as a sign that He is prepared to help Gideon save Israel. Gideon's subsequent prosperity consists of slaying the Midianites, erecting an ephod made from the gold earrings of the defeated, and producing seventy sons — activities which have nothing whatsoever to do with the fleece or, for that matter, with the Pardoner's sheepbone.

In addition to the problem regarding the identity of the Holy Jew, there is a difficulty concerning the sheepbone itself. The Pardoner does not ascribe to it the properties commonly attributed to a magic shoulderbone, The shoulder-bone of a sheep is widely used in scapulomancy, an activity specifically denounced by the Parson:

> But lat us go now to thilke horrible sweryng of adjuracioun and con-juracioun, as doon thise false enchauntours or nigromanciens in bacyns ful of water, or in a bright swerd, in a cercle, or in a fir, or in a shulder-boon of a sheep. (*ParsT*, x, 603).

Arising in the East in ancient times, the art consists of reading the fissures on the shoulder blade of a sacrificial animal. A lengthwise split in the blade is informative on big issues, while cross-cracks on the left and right augur varying kinds and degrees of good and bad fortune. Although the practice was periodically condemned, it appears to have been well understood by medieval translators of the Bible. The Wyclifite Bible gives Deuteronomy 18:10 as 'Dyvynouris that dyuynen aboute the auteris,' and Isaiah 44:25 as 'Dyuynours, that dyuynen by sacrifices offrid to feendis,' and such an interpretation is not surprising in view of the extent of the practise in medieval times. John of Salisbury strongly condemns such activities in his *De nugis curialium* (ii, 27). Giraldus Cambrensis describes the shoulder bone as being boiled by the Welsh and being used to discover anything from a wife's infidelity to a country's impending doom (*Itin. Kamb.*, 1, xi). A famous French pirate called Eustace the Monk was a practitioner in the same century and among more recent exponents is a young lady from Wakefield in the nineteenth century and the descendants of the Flemish weavers in Wales in this century, whose young women discover the identity of their lovers by means of a shoulder of mutton.[16] Divination, however, is not the property assigned by the Pardoner to his sheepbone. In fact, with regard to cuckolded husbands, the sheepbone by eradicating justifiable jealousy might be said to give rise to delusions rather than a revelation of truth.

The Pardoner implies that his sheepbone is in the nature of a relic (347–351). Relics are, of course, primarily the bones of saints used for healing the sick. For lack of the saint whose presence will induce the cure, the relic is used by his ecclesiastical representative. Many preachers of Chaucer's day actively promoted relics, urging peasants to give up pagan charms for benefits accruing from a glimpse of St Winifred's bones in Shrewsbury Abbey or of St John the Evangelist's ring at Westminster.[17] Fragments of the True Cross were particularly efficacious, and when the Miller's Wife, in bed with young clerk John, invokes the holy cross of Bromeholm (*RvT*, 1, 4286) she is referring to a piece of the Cross brought from Constantinople in 1223 to Bromholm Priory, some seventy-five miles from Trumpington.

It has often been remarked that the Pardoner's sheepbone has the properties of magic charms or stones. More probably the Pardoner, always with a view to his own commercial advantage, gives to the sheepbone the attributes suited to the occasion, at the same time availing himself of any supernatural association which may add conviction to his claim. By using well water he disseminates the bone's beneficial properties in the widest possible way thereby increasing his own earnings. All that is required in the water, either as a mouthwash or a potion, to multiply cattle or cure them of their diseases, and to persuade a cuckold that his wife is faithful, Such benefits have a slight connection with scapulomancy. Kirk, a Scottish minister in the seventeenth century, states in *the Secret Commonwealth*: 'by looking into the Bone they will tell if Whoredom be committed in the Owners House . . . and if any Cattel there will take a Trake, as if Planet-struck.'[18] They have some connection with Saints' relics in as much as water, particularly well water, in which the bones of saints are dipped, has curative powers. The Pardoner also appears to be making use of the fact that animal bones since antiquity have been favored with magical properties. For centuries a sheepbone warded off fairies and witches, and the patella in particular was worn as near to the skin as possible and put under the pillow at night as a protection against 'cramp.' Even in this century Manx people are reported to carry the lucky bone of a sheep in their purse.[19] The Pardoner would also know that his audience was familiar with the custom of drinking a potion as a test for sexual morality. In the so-called *Ludus Coventriae* the Summoner has Joseph and Mary hauled before the Episcopal Court to undergo such a test. The practice was probably standard and seems to derive from the test for adultery laid down in Numbers 5, whereby a draught of holy water mixed with tabernacle dust makes a guilty woman's thighs fall away and her body swell.

It is possible that the Pardoner's hocus-pocus about the sheepbone arises from a difficulty inherent in his profession. Chaucer identifies his sacred relics as pigs' bones (*Gen Prol*, 1, 700) yet the Pardoner is expected to have his own travelling display case of such items. He is probably hard put to find relics that even looked genuine and yet he must know that a Pardoner without his saint's bone is without his most important stock in trade. His problem is to make the sheepbone do the kind of work his customers will expect from a holy relic. Even the simplest peasant is unlikely to attribute the shoulderbone of a sheep to the anatomy of a saint. But a large bone, such as he might pick up near a village from the common pasture, has advantages from the point of view of showmanship. By producing the fiction of the Holy Jew's sheep he is able to account for it and make use of a confusion of ideas associated with Holy Men, wells, saints' bones, lucky sheep bones and charms.

The sheep is, of course, specifically associated with Jewish sacrifice from earliest times. The Hebrews of the patriarchal age were nomadic shepherds and, significantly, the mother of the house of Joseph was called Rachel — 'mother sheep.' It was the animal on which their life depended. Tacitus in his history implies that a basis for Roman enmity towards the Jews was the fact that they sacrificed a ram, a practise which the Romans regarded as an insult to Jupiter Ammon (v, 4). The shoulder blade was the portion heaved up for divine acceptance, and as is evident from Deuteronomy 18:3, it was assigned to the priest. It follows that the priest could use the blade for purposes of divination. The nature of the Jewish sacrifice was stressed by the encyclopedists. 'Aries,' says Bartholomew, as translated by Trevisa, 'comyth of Aris/ awters/ for, as Isyder sayth, this beest was fyrste offryd on awters amonge nacions, and so the ramme hyght Aries for he was slayne by Aaron at the awter. And soo by Moyses lawe the ramme was pryncypally a clene beest both to sacrifyce and to meate' (cccv). It also formed one of the most dramatic episodes in the Mystery Cycles, the story of Abraham and Isaac. Both the learned and the laity would know about this miraculous beast. Just as its creation had been extraordinary so was the use to which its carcass was put. Its ashes formed the foundation of the inner altar used for the expiatory sacrifice offered once a year on the day of Atonement, the day of Abraham's sacrifice. Of its sinews David made ten strings for his harp. Elijah used the skin for a girdle. One horn was sounded at the end of the revelation on Mount Sinai and the other will proclaim the end of the Exile.[20] Even after the destruction of the Temple when the Passover became a sacrament observed at home, a roasted bone was placed on the table in memory of the rite.

Had Chaucer meant Abraham as the holy Jew he surely would have named him. If the reference in general, as it seems to be, I would suggest that he is referring to one of a dedicated sect, a holy man. Such were the Levites who, during the period of their dedication, observed various rituals, wore their hair long and abstained from alchohol. As a sect, they were not great priests or prophets but because of their self-discipline they were popularly credited with extra-sensory powers and considered to be minor seers. The Rev.

Robert Kirk, remarking that in scapulomancy the knife must never be applied to the bone, observes that the Nazarites of old were aware that 'iron hinders all the operations of those that travell in the intrigues of the hidden Dominions [future events].'[21] The Pardoner, who also wears his hair long, twice refers to the most famous Nazarite, Samson, appears to be obsessed with the idea of abstinence and may have had a particular interest in this sect. What is certain is that the Nazarite, at the end of his period of dedication, observed an elaborate ritualistic sacrifice. Whereas other early sacrifices also included various cattle, the Nazarite offered only a lamb, a ewe and a ram, and the ram's shoulder was the object of various ceremonies (Numbers 7:13–20). By ascribing his sheepbone to a holy Jew the Pardoner gives it an aura of sanctity and magic.

Chaucer makes skilful use of the sheep both as an animal in daily life and as a symbol. Details of sheep's diseases given by the Pardoner, the brief references to the sheep of the Reeve's master and of the poor widow, the allusion the Noah's 'wetheres blake,' and even the Pardoner's sheepbone, all reflect aspects of the contemporary scene and give concreteness to the situations. Traditional concepts of the sheep's meekness and stupidity are used perfunctorily in *The Knight's Tale* and in *The Second Nun's Tale*, but in *The Prologue to the Wife of Bath's Tale* and *The Miller's Tale* proverbial expressions give vitality to the characters. The symbolism of the sheep and the shepherd in the portrait of the Parson in *The General Prologue* and that of the lamb in *The Clerk's Tale* provide images of religious connotation and create a high seriousness of tone. While Chaucer knows that sheep suffer from 'pokkes,' scabs and sores, and cower in their fold, he is not sufficiently interested in the animal to draw attention to it on its own account.

X. The Dog

T HERE have been two conflicting attitudes towards the dog from com-
paratively early times.[1] While the Egyptians regarded it with great
veneration, even shaving their heads as a mark of respect when a dog
died, the Jews termed it unclean and spoke of it with abhorrence. The Greeks
praised it for its affection, fidelity, long memory and intelligence but used
κύων and related words as terms of abuse, particularly for women of ill-
repute. The Romans called it *sagax* and associated it with supernatural powers.

The stories popularized by the encyclopedists and bestiarists derived
mainly from Pliny and told of cures effected by dogs and of sacrifices made by
dogs for their loved ones. They were a favorite subject for spirited illustrations and typical of these is a series of panels in a thirteenth-century English
bestiary. One, captioned *de fidelitate cani*, shows an intruder hurled violently
to the ground by two mastiffs. Another presents a shepherd dozing confi-
dently among his flock while his dog stands on guard with ears cocked. In the
most dramatic of the panels a hound sits on its haunches howling beside its
slain master while a second hound holds the murderer by the throat.[2] Such
illustrations, in testifying to the estimable qualities of the beast, also suggest
a carnivorous ferocity, a quality probably only too evident in the half-wild

creature common in daily life and convincingly demonstrated by a short-eared, short-legged brindled mongrel gnawing the leg of a tinker in the *Luttrell Psalter* (fol. 70v).

It is only in recent times that not to love dogs has come to be the mark of an ignoble nature. Some idea of the attitude towards dogs can be gauged from the fact that a law existed, probably originating with the Normans and certainly in force during the reign of Henry I, which subjected all dogs found in the royal chases and forests, except those belonging to privileged persons, to be maimed by having the left claw (*sinistro ortello*) cut from their feet, unless they were redeemed by a fine.[3] In the house, children were requested to stop clawing the dogs at mealtime and stewards to clout them if necessary to drive them from the master's bedroom. In the villages and on the highways dogs roamed half-wild. Their appearance was villainous, and according to *The Master of Game* rabies was a constant threat. Some cities took measures to restrain the animals. In fourteenth-century Bristol no large dogs were allowed to roam the streets without chains but in other cities even in the fifteenth century dogs were not leashed. Hunting dogs and pet dogs of the nobility were another matter, and the appearance of such dogs on fourteenth-century brasses and sculptures at the feet of their masters or mistresses suggests that they were highly prized for their loyalty and affection. Ladies who were so infatuated with their dogs that they brought them to church were frequently denounced by satirists and homilists, and the *Luttrell Psalter* shows ladies travelling in a wagon with pet dogs and squirrels (fol. 181v). Wyclif was particularly insensed because friars gave women 'smale gentil houndis, to gete love of hem,'[4] and Langland was even more scathing of the cleric who 'priked a-boute on palfrais . . ./ An hepe of houndes at hus ers · as he a lord were' (c, vi, 160–161).

Boethius likens the dog to the man who 'ferox atque inquies linguam litigiis exercet,' and Chaucer translates the passage: 'If he be felonows and withoute reste, and exercise his tonge to chidynges, thow schalt likne hym to the hownd' (iv, pr. 3, 107–110). This pejorative view, reinforced by Biblical reference, appears to have been largely favored by the Church. In illustrations of the seven deadly sins the dog came to represent envy. Its mystical powers were associated with evil rather than with good; the Christian attitude seems to have turned the hounds of pagan gods and goddesses, such as those belonging to the Celtic huntress whom the Romans equated with Diana, into the familiars of witches and devils, giving rise to folklore beliefs, some of which persist into this century, in sinister, hunting ghost-hounds, in the devil appearing as a dog, and in dog-vampirism. There are a few instances of the dog appearing as a magic, tutelary animal: a 'blak brachette sekyng in maner as hit had bene in the feaute of an hurte dere' leads Sir Lancelot to a dead knight and a distressed lady.[5] But in saints' legends the dog rarely appears, and when it does, its presence is usually disturbing. Saints such as St Dunstan and St Waltheof were troubled by the devil appearing to them as a dog, and the mothers of Bernard, Dominic, and Vincent dreamed they had little dogs in their wombs. Nor does the virtuous dog lose its savagery. A Jew's dog refused to eat the Host, and when the Jew attempted to force it the dog 'stirte vp to is þrote and voried hym.'[6]

The Biblical use of *hound* as an epithet of contempt is common among the writers of romances. The hound in a heathen in Layamon's *Brut* (16623) and a Saracen in *King Horn* (1465). In early Middle English the word *dogge* is usually depreciatory, and an unequivocally pejorative meaning is attached to *dogged*, *doggedli*, *doggi* and *doggish* throughout the period. Among the didactic writers the dog is even more repulsive. In the *Ancrene riwle* the Devil is a dog who comes 'snakerinde wit his blodi flehen of stinkinde þohtes', and in *Jacob's Well*, the flatterer 'faryst as an hounde þat lyckyth an-oþer hound, whanne he metyth hym, behynde in þe ers, in þat vnclene membre.'[7] The sexual life of the dog appears to have impressed itself on the imagination. A typical punishment in hell for adulterous intercourse involves the joining of lovers *quomodo canis* for all eternity.

Chaucer uses conventional ideas about the dog which are wholly pejorative. Except when they are non-committal, his references are harsh, and when he applies a proverbial phrase or an image from a literary source, he frequently selects those with derogatory connotations.

The dog in the hunt he alludes to several times but the lack of detail suggests that he takes it for granted and has no special interest in describing it. Of specific types of hunting dogs, he mentions *lymeres* (*BD*, 362, 365), which are tracking hounds, the Monk's swift greyhounds (*Gen Prol*, 1, 190), the spaniel (*WB Prol*, 111, 265–268) and the alaunts 'as grete as any steer' which accompany Lygurge (*KnT*, 1, 2148–2152). Probably related to the Great Dane, *alaunts* are the only dogs to which Chaucer ascribes a hue, presumably with the intention of enhancing the effect of pageantry. They are supposed to have been brought to western Europe by a Caucasian tribe called Alains or Alani, who, in the fourth century, invaded Gaul and then Spain. During the Middle Ages the best alaunts were obtained from Spain, and Gaston de Foix, living on the Spanish borders, gives a description which exactly tallies with that given in *Libro de la Monteria*, a fourteenth-century hunting treatise by Alfonso XI.[8] Chaucer's alaunts accompany Lygurge in *The Knight's Tale*, and they are white:

> Aboute his chaar ther wenten white alauntz,
> Twenty and mo, as grete as any steer,
> To hunten at the leoun or the deer,
> And folwed hym with mosel faste ybounde,
> Colered of gold, and tourettes fyled rounde.
>
> (2148–2152)

According to *The Master of Game*, 'though there be alauntes of all hues, the true hue of a good alaunte, and that which is most common should be white with black spots about the ears, small eyes and white standing ears and sharp above.'9 There are three kinds of alaunts: *alauntes gentle, alauntes veutrères* and *alauntes of the butcheries*. The large size of Chaucer's alaunts suggests that they are *alauntes veutrères*, good for baiting the bull and for hunting the wild boar. All alaunts will hold any animal but the *alauntes gentle* appear to be smaller than the *alauntes veutrères*, and the *alauntes of the butcheries* are used mainly by butchers to bring in cattle bought in the country. Since all types are vicious, the fact that Chaucer's alaunts wear muzzles is not significant. *Colered* is a heraldic term, but while 'Colered of gold, and tourettes fyled round' is appropriate to the glittering pageantry of the general description of Lygurge, such details may derive from contemporary life. The collars of hunting dogs were often ornate and expensive. Chaucer describes the dogs in detail probably to fit in with the general brilliancy of the spectacle, rather than because they were unfamiliar to his audience. (The writer of *The Master of Game* gives the impression that alaunts were not uncommon in England, for he adds to Gaston de Foix's account the fact that they were used in bull-baiting as well as in boar hunting.)

Under the name greyhound a whole group of dogs was included in the Middle Ages, such as the large Irish wolfhound, Scottish deerhound and the smaller, more elegant Italian greyhound. The Scottish deerhound may have been used for pulling down deer, but for the Monk's hare the smaller, nervous harehound, described in France as *petit levrier pour lièvre*, was probably used. Hounds of the greyhound group were not restricted to the kennels. They were the constant companions of their masters on journeys, in wars and at home. A Welsh proverb declared that a gentleman might be known 'by his hawk, his horse and his greyhound,' and by the laws of Canute the greyhound was the companion of a gentleman only and could not be kept by anyone of inferior rank.'10

As might be expected, Chaucer's various descriptions of the actions of dogs in the chase are in accordance with the practices of his age. In *The Franklyn's Tale* (1193) by the magician's art, Aurelius sees a hundred harts 'slayn with houndes,' denoting the English practice, described in *The Master of the Game*, of running down the deer with hounds; in *The Book of the Duchess* the hounds, after being uncoupled and quickly pursuing the hart for a long time, overrun the scent: 'The houndes had overshote hym alle,/ And were on a defaute yfalle' (383–384), and in accordance with the correct custom, the *forloyn* is sounded. With regard to Theseus' hounds in *The Knight's Tale*, Chaucer's phrase 'han a cours . . . with houndes' is a further illustration of a familiarity with specific hunting terms. But it is possible to overstress Chaucer's concern with hunting practices. In *The Book of the Duchess* he states:

> And as I lay thus, wonder lowde
> Me thoght I herde an hunte blowe
> T'assay hys horn, and for to knowe

Whether hyt were clere or hors of soun.
And I herde goynge, bothe up and doun,
Men, hors, houndes, and other thyng;
And al men speken of huntyng.
(344–350)

It has been suggested that in referring to 'other thyng' he was no doubt thinking of preparations such as those cited in the chapter entitled 'how the assembly that men call gathering should be made both winter and summer after the guise of beyond the sea' in *The Master of Game*. But a similar phrase occurs in Barbour's *Bruce* (I, 207) — 'As hors or hund or other thing' — where it refers not to hunting but to pillaging in battle, and Chaucer may be merely using a tag for the purpose of rhyme.

In the description of the preparations for the hunt in the story of Dido in *The Legend of Good Women*, Chaucer medievalizes the scene and gives it focus, by bringing the hounds into court (iii, 1194), in contrast to Virgil's 'Massylique ruunt equites et odora canum vis' (*Aeneid*, iv, 132). Instead of huntsmen waiting for Dido at the palace door, mounted knights, women and dogs all hover about the queen. A similar tendency to medievalize is seen in the description of the hunt itself, where he uses the correct hunting term 'a herde of hertes' (1212), gives English hunting cries and omits Virgil's wild goats. But the scene is less descriptive than Virgil's, and Chaucer is not so anxious to anglicize it consistently as to omit the lion, nor does he hesitate to substitute a bear for a boar, apparently for the purposes of rhyme.

In all the references cited so far the attitude is non-commital: the animal simply belongs to a descriptive scene which serves as a back-cloth for the human drama. Elsewhere, with the exception of Diana's 'smale houndes al aboute hir feet' (*KnT*, I, 2076), which are not described further, the houndes briefly referred to by the Wife of Bath (*WB Prol*, III, 285), and Colle, Talbot and Gerland (*NPT*, VII, 3383–3386), whose only harm is to frighten the hogs with their barking, Chaucer's dogs, at best obsequious or pampered, are associated with distasteful ideas.

In a single reference to the spaniel, the idea of the hunting animal is applied to woman in pursuit of man:

And if she be foul, thou seist that she
Coveiteth every man that she may se,
For as a spaynel she wol on hym lepe,
Til that she fynde som man hire to chepe.
(*WB Prol*, III, 265–268)

The Wife of Bath is giving a demonstration of the efficient way she copes with a complaining husband. The husband has apparently implied that the ugly woman is a nymphomaniac who solicits boldly until she meets with success. The question arises why an ugly woman should be compared to a spaniel. According to *The Master of Game*, a spaniel has a great head and a great body; its nature is demonstrative but its affections appear to be confined to one master.[11] Since spaniels can be good hunters and are fighters and great barkers if taken among running hounds, Chaucer may simply be suggesting predatory, aggressive and noisy qualities in an ugly woman. According to *The Master of Game* spaniels are particularly useful for taking quail, the game bird to which Chaucer compares the husband in the Clerk's ironic envoy (1201–1206).

It is tempting to suppose that Chaucer may have had in mind some proverbial comparison. Current in the sixteenth century was the saw: 'A spaniel, a woman and a walnut tree / The more they're beaten, the better still they be,' but I have found no instance of its earlier use. Chaucer may also have been ascribing to woman the lustful propensities customarily attributed to the dog, as well as the obsequious, fawning propensities traditionally ascribed to the spaniel. Often repeated was the idea that by Mosaic Law the offering of the price of a dog was accounted unclean, as the price of a common woman: 'for such wretched persons serve in al lechery as hounds doe,' and according to Caxton 'Seneca sayth that the women that have evyll visages be gladly not chaste.'[12]

Hunting terms to do with dogs have a derogatory connotation when Chaucer uses them metaphorically. Of the Summoner in *The Friar's Tale* Chaucer writes:

> For in this world nys dogge for the bowe
> That kan an hurt deer from an hool yknowe
> Bet than this somnour knew a sly lecchour,
> Or an avowtier, or a paramour.
>
> (1369–1372)

A similar metaphor is applied to Damyan in *The Merchant's Tale*, who goes to January 'as lowe / As evere dide a dogge for the bowe' (2013–2014). The dog referred to would be the greyhound, capable of pulling down the deer in readiness for the bowman's arrow. In the first example, the metaphor appropriately illustrates the Summoner's ability to hunt down sinners in preparation for subsequent punishment by the archdeacon. In the second instance, Damyan has just received a letter from May and has high hopes of cuckolding the antlered stag, January. The metaphor suggests his eagerness and readiness. It is not continued further, but there may be an ironical hint of it in the later remark of the victim when he is unwittingly contributing towards the final consummation: 'Mighte I yow helpen with myn herte blood' (2347).

On the domestic scene, the dog is a creature which eats corpses or children. When Creon conquers Thebes, he refuses to allow the dead to be buried but 'maketh houndes ete hem in despit' (*KnT*, I, 947). The aged January would prefer the most ignominious of deaths, that dogs should eat him (*MerchT*, IV, 1438), rather than that on his demise his property should pass to a stranger.

In *The Clerk's Tale* (IV, 1095) Griselda says that she was afraid that cruel hounds or some foul vermin had eaten her children. In the first passage Chaucer substitutes dogs for the more general reference to animals which appears in the corresponding passage in *Teseida* (ii, 31). Later, in the same tale (2204–2205), he omits the commendatory force of *usavano e diletto* occurring in *Teseida* (vi, 8), but the reason may be simply that he is making use of the rhetorical device of *occupatio* and is avoiding Boccaccio's grand manner.

Used figuratively, the dog evokes a variety of unpleasant images. A good ruler has the tolerance of a lion, not the vengeful disposition of a cur (*LGW*, F, 396, G, 382); the disreputable Friar indulges in puppy-like frolics (*Gen Prol*, I, 257); quick-tempered Goodelief, according to her husband, refers to the servants as dogs, and suggests he should kill them (*Mk Prol*, VII, 1899); the sinister beast of which Chauntecleer dreams is 'lyk an hound' (*NPT*, VII, 2900), and Pertelote, diagnosing that the dreams are due to an excess of red choler, includes 'whelpes grete and lyte' (2932) among the disagreeable items, arrows, fire with red flames, red biting beasts, and warfare, which appear in such dreams (2930–2932). The wedded man in the morning cowers like the weary hare harassed by dogs (*ShipT*, VII, 103–105); 'olde dotarde holours' (857) are compared to the dog vainly going through the gestures of urinating 'whan he comth by the roser or by othere beautees [Robinson: bushes]' (*ParsT*, x, 857–858).

When Chaucer draws upon proverbial material repellent images still predominate. Pandarus sees himself and his relatives lying like dogs dead in the street, 'thorughgirt with many a wid and blody wownde' (*Tr*, iv, 627); the sinner returning to his wickedness is like the dog returning to its vomit (*ParsT*, x, 137–139), and the damned whom God will consign to hell are like dogs who are given bones and not meat (*ParsT*, x, 221).

Of two further proverbial expressions connected with the dog, one presents an image of flagellation, the other hints at the potential violence of the dog. The falcon in *The Squire's Tale* says to the sympathetic Canacee:

> 'But for noon hope for to fare the bet,
> But for to obeye unto youre herte free,
> And for to maken othere be war by me,
> As by the whelp chasted is the leon,
> Right for that cause and that conclusion,
> Whil that I have a leyser and a space,
> Myn harm I wol confessen er I pace.'
> (488–494)

Its sententiousness is not particularly suited to the falcon nor to the teller of the tale. Its origin may be either factual or literary, for it was the practice to discipline the lion by beating a dog, and it had already given rise to proverbs in Latin, French and English by Chaucer's day.[13] In his sketchbook, Villard de Honnecourt, the thirteenth-century architect and artist, describes the practice and shows a ferocious lion and trainer with dogs straining at the leash (fol. 46). The *Queen Mary's Psalter* has a vigorous illustration of a man whipping a dog before a crouching lion (fol. 185).

The second proverb occurs in *Troilus and Criseyde*. It is admirably suited to the character of the person who cites it. Its use and application illustrate Chaurce's art at its most mature:

> Quod tho Criseyde, 'let me som wight calle!'
> 'I! God forbede that it sholde falle,'
> Quod Pandarus, 'that ye swich folye wroughte!
> They myghte demen thyng they nevere er thoughte.

> 'It is nought good a slepyng hound to wake,
> Ne yeve a wight a cause to devyne.
> Youre wommen slepen alle, I undertake,
> So that, for hem, the hous men myghte myne,
> And slepen wollen til the sonne shyne.
> And whan my tale brought is to an ende,
> Unwist, right as I com, so wol I wende.'
>
> (iii, 760–770)

There is an unusual amount of aphorisms, saws, axioms, 'ensaumples' and other proverbial material in *Troilus and Criseyde* which is not found in *Il Filostrato*, and, apart from the narrator, Pandarus is the main user of such material. The use of the proverb in the passage cited is psychologically very astute. Pandarus' arrival in Criseyde's bedroom *via* the trap-door makes Criseyde uneasy and she wants to call one of her companions, the custodians of her honor and reputation. By drawing upon the wisdom of the ages, Pandarus is able to make her sensible suggestion seem like folly, implying that her sleeping attendants are not friendly watchdogs but hounds which attack when wakened. In a brief phrase, he conjures up the world of which Criseyde is always afraid, and, not surprisingly, successfully silences her.

Similarly unsparing are Chaucer's allusions to the dog when he follows a source. Two images of violence occur in the *Tale of Melibee*. In one image, given by Prudence when advising her husband not to underestimate his enemies, Chaucer's source, *Le livre de Mellibee et Prudence* has 'le chien, qui n'est pas moult grant, retien bien le sanglier,' whereas Chaucer has 'an hound wol holde the wilde boor' (1326). By omitting the reference to size, he robs the maxim of some of its force. The second image is merely proverbial, and is cited in Chaucer's source: the meddler is likened to the man who takes a strange dog by the ears and is subsequently bitten (1541). Another proverbial idea occurs in *The Parson's Tale*: those who commit incest are like 'houndes, that taken no kep to kynrede' (907). Peraldus has the same image: 'canis enim in opere illo non observat.'

Sometimes Chaucer will go outside his immediate source to add an unpleasant image. In *The Knight's Tale* he introduces the Aesopian fable of the kite and the dogs, implying that the lovers can be compared to the dogs for stupidity and quarrelsomeness (1177–1180), and later in the same tale he takes from Ovid the story of Actaeon who, having been turned into a stag by Diana, was eaten by his hounds;

> Ther saugh I Attheon an hert ymaked,
> For vengeaunce that he saugh Diane al naked;
> I saugh how that his houndes have hym caught
> And freeten hym, for that they knewe hym naught.
>
> (2065–2068)

Later Emily implores the goddess of chastity 'keepe me fro thy vengeaunce and thyn ire/ That Attheon aboughte cruelly' (2302–2303), implying that these dogs symbolize the sexual passion which she fears.[14] A most curious allusion occurs in *The Parson's Tale* where those who condone wickedness in their menials are likened to dogs following carrion (441). Chaucer appears to be translating Peraldus' treatise on the Vices but whereas Peraldus writes: '. . . mel musce sequunter, cadavera lupi' (20), Chaucer writes: '. . . the flyes that folwen the hony, or elles the houndes that folwen the careyne.' Since the wolf was 'a common beast enough' throughout the medieval period, there seems to be no obvious reason for the substitution. It would seem that Chaucer equates the dog with the wolf, an animal which, both in terms of medieval symbolism and modern psychiatry, epitomises aggression, rapacity and dissimulation.

In all his allusions to the dog Chaucer does not employ a single commendatory adjective. He seems unaffected by the strong tradition which praised the dog for its affection, fidelity, long memory and intelligence, and his one dog lover, whose charity caused her to weep if her pets were ill-treated, tells a viciously anti-semitic tale violating the deepest sense of charity.[15]

What of the whelp in *The Book of the Duchess*? Critics, in general, have found it attractive. Steadman regarded it as a symbol of marital fidelity, although Chaucer never uses the long tradition of the dog's faithfulness and affection elsewhere; Donaldson termed it 'a most pleasing symbol of the sympathy that pervades Chaucer's dream world.'[16]

Such interpretations seem to be based on the assumption that Chaucer, like ourselves, regards dog-loving as a virtue, but the nature of Chaucer's other allusions to dogs do not support this assumption. The language Chaucer uses here to describe the whelp is equivocal, and the scene itself seems best explained when fully integrated in the dream sequence.

The dog appears in the dream after the hart has escaped and the *forloyn* has been sounded:

I was go walked fro my tree,
And as I wente, ther cam by mee
A whelp, that fauned me as I stood,
That hadde yfolowed, and koude no good.
Hyt com and crepte to me as lowe
Ryght as hyt hadde me yknowe,
Helde doun hys hed and joyned hys eres,
And leyde al smothe doun hys heres.
I wolde have kaught hyt, and anoon
Hyt fledde, and was fro me goon;
And I hym folwed, and hyt forth wente
Doun by a floury grene wente.
(387–398)

Although Chaucer borrows phrases from Machaut for his description of the dog's behavior, he makes certain omissions which may be significant. The little dog in the *Dit du Roy* faithfully follows the mourning lady, and the amiable lion in the *Dit dou Lyon* submits to petting. Chaucer's whelp, with its docility and obsequiousness, demonstrates those very qualities proverbially regarded as being most deceptive in the dog. *Fawn* in Middle English means not only 'to show delight or fondness' but 'to court favor by cringing' and is frequently used in the pejorative sense in connection with the dog. The Devil is likened to a fawning dog; a hound approaching a man 'fawnyth hym wyth his tayl and behynde him byteth hym'; 'covert fraude' is described as 'berkyng behynde, ffawnyng in presence.'[17] Trevisa, in his translation of Bartholomew's *De proprietatibus rerum*, which gives the dog's virtues as well as its faults, states that the dog is 'gyleful . . . he fikeleþ and fawneþ wiþ his tail on men þat passeþ . . . as þough he were here freend, and biteþ hem sore' (xxvii).

Much discussion has centred on what the Dreamer intended to do with the dog had it not run away. Kittredge suggests that when the Dreamer states 'I wolde have kaught hyt,' he is indicating that he wished to take it in his arms. If the Dreamer's intention can be so construed, and was not simply to hold the dog by its collar, than the animal must have been portable. Most critics think that the dog is small. They refer to 'the little whelp,' 'the little dog,' and on this premise build up an appealing image of a tiny, helpless creature. In fact, Chaucer does not mention size, and according to Pertelote (*NPT*, VII, 2932) whelps are both 'grete and lyte.' Neither does Chaucer seem to associate the whelp with pleasant ideas. Not only does it appear in nightmares but it resembles a greedy profligate friar, a love-betrayed falcon, and, in *The Second Nun's Prologue* (60), in a reference to Matthew 15:27, it is the despised dog of the Jewish community, scavenging for crumbs.

The text then, provides no firm support for the view that man and beast are shown in mutual sympathy. All that Chaucer's accounts tells us of motivation is that the dog 'koude no good' — did not know what to do. It followed the Dreamer, behaving as if it knew him and wanted to be caressed. The Dreamer would have taken hold of it but it fled. In view of the ambiguity of the passage, the nature of Chaucer's other allusions to the dog may be relevant. If the whelp in *The Book of the Duchess* is intended to be an endearing figure, then Chaucer has divorced the animal from qualities such as greed, lechery or ferocity which he gives it elsewhere whenever he associates it with some specific psychological trait.

It is possible that in *The Book of the Duchess* Chaucer selected a dog from all the other magic tutelary creatures which he might have chosen because of its appropriateness to the hunting scene in an English forest. It may be that the dog is a simple structural device to effect a transition from the hunt to the elegy, and nothing more. It is also possible that Chaucer was thinking of the dog in its ancient role of guide from this world to the next. Such it was to the Amratians in the high-neolithic period in Egypt, to the Arabs who gave its name to the guiding star Sirius, and to the Greeks who regarded it as the representative of Mercury, keeper of the boundary between life and death.[18] Yet such explanations do not seem to account for the peculiar effectiveness of the dog's appearance; for the artistic rightness of the scene. If the whelp has a deeper meaning which is not inconsonant with the considerations already stated, it may be dependent on the fuller context of the passage.

The psychological circumstances which contribute to the dream are explicit. The narrator experiences a brooding melancholy due to persistent sleeplessness, and he has suffered thus for eight years without relief. To while away the sleepless hours, he reads the story of Alcyone, the unhappy queen who could learn nothing of the fate of her absent husband nor get respite from her longing. The narrator, finding his own grief imaged in that of the mourning wife, dwells on her sorrow in sympathetic detail. Unlike Gower, he omits the happy sequel whereby husband and wife are metamorphosed into birds and reunited. Instead, he prays to Morpheus, who was instrumental in bringing Alcyone's dead husband to her in a vision and confronting her with the truth, and invokes his aid for sleep. His wish is immediately granted. He falls asleep, his book still in his hand:

> ... and therwith even
> Me mette so ynly swete a sweven,
> So wonderful, that never yit
> Y trowe no man had the wyt
> To konne wel my sweven rede;
> No, not Joseph, withoute drede,
> Of Egipte, he that redde so
> The kynges metynge Pharao,
> No more than koude the lest of us.
> (275–283)

But if the dominant emotion experienced by the narrator prior to sleep is a protracted and unsatisfied love-longing, as seems to be suggested, the kind of dream which ensues should be of the anxiety type. Although Chaucer's artistic intentions preclude his presenting such a dream, he appears to make use of certain features which are characteristic of the nightmare. As we have seen in connection with the horse, the hunt, in the *Book of the Duchess*, with its quickness of pace, compulsive participation, strange duration from early morning to midnight, its legendary leader Octavian, contains traces of the *angstvolle Traumfahrt*. Closely linked with the nightmare ride is the superstition of the spectral huntsmen who, particularly on stormy nights or when the moon was full, could be heard riding past with horns blowing and dogs baying. So important were the dogs, with their eyes aflame and their unearthly howls, that separate legends arose about them. In Northern England there were Gabriel's hounds — the name originally probably having nothing to do with the archangel but being a variant of a Yorkshire word *gabble*: a corpse; in the south there were the Yeth or Wisht Hounds believed to range over the moors of Devon and Cornwall. Like the dog in ancient times, the hound of the Wild Hunt was the conductor of souls to the after-life. It was, as the lingering superstition regarding the howling dog indicates, the presager of death, or the snarling emissary of hell.[19]

But from the beginning of the dream, literary conventions — the May morning of the Garden of the Rose, the windows depicting the story of Troy, the walls on which are painted scenes from the *Roman de la rose* — are interwoven with a seemingly genuine dream fabric, and with the escape of the hart the poet reveals his intention to develop his main theme. Instead of a hound of hell, an inexperienced hunting dog approaches the Dreamer.

Chaucer has frequently been praised for the knowledge of dream psychology displayed both in the strange way in which one incident flows into another and in the manner in which the attitude of the Dreamer is consistent with what has gone before. In a real dream, the Dreamer often splits into two: he sees his *alter ego* move and talk. Chaucer makes use of the same authentic phenomenon in his poem. The Dreamer and mourner are remarkably similar to each other. They are both stupefied by grief (6–13, 509–511), have lost their vital spirit (25–26, 489) and are astonished that they are still alive (16–21, 467–469). Even the age assigned to the Man in Black appears to be that of the narrator rather than that of John of Gaunt. Although the narrator identified himself with the 'I' of the dream, he is also represented by the other person in his dream. The dichotomy is anticipated by the counter moves of animal and Dreamer: the dog approaches; the Dreamer intends to catch it; the dog flees in the direction of the mourner; the Dreamer pursues it. The Dreamer is, in fact, about to split into two roles, that of observer and that of participant, and the lesson which emerges for the Man in Black is one which the narrator has already advised for himself: 'But that is don . . . that will not be mot nede be left' (40–42).

The whelp is splendidly appropriate as the agent to effect the transition. It is a figure which arises naturally from the psychological circumstances of the dream hunt. Transformed though it is from the evil creature of the nightmare into a young English hunting dog, its role is not sentimental as is often suggested. It serves both to illustrate the dichotomy about to take place in the Dreamer himself and to give meaningful continuity to the hunt.

Bartholomew devotes a chapter to the 'unclene and lecherous' propensities of the dog, and attributes to Aristotle the idea which is also expressed by Chaucer's Parson that 'houndes bothe male and female use lychery as longe as they ben alyue, and yeue them to vnclennesse of lechery, that they take noo dyuersyte bytwene mother and sister, and other bytches, towchynge the dede of lechery' (xxvii). But he also praises the dog's courage and loyalty, qualities which Chaucer chooses to ignore. In his works, excluding the translations of the *Roman de la rose* and Boethius' *De consolatione philosophiae*, Chaucer refers to the dog nearly fifty times, either concretely in description or figuratively for the purpose of throwing light on human behavior. But he is not interested in the animal for its own sake. He is non-committal when he refers to it as part of the local scene, and when he uses it for purposes of illustration he applies conventional ideas which are almost wholly pejorative. He enhances the impact of the stereotype by skilfully adapting his knowledge of current practices to the situation immediately before him. The effect is to startle the reader with a brief but unsparing reflection of man's depravity or lack of dignity. All this is achieved with seeming naturalness and spontaneity — qualities which are not the result of simplicity but of an art so practised that it conceals itself.

Conclusion

WE have seen that, from primitive times, animals acquired specific traits which remained almost unchanged over the centuries, despite wide divergencies in the motivations of those who used them. Different as the approaches of the early natural historian and the hermeneutical writer were, for example, the one seeking to compile a factual account of natural phenomena, the other regarding the visible world as wholly emblematic, serving to instruct man in the abstract truths which lay behind the physical manifestations, they both reiterated the stereotyped characteristics of animals found in many other kinds of literature as well as in popular lore. Chaucer uses the same conventional ideas. When he alludes to the fierceness of the lion, the rapacity of the wolf, and the craftiness of the fox, he is referring to widely accepted attributes. Also traditional is the general use to which he puts the animal. Regarding the animal as important for its similarities to man, he makes it serve to throw light on human character and action.

It might be observed that Chaucer's imagery in general reflects the peculiar conditions of oral delivery. The medieval listener could not go back over something he failed to grasp: he appreciated a surface simplicity, familiar phrases, repetition, alliteration, onomatopoeia. It is because Chaucer's figurative language consists largely of proverbial expressions and formulaic groups of words expressing essential, accepted ideas that we have so many allusions to animals in phrases which, by his day, were frequent in everyday speech. But the very qualities which would cause such allusions to seem trite in a lesser poet, Chaucer turns into an advantage. The platitudinous nature of so many of his phrases enables him to disguise point of view, to obscure moral alignment and to make the narrator seem uncommitted. The apparent objectivity is appropriate to the oblique approach and it heightens the impact. The reader is ultimately startled to discover the intensity with which a figure may be realized.

An animal figure, seemingly perfunctory and serving only a very immediate purpose, may illuminate a passage or even a whole work. At its most powerful it is organic; it sets up a series of responses and functions organically within the aesthetic whole. It can illustrate theme, complexity of character, action, or even be part of a pattern in an ironic sub-structure.

All this can be achieved when the actual allusion consists of some factual detail about the animal, with the symbolism implied but not stated. In *Troilus and Criseyde* the symbolic quality of timidity is suggested in Pandarus' comparison of Criseyde to a deer:

'Lo, hold the at thi triste cloos, and I

CONCLUSION

Shal wel the deer unto thi bowe dryve.'
(ii, 1534–1535)

The figure also presents a graphic visual image arising from actual practises in the hunt. But since it proposes that Criseyde is an animal to be caught, that Pandarus is the beater using craft and experience to drive the animal into a trap, and that Troilus is the bowman lying in wait to kill the quarry, it is a subtle device for illustrating the roles of the protagonists as Pandarus sees them. In *The Parson's Tale*, while the basic symbolism of the ape as being imitative and lascivious is appropriate to the indictment of the fashionably dressed man, the physical appearance of the she-ape at *oestrus* also offers opportunity for a more detailed comparison. The passage gains even further dimension from the fact that the ape represents pride, the sin which the Parson is denouncing.

In other powerful figures the associational values are exploited with even further subtlety and thoroughness. When the hare is applied to the Pardoner and the weasel to Alison, an apparently swift simile adumbrates an extremely complex presentation of character in which considerations of the animal's symbolism, folklore and physical appearance are all taken into account. The first reveals that the Pardoner is a hermaphrodite, the second indicates that, for all her countrified charm, Alison is both the traditional creature of ill-luck, possessing many of the qualities attributed to the weasel in folklore, and the fierce little animal of the heath.

An examination of the kind of image used suggests that to Chaucer, the animal embodies the least attractive qualities of man. The implications are frequently pejorative, whether the images are derived from his own experience, the natural histories and other compilations, the fables, or from proverbial lore. To passages in which he appears to be following a literary source fairly closely, he sometimes even adds an image of violence or of sexual licence, and his two longest passages on animals, which occur in *The Manciple's Tale*, illustrate man's 'likerous appetit.'

While Chaucer's views are in accordance with the teachings of Boethius and of the Church, they may seem surprisingly harsh in one so sharply conscious of the poignant appeal of 'this world, that passeth soone as floures faire.' But medieval man did not need to reconcile the abstract and the actual. Chaucer shares the double vision of the Gothic world, and from it arise some of the complexities of his most successful animal figures. The Wife of Bath, the promiscuous lioness, can be triumphant in her claim for the natural life; Alison, the untamed weasel, can emerge unscathed. Excused from moral obligations by their creator, they exemplify the unlicensed vitality of the animal world, a quality simultaneously attractive and repellent, producing images of both the skipping kid and the prancing ape.

For all his delight in him, Chaucer knows that man is but a poor, bare, forked animal, only rising above the brute when the soul is in control of the body. The animal is, in fact, a kind of Yahoo, a creature of which it may be said:

> Lo, heere hath lust his dominacioun,
> And appetit fleemeth discrecioun.
> *(Manc T*, ix, 181–182)

Notes to the Text

Chapter I. The Traditions

page

3 1 *HA*, ii, 1, 4; ix, 5, 4; v, 19, 13. For Pliny, see *NH*, x, 67, 86; xxiv, 4, 23.

3 2 Dio, *Epit.*, lxxv, lxxci; for Aelian see *De nat*, iv, 31; xii, 46; ii, 31.

5 3 Hervieux, iv, 287; cf. de Vitry, p. 87. Owst calls the tale 'a hoary commonplace of our pulpit,' p. 389.

5 4 *Jacob's Well*, p. 262; Bromyard, *Adulterium*, A xv; *Ayenbite*, p. 438.

5 5 *Rev. of S.B.* pp. 108–109.

7 6 *Jacob's Well*, p. 263; *Cursor Mundi*, 18639–18660; *Orm.*, 5830–5831; *Ayenbite*, p. 61; cf. Shoreham, p. 262.

7 7 Mand., p. 175.

7 8 *Pol. Poems*, 1, 123–215.

8 9 *Ibid.*, 1, 363–366.

8 10 *Pol. Songs*, 195–205.

8 11 See Raven, *passim*.

8 12 BM Arund. MS 83, fols. 124, 131.

9 13 Magd. Coll, Camb. MS. 1916.

9 14 See Christie, pls. lxxvi, lxxvii, cxix.

9 15 Bond, *Engl. Churches*, 1, 27–28; cf. Univ. Lib. Camb. MS Ii–4–26, fol. 7; BM. Harl. MS 4751, fol. 9.

10 16 Bodl. MS 264, fols. 70, 181v; Chambers, *Med. Stage*, 1, 275, 391–392; Welsford, *Court Masque*, pp. 42–43.

10 17 See Anderson, *Brit. Churches*, p. 21.

Chapter II. Aspects of Chaucer's Use of Animals

13 1 John of Gaunt's *Reg.*, 11, 98; Rolls, 111, 501.

13 2 See BM. Slo. MS 2435 fol. 48v; BM. Roy. MS 2 B vii, fol. 145; see also Anderson, *Brit. Churches*, p. 265; *Med. Carv.*, p. 37.

13 3 *Régime*, pp. 127–128.

14 4 *Roman de Brut*, 10889; *De gestis*, p. 161; *De nat.*, 1, 23, 11, 165–166.

14 5 T. Wright, *Voc.*, p. 136; Loftie, *Hist. of London*, 11, 146; *Magenta*, 1, 117; *EB*, xxviii, 1018; Poole, p. 608; Haskins, *12th Cent.*, p. 328; Anderson, *Med. Carv.*, p. 147.

14 6 E. A. Bond, 'Lib. Rolls,' p. 316; Cook, *Trans.* p. 174; n. 1.; Toulmin Smith, *Derby Accts.* p. lxv.

page

14   7 Skeat, *Works*, I, 545, cit. V. de B's *Spec. Nat.*, xix, 63; Pliny, *NH*, xxviii, 8. On the hyena as detractor, see Holcot's *Wisdom*, Lectio ix. See, too, Robertson, *Preface*, p. 307.

15   8 *An. Creat.*, I, 131.

15   9 *Cal. Pat. Rolls*, 1385–1389, pp. 170–171; *Manners and House Exp.*, xliii; *Iss. Excheq.*, 8 Ed. II, June 14.

16   10 See Bennett's comments, *Parlement*, p. 79.

16   11 Lowes, *PMLA*, xix, 627.

17   12 Shook, *Companion*, p. 349; Bennett, *Book*, p. 51; Jaeger, *Paideia*, p. 220; Wilson, *QJS*, L, 153–158. On the iconographic significance of the eagle, see also Koonce, *Fame*, pp. 85–86, 143ff; Teager, *PMLA*, xlvii, 410–418.

17   13 Robertson and Huppé, *Fruyt and Chaf*, p. 46, see these birds singing in 'solempne servise' as performing a symbolic action; Rodney Delasanta, *PMLA*, lxxxiv, 249–250, regards them as initiating 'a process of spiritual epiphany in the dreamer.' On the other hand, many earlier critics, including John Lawlor, *Spec.* xxxi, 626–648, treat the birds as part of the courtly love tradition, which Chaucer revitalizes 'in all its brightest colours.'

18   14 See Baker, *Companion*, p. 363.

18   15 Birney, *Anglia*, lxxviii, 207–208.

19   16 Bacon, *Opus*, II, 264; *AR*, pp. 89–90; cf. Silvestris, *Comm.*, p. 62; Hervieux, IV, 216; *Secreta Secretorum*, I, 104; Robertson, *Preface*, pp. 153–154.

19   17 See D. T. B. Wood, *Burl. Mag.*, xx (1911–1912), 210–222, 277–289; *Mel. d'Arch.*, II, 21–27 (MS franc, 70113.3); Bodl. MS Douce 366, fols. 72, 109; BM. Ad. MS 28162, fol. 3v.

20   18 Camb. MS Univ. Lib. Gg 4.27 fols. 432, 433; Furnivall, *Harl.*, append. 4; Manly and Rickert, *Text*, I, 593–596.

22   19 Marckwardt, *Characterization*, pp. 1–23.

23   20 *cf.* Muscatine, *Chaucer*, pp. 205–206.

24   21 Maynard, *Vocal Organs*, p. 45; Carr, *Pigeons*, p. 138.

24   22 T. H. White, *Bestiary*, p. 144. See also 'Allegoriae,' *PL*, cxii, col. 899.

25   23 For further comment see Biggins, *MAE*, xxxiii, 200–203; Rowland, *ChauR*, II, 159–165.

25   24 Bodl. MS Lat. Th. d. i, fol. 88v.

25   25 Zuckerman, *Monkeys*, p. 142. See Robertson, *Preface*, p. 263. and fig. 110, for a possible connection between apes and the hunt of Venus.

25   26 Carmody, *Versio Y*, p. 122; McCulloch, *Best.*, p. 86.

25   27 Ruggiers, *Art*, p. 59, finds the animal imagery suggests 'either an irresponsible and unburdened pastoral innocence, or more specifically the barnyard world . . . ,' similarly, Jordan, *Shape*, p. 190, speaks of Alison's 'incomparable . . . natural freshness and animal vigor.' For various discussions of imagery in the tale see Donaldson, *EIE*, 116–140; Beichner, *MS*, xii, 222–233; Birney, *Neophil*, xliv, 333–338; Kaske, *SP*, lix, 479–500; Dean, *MS*, xxi, 149–163.

26   28 Neckam, *De nat.*, pp. 201–202; BM. MS 12F xiii, fol. 44; cf. *Palladius*, p. 9; Giraldus, *Itin. Kambriae*, xii.

26   29 *Hist. of Earth*, I, 414; J. G. Wood, *An. Creat.*, I, 290.

26   30 Lydekker, *Nat. Hist.*, II, 654; Drimmer, *An. King.*, I, 494.

27   31 Bannerman, *Birds*, III, 376; Witherby et al., *Brit. Birds*, II, 227.

27   32 pp. 67–68.

27   33 Drabble, *Weasel*, p. 190. See also Cuvier, *An. Kingdom*, II, 285; *Brehm's Tierleben*, IV, 404; Moore, *Pets*, p. 374.

28   [34] Walker, *Animals*, p. 120.

28   [35] Daniel, *Rural Sports*, I, 338.

29   [36] p. 12.

29   [37] Apuleius, II, xxv, 6; Kittredge, *Witchcraft*, p. 174; Wimberly, *Folklore*, p. 12; Moore, *Pets*, p. 104.

29   [38] Duncan, *Weasel*, p. 44; *Hist. of Earth*, I, 414.

29   [39] *Rural Sports*, p. 338.

29   [40] Duncan, *Weasel*, p. 59.

29   [41] See Paul Olson, *MLQ*, XXIV, 227–236; Bentley, *SAQ*, LXIV, 247–53. Cf. Craik, *Comic Tales*, p. 6.

Chapter III. Animals Mainly from Tradition

32   [1] BM. Roy. MS 18 B XXIII, fol. 110v; cf. BM. Harl. MS 1288, fol. 44v.

34   [2] *Rel. Ant.*, II, 196.

35   [3] Ginzberg, I, 168; cf. *Gesta*, clix.

36   [4] *Laches*, 196E.

36   [5] Drimmer, *An. King.*, I, 176.

37   [6] Robinson, p. 753; Shaver, *MLN*, LVIII, 106, n. 4, 107.

38   [7] Artemidorus, III, lxv, 194; cf. II, xii, 104; IV, lvi, 235; see also *Berakoth*, 57b; Suetonius, *Nero*, xxxxiv, 1.

39   [8] BM. Ad. MS 38818, fol. 229v; see also illus. in Cave and Borenius, *Arch.*, LXXXVII, 297–309; Millar, pl. 100; Phipson, p. 25; Anderson, *An. Carv.*, p. 58; J. Evans, *Nature*, fig. 63.

39   [9] See Aelian, x, 37; Pliny, x, 12, 16; Plutarch, *Moralia*, VII, 18A; Carmody, *Versio* Y, p. 121; McCulloch, p. 87.

39   [10] BM. Ad. MS 42130, fol. 124v; BM. Ad. MS 47682, fols. 30v, 31, 31v, 32, 32v.

39   [11] *Physiologus*, p. 85; MS Sion Coll. $\frac{\text{L40.2}}{\text{L28}}$ fol. 33.

40   [12] BM. Roy. MS 12F XIII, fol. 62; BM. Ad. MS 42130, fol. 128v; Isidore, xii, 7, 39; see also Anderson, *Med. Carv.*, p. 135; *Misericords*, p. 15.

40   [13] Hildegard, *PL*, CXCVII, col. 1329; 'Allegoriae', *PL*, CXII, col. 871; see also Koonce, *MS.*, XXI, 176–184; Janson, p. 180.

40   [14] Arundel MS 83, fol. 14.

40   [15] E. P. Evans, *Eccl. Arch.*, pp. 295–296.

40   [16] Bodl. MS Douce 151, fol. 26; for primitive punishment see B. D. H. Miller, *N&Q*, CCVI, 412–414; CCVIII, 366–368.

41   [17] Mustanoja, p. 160, E47.

41   [18] See *Eranos Archive*, 105; Matthews, *Mazes*, pp. 60–75, 175, 176.

41   [19] Dawson Turner, *Normandy*, II, 206–207; Matthews, *Mazes*, p. 67; see also Crisp, *Med. Gardens*, p. 70.

43   [20] BM. Roy. MS 2 B VII, fol. 96v; BM. Harl. MS 624, fol. 128v; Bodl. MS 602, fol. 10v; see also E. P. Evans, *Eccl. Arch.*, pp. 314–316; Anderson, *Med. Carv.*, p. 100.

43   [21] Strzygowski, pl. 2.

43   [22] BM. Harl. MS 45, fol. 146v.

page

43   ²³ E. P. Evans, *Eccl. Arch.*, pp. 314–316; Anderson, *Med. Carv.*, p. 100.

44   ²⁴ BM. Harl. MS 3244, fol. 43v.

45   ²⁵ Cook, *Old English*, p. xlix; Hervieux, IV, 187.

45   ²⁶ S. Ambrose, *PL*, XVI, cols. 519; Pseudo-Ambrose, *PL*, XVII, 575; St Augustine, *PL*, XLIV, 543; 'Allegoriae,' *PL*, CXII, col. 862; Pseudo-Hugo, *PL*, CLXXVII, cols. 48, 54.

47   ²⁷ Mandeville, p. 179; Druce *Notebooks*, C 101; F 157; St John's, Oxford, MS 178, fol. 161.

47   ²⁸ J. G. Wood, *An. Creat.*, III, 27.

47   ²⁹ Gutch, 11, pl. opp. p. 349; Gale, *Archaeol.*, 1 (1779), 199.

48   ³⁰ Garver, *Burlington Mag.* (1918), 157–158; Collins, *Symbolism*, p. 186; Busch, *Romanesque*, p. 55; Christie, pp. 71, 79, 183; *Cal. In. Misc.*, V, 28; Boase, *Eng. Art*, p. 90.

49   ³¹ See illus. *MD*, IV, 108.

49   ³² Berchorius, fol. 134v.

50   ³³ See B. White, *Neophil*, XXXVII, 113–115; Baum, *PMLA*, LXXIII, 167.

50   ³⁴ Katzenellenbogen, p. 76, n. 1.

51   ³⁵ *Relation*, pp. 11, 62, 63.

53   ³⁶ BM. Slo. MS 2435, fol. 48v; BM. Roy. MS 2 B VII, fol. 100v; Bodl. MS 264, fol. 76; see also Strutt, p. 214; Anderson, *Med. Carv.*, p. 37; *Brit. Churches*, p. 265.

53   ³⁷ 1, 546–548.

53   ³⁸ Stith Thompson, p. 357.

54   ³⁹ BM. MS 12 F XIII, fol. 80. For illustrations see Westminster MS 22, fol. 47; see also Camb. Univ. Lib. MS Kk–4–25, fol. 80v; BM. Harl. MS 4751, fol. 55v; BM. Ad. MS 11283, fol. 23; BM. Slo. MS 3544, fol. 57; cf. Isidore, xii, 7, 50; see also E. Salter, *E&S*, XXII, 19, for associations with 'courtly painting of elaborate French style.'

55   ⁴⁰ Boone, *MLN*, LXIV, 78–81; Hotson, *PMLA*, XXXIX, 774; Dahlberg, *JEGP*, LIII, 282; Robertson, *Preface*, p. 252. See Miller, *Companion*, pp. 268–290 and Ramsay, *ibid.*, pp. 291–312 for useful discussions of allegory and irony in the *Tales* generally.

55   ⁴¹ *Mactacio Abel*, ll. 84–86; see also Robbins, *Lyrics*, p. 44 and illus. in Anderson, *Misericords*, pp. 21–22; Varty, *JWCI*, XXVI, 347–354; Clayton, *Arch. Journ.*, LXIX, 61.

55   ⁴² Wildridge, *Grotesque*, p. 196.

56   ⁴³ BM. Ad. MS 11695, fol. 157.

56   ⁴⁴ For various interpretations see Donovan, *JEGP*, LII, 498–508; Broes, *PMLA*, LXXVIII, 156–162; Lenaghan, *PMLA*, LXXVIII, 300–307.

Chapter IV. Animals Mainly from Nature

58   ¹ Robinson, p. 795; Swainson, *Prov. Names*, p. 4.

58   ² Harrison, p. 40, quoting 'Bombadier,' p. 125; see also Skeat, *Works*, I, 519.

58   ³ Bannerman, *Birds*, VI, 187; for swan, see also Witherby et al., *Brit. Birds*, III, 169, 171, 177–178.

59   ⁴ Witherby, I, pp. 58–60; cf. Bannerman, I, 104–105.

page	
60	⁵ *Hist. of Earth*, II, 185; cf. J. G. Wood, *An. Creat.*, IV, 544.
60	⁶ BM. Ad. MS 41321, fol. 98.
61	⁷ Barclay-Smith, pp. 13–14; see also Bannerman, *Birds*, VI, 180. On the *SumT*, 1929–1931, see Silvia, *ELN*, I, 248–250, and Hartung, *ELN*, IV, 175–180.
62	⁸ On the character and iconography of Theseus, see Ruggiers, *Art*, pp. 161–162, and Robertson, *Preface*, 260–266. See Severs, *Companion*, pp. 229–233, 242–243, for a useful introduction and bibliography to the *Knight's Tale*.
63	⁹ Froissart (Berners), V, 279, 282; see also Mandeville, p. 156.
64	¹⁰ For a most comprehensive treatment of animal imagery in *Tr.*, especially for images of snaring and fowling, see Meech, *Design*, III, 6. See also Payne, *Remembrance*, pp. 196–201, for patterns of imagery.
64	¹¹ BM. *Ad.* MS 18850, fols. 65, 83; BM. Slo. MS 2435, fol. 48v; Camb. FitzW. MS 242, fol. 29; BM. Ad. MS 36684, fol. 69; cf. Bart. Ang., lxviii.
64	¹² For ref. to conies, see *Cal. Pat. Rolls*, 1266–1272, p. 285; *Cal. Close Rolls*, 1237–1242, p. 381; *Cal. Lib. Rolls*, 1240–1245, pp. 120, 228; *Cal. Pat. Rolls*, 1327–1330, pp. 157, 208, 209, 355, 429, 568, 569; *Cal. Pat. Rolls*. 1381–1385, p. 302; *Cal. Pat. Rolls*, 1334–1338, p. 435; Barrett-Hamilton, II, 180–196; Rogers, *Hist. of Ag.*, I, pp. 340–341; Veale, pp. 209–214.
66	¹³ Veale, p. 61.
66	¹⁴ See Barrett-Hamilton, II, 578.
67	¹⁵ p. 118.
67	¹⁶ *Brehm's Tierleben*, II, 134; Skeat, *Stud. Past.*, p. 103.
69	¹⁷ Jacques de Vitry, pp. 87–88; Hervieux, IV, 391. See also Matheolus, I, 1939; Robinson, p. 700.
69	¹⁸ Drimmer, *An. King.*, I, 560.
71	¹⁹ *Rel. Ant.*, I, 247–248; *Proc. contra Templarios*, I, 141; Scot, *Discoverie*, pp. 25, 36, 37; Champier, *Dyalogus*, iii, 3, sig. bij; Wilkins, *Concilia*, II, p. 331; Wright, *Contemp. Nar.*, pp. vi, 23, 32.
71	²⁰ *MG*, p. 71; for Odo, see Hervieux, IV, 254.
71	²¹ Walsingham, II, 250–251, 351–352; Capgrave, *Chron.*, p. 279; J. de Trokelowe, *Annales*, pp. 343–344.
72	²² Luther, *Tischreden*, II, no. 1557; E. Jones, *Nightmare*, p. 176; Bourke, *Scat. Rites*, pp. 163, 444. Braddy, *SFQ*, xxx, notes examples of scatalogical word-play, e.g. *ferthyng/fert*; *odious meschief/arsmetrike*.
72	²³ Druce, *Notebooks*, F101.

Chapter V. The Boar

74	¹ Fitzstephen, III, p. 3; *MG*, pp. 48, 264–265.
75	² *Liber Albus*, pp. 235–236, 509.
75	³ See *Examiner* (DCLXIV), 608.
75	⁴ *Pol. Poems*, p. xxi; Salter, *Oxford*, p. 46; Agnel, pp. 7–12.
77	⁵ Skeat, *Proverbs*, p. 129.
77	⁶ *Merlin*, p. 421.
77	⁷ On various aspects of boar symbolism see excellent article by Marcelle Thiébaux, *RP*, XXII, 281–299, published too late for reference in my study. See also Robertson, *Preface*, p. 154; Friedman, *ChauR*, II, 17–18. On

page

sow and bagpipe imagery in the Miller's portrait, see Scott, *RES*, xviii, 287–290.

77　8 p. 159.

79　9 Allen, pp. 152–159; M. Gray, p. 5.

80　10 *Prosalegenden*, p. 174.

82　11 Gratian, *Decretum*, xxv, 2, 3, 4; Gregory IX, *Decretals, Extra*, iv, 14.

83　12 See Dronke, *Med. Lyr.*, pp. 176–177, for interesting anticipation of Pandarus' watchman role in an early thirteenth-century *alba*.

84　13 p. 430.

86　14 See Coghill, p. 162; Gerould, p. 71; Bronson, p. 182; Brewer, *Chaucer*, p. 159, for explanations of the intensity of the host's reaction.

Chapter VI. The Hare

87　1 *Vénerie*, p. 44; *MG*, p. 14; *Bk. of St. A.*, sig. eii.

88　2 *Vénerie*, p. 51; *MG*, p. 22; *Short Treatise*, sig. biii.

88　3 *Piers Plow.*, B, iii, 315; B, v, 423; C, iv, 470; C, vii, 31ff; Wright, *Polit. Songs*, p. 329, 11. 121–122. See also Thiébaux, *Spec*, xlii, 264.

88　4 Anderson, *Med. Carv.*, p. 130.

89　5 A similar point is made by Robertson, *Preface*, p. 113, and Abraham, *SP*, lx, 592–595.

89　6 *Mon. Order*, 1, 460, n. 1; see also Ley, *Lungfish*, p. 73; Mitchell and Leys, p. 61.

89　7 Stow's *Survey*, 11, 7; see also Larwood, p. 5.

90　8 *Nug. Poet.*, p. 6; Bodl. MS Rawl. C 86, fol. 109v.

90　9 *Cal. Pat. Rolls*, 1370–1374, p. 240. See Reiss, *ChauR*, 11, pt. 2, 19–21, on the swan as a powerful image of deception.

90　10 See Tucker, *RES*, x, 54–56.

91　11 See McCall, *MLN*, lxxvi, 201–205.

91　12 E. P. Evans, *Eccl. Arch.*, p. 228.

91　13 Ross, *Proc. Leeds*, iii, 365.

92　14 *Rom. Rev.*, xiii, 147, n. 36.

93　15 *Noble Art*, ch. 59, p. 165.

93　16 Hervieux iv, 263.

95　17 p. 676; cf. Hinckley, p. 76.

95　18 Drimmer, *An. King.*, 1, 241.

96　19 Lumiansky, *PQ*, xxvi, 318.

96　20 See *MG*, p. 16; Robbins, *Sec. Lyrics*, p. 107; Anderson, *Med. Carv.*, p. 34, pl. 111a; cf. BM. Roy. MS 2B vii, fols. 170v, 171.

97　21 Mayers, p. 235.

97　22 Ross, *Proc. Leeds*, iii, 350–351; cf. pp. 374–375. See also M. R. Cox, *Introd. to Folklore*, pp. 91, 109.

97　23 p. 110.

97　24 Lumiansky, *PQ*, xxvi, 318–320.

98　25 Heinrich, p. 155.

98　26 Gener, 11, 230; Murisier, pp. 148–151.

99　27 Curry, *Med. Sciences*, p. 59; Sedgewick, *MLQ*, 1, 431; R. P. Miller, *Spec.*, xxx, 180–199.

99   [28] Barrett-Hamilton, II, 229. For a discussion of the Monk's glaring eyes, see Reiss, *ChauR*, II, 269–271; III, 13–19.

100   [29] Cuvier, IV, 299.

100   [30] *Ancient Laws*, I, 735.

100   [31] *Vénerie*, p. 44; *MG*, p. 14.

100   [32] Ross, *Proc. Leeds*, III, 357. For further evidence see Schweitzer, *ELN*, IV, 247–250.

100   [33] Aelian, iv, 11; Albertus Magnus, vi, 99 — 'et equam ideo vocamus feminam luxuriam appetem.' See also E. Jones, *Nightmare*, p. 245.

100   [34] See *Price's Textbook*, p. 521.

100   [35] *Price's Textbook*, 515.

101   [36] D. J. West, *Homosexuality*, p. 105.

101   [37] Grennen, *NM*, LXVII, 118–119, suggests that the idea may derive from la Tour-Landry, from his chapter on Samson and temperance.

Chapter VII. The Wolf

103   [1] Villon, pp. 9, 32; *Bk. of St. A.*, sig. eii; see also *MG*., pp. 54, 61–63, 256; Blount, *Frag. Ant.*, p. 94; *Relat. Is. Eng.*, p. 10; Salzman, p. 53; Veale, pp. 57, 59.

104   [2] de Lamothe-Langon, II, 614.

104   [3] Hervieux, IV, 195–197, 270, 216, 449; Langland, *P.Pl.*, C, x, 265; Matheol., I, 2644–2648; Wycl., *Engl. Works*, p. 32; Owst, *Lit and Pulpit*, p. 373 (Ryl. Libr. Manch. Lat. MS 367, fol. 299v).

105   [4] Ramsay, II, 251–261.

105   [5] BM. Harl. MS 2276, fol. 113; cf. Hervieux, IV, 449.

105   [6] *Acquisitio Mala*, A xii.

107   [7] Ovid, iii. 419–422; Matheol., I, 973; *Roman de la rose*, III, 7764–7766; Latini, *Trésor*, p. 247; *MG.*, p. 55.

109   [8] Pseudo-Hugo of St Victor, *PL*, CLXXVII, col. 67; McCulloch, p. 188; Hervieux, IV, 264; Map, ed. Wright, p. xliii; see also DuCange, sv., *lupa, lupor, lupanar, lupanaria*.

109   [9] See Seznec, figs. 74–77.

110   [10] See Liebeschütz, p. 117, fig. xvii.

110   [11] Reinaert, II, 3994ff; see also *Fables*, ed. Jacobs, II, 157–158; Baum, *MLN*, XXXVII, 350–353.

Chapter VIII. The Horse

113   [1] See Cook., *Trans.*, p. 168, n. 11. On the subject of horses generally see Dent, *Leeds*, IX, 1–12; Dent and Goodall, *Epona, passim*; Fisher, *SAQ*, LX, 71–79; Bowden, *Commentary*, passim; Delasanta, *ChauR*, III, 29–36.

page

113   2 See Strange, *ChauR*, 1, 167–180 for a brilliantly suggestive analysis of the structure of the Monk's tragedies. On the Monk's tale as 'limited' and 'mechanical,' see Ruggiers, *Art*, pp. 184–185.

113   3 *Chronicon Novaliciense*, 11, 7, pp. 13–15. Translated also by Coulton, *Life*, IV, 39–40.

114   4 Kirby, *Companion*, p. 220. For medieval amulets see Wright, *Gen. Powers*, p. 63; Reiss, *ChauR*, 11, 260.

114   5 V. de B., *Spec. Hist.*, xxx, 85; Wycl., *Works*, ed. Arnold, 111, 519–520; see also Peterson, *Sources*, p. 39; Owst, *Lit. and Pulpit*, pp. 250–283.

114   6 *De Nat.*, p. 239.

117   7 *SE Leg.*, 11, 1179–1180.

117   8 *GGK.*, 303; *Sir Beues*, 757; Manning, 11422; Dunbar, *Flyting*, 228; Ed. I. *Ward. Acct.*, p. 172; Froissart, ed. de Lettenhove, 11, 133–144.

117   9 p. 9, 17.

118   10 R. *de B.*, xxvii, 28; Weber, ii, 343.

118   11 BM. MS Cot. Cleo. C. viii, fol. 10v; BM. MS Cot. Claud. B. IV, fols. 25v, 46, 49, 78v.

118   12 See Druce, *Notebooks*, K 96, pl. I; Boase, *Eng. Art*, pl. 57a; BM. Reg. MS 20C vii, fol. 185v; cf. BM. Roy. MS 2B vii, fol. 25v; BM. Harl. MS 4431, fol. 81; BM. Ad. MS 38120, fol. 225.

119   13 p. 15; see also illus. BM. Harl. MS 603, fol. 51v; BM. Ad. MS 42130, fol. 170; BM. Ad. MS 28162, fol. 8v; *EB* (11th ed.), xiii, 718.

120   14 Skeat, *Proverbs*, p. 208.

121   15 *PPL*. A, v, 161; B, v, 318; C, vii, 365, 378, 391; Riley, *Mem.*, p. 63 (1308).

121   16 *Leechbook*, p. 120.

123   17 *Trev. Bart.*, xviii, xxxix; Berthelet, cccxxviii; Batman, fol. 361; Blundeville, 1, fols. 7v, 8; 11, fol. 50.

125   18 Batman, fol. 361v; see also McCulloch, *Best.*, p. 102.

126   19 See Richardson, 'Imagery,' p. 96; Friedman, *ChauR*, 11, 8, 9, 11; Ruggiers, *Art*, p. 76.

127   20 *EB* (11th ed.) xxiii, 96.

129   21 For tale, see G. W. Cox, *Myth. Ar. Nat.*, 1, 151–154.

130   22 *Opera*, 11, 15–19; see also Plato, *Phaed*, 247, 248, 253–256; St James 3: 2–3; Plutarch, *Moralia*, vii, 420, 3; Clement, *PG*, ix, col. 84; St Augustine, *PL*, xxxii, col. 1313; Bardenhewer, *Hermetis*, p. 105.

130   23 'Ambulatio,' A xix; see also 'A Tretyse . . .' ii, 241; 'Love god . . .' 1.85; 'Blessid god,' 1.17; *Dan Michel*, p. 254.

130   24 ed. W. Linow, *EB*, 1 (1889), 25–65.

130   25 See Guillaume d'Auvergne, 1, 1066; Gervase of Tilbury, *Decisio* iii, 62, 92; Scot, *Discoverie*, p. 37; see also Nork, *Myth.*, p. 22; Hopf, *Thierorakel*, pp. 58, 59, 70; Henderson, *Folk-lore*, p. 389; E. Jones, *Nightmare*, p. 267; Kittredge, *Witchcraft*, pp. 244, 548; Robbins, *Encycl.*, pp. 511–514; Stith Thompson, p. 257.

131   26 See illus. Allen, *Reliq.*, 1, 224–225; Oakeshott, *Med. Art.*, pl. 50.

131   27 See Skeat, *Proverbs*, p. 129; Jähns, *Ross and Reiter*, 1, 77; Wycl., *Eng. Works*, p. 435; cf. Blount, *Frag. Ant.*, p. 153.

131   28 p. 65.

131   29 See Jewett, *Reliq.*, 1, 65–78; xiii, 193–194; Gutch, *County Folklore*, 11, 298–300.

132   30 *PL*, ccxii, col. 734; V. de B, *Spec. Hist.*, xxix, 120; *Lai du Trot*, pp. 71–83; *Conseil d'amour*, 11, 50–51; Gower, *Works*, 11, iv, 1244–1446.

132   31 See Dent and Goodall, *Epona*, pp. 8, 9, figs. 11, 12.

page

132   [32] Peterson, *Sources*, p. 39; Wycl., *Eng. Works*, pp. 32, 434.

133   [33] But see Severs, *PQ*, XLIII, 33–34 for view that the cause of sleeplessness is unimportant. [C. B. Hieatt's study arrived too late for consideration in this chapter.]

133   [34] Pausanias, I, i, 32, 4; Map, *Dist.*, IV, 13.

134   [35] See Hadfield, *Dreams*, pp. 14, 81, 83, 144; Freud, *Traumdeutung*, Bd. II, 412; for puns see Baum, *PMLA*, LXXI, 239.

135   [36] See Grennen, *MLQ*, XXV, 131–139, for a biological and psychological reading of the heart/hart ambiguity and for the view that the hunt allegorizes the discomfiture of 'the powers arrayed against the heart of the Black Knight'; also Delasanta, *PMLA*, LXXXIV, 245–251, who finds that the hunting scene and the ambiguity 'suggests through the echoic use of resurrectional diction from the Canticle of Canticles further Christian affirmation about the mystery of immortality'. A similar pun in *KnT* is noted by Van, *ChauR*, III, 71. Theseus, hunting the hart, is likely to prove 'the grete hertes bane' (1681) to the lovers.

135   [37] Jordan, *Shape*, p. 74, sees Chaucer as having his narrator commit a comically 'woeful failure of taste' in comparing Troilus to Bayard.

136   [38] See McCall, *Companion*, pp. 370–384, for a cogent summary of critical approaches to *Tr*.

137   [39] Matheol. (Le Fevre), I, i, 1147–1148; cf. 'Lai d'Aristote,' V, 258; *Rom. de la Rose*, IV, 14528–14530.

137   [40] pp. 112–113.

138   [41] p. 15. See Robbins, *Encycl.*, pp. 551–553, for account of the belief in sixteenth and seventeenth centuries.

139   [42] See BM. MS Nero CIV, fols. 38, 39; BM. Ad. MS 17333, fol. 28; Brand, *Antiq.*, p. 103; Druce, *Arch. Journ.*, LXXII, 152–153.

139   [43] Also on the irony of the wife's 'triumph,' see Jordan, *Shape*, p. 226, who suggests that 'though the Wife of Bath may have won a skirmish, the Wife of Bath's *Prologue* is a dazzling victory for antifeminism'.

Chapter IX. The Sheep

142   [1] Towneley, p. 101; Chester, pp. 133, 135; see also Fitzherbert, p. 46; Sabine, *Spec*, VIII, 339.

142   [2] Power, *Wool*, p. 29.

143   [3] p. 3.

143   [4] Pelham, p. 134.

145   [5] See *Sources*, pp. 302–303.

146   [6] See Gollancz, *The Caedmon MS*, p. 66; *Newcastle Play* in *Non-Cycle Myst. Plays*, pp. 19–25; BM. MS 2 B VII; fols. 5v, 6; James, *Apocrypha*, p. 12; see also Anderson, *Drama*, pp. 107–108; Utley, pp. 59–91.

147   [7] *A.S. Dict.*, p. 5; *Etym. Dict.*, s.v. *Wether*; Wright, *Voc.*, p. 177; *Prompt. Parv.*, p. 519.

147   [8] *Non-Cycle Myst. Plays*, pp. 33, 50.

147   [9] See Hazlitt, *Proverbs*, pp. 3, 267–268; Tusser, p. 119; *Chrestoleros*, IV, 90.

148   [10] Low, p. 659.

page
148 11 Zeuner, pp. 167–170; Fraser and Stamp, p. 120; Zavadovskii, p. 25; Lydekker, *Sheep*, pp. 186–189; Ryder, pp. 1–2; Guthrie, pp. 4–9; Low, p. 682.

148 12 BM. Ad. MS 47682, fols. 13, 26; BM. Roy. MS 2 B VII, fols. 4v, 9, 10v, 11v, 14v, 74, 104v; BM. Slo. MS 3544, fol. 37, 44, 45; BM. Ad. MS 42130, fol. 124; Camb. Univ. Lib. MS Ii-4-26, fol. 22; Camb. Univ. Lib. MS Gg-6-5, fol. 24v; Westminster MS 22, fol. 13.

148 13 Fraser, *Sheep Husbandry*, p. 153.

148 14 Régime, p. 124; cf. BM. Slo. MS 2435, fol. 47v; Gras, *Econ. Hist.* p. 43.

149 15 Skeat, *Works*, v, 271; Rutter, *MLN*, XLIII, 536.

150 16 Rhys, p. 80, n. 1; Henderson, *Folk-lore*, p. 175; Dalyell, *Superstitions*, pp. 517–519.

150 17 Myrk, *Festial*, pp. 100–101, 149, 178–180.

150 18 p. 85.

150 19 Gosset, pp. 313–314.

151 20 Ginzberg, I, 283.

152 21 p. 85.

Chapter X. The Dog

153 1 See *EB*, VIII, 374; Wright, *Hist. of Dom. Manners*, p. 161; E. P. Evans, *Eccl. Arch.*, pp. 89–90; Campbell, *Masks*, p. 423; Burriss, *Class. Phil.*, xxx, 33–42; see also I, Kings, 14:11; Psa. 22:16; Homer, *Odyss.*, xvii, 296; *Iliad*, vi, 344, 356; viii, 283, 423; ix, 373, x, 503; Aristotle, *HA.*, I, i, 14; IX, i, 2; Pliny, *NH* viii, 40, 61; Aelian, *De nat.*, vi, 62–63; vii, 10; pseudo-Hugo de S. Victore, *PL*, CLXXVII, col. 86; McCulloch, *Bestiaries*, p. 111

153 2 BM. Harl. MS 3244, fol. 44v; cf. Bodl. Ashmole MS 1511, fol. 25.

154 3 Blount, *Frag. Ant.*, p. 141.

154 4 *Engl. Works*, p. 12; see also *Boke of Nurture*, p. 66; *Boke of Curtasye*, p. 179; *Rel. Ant.*, I, 155; *Visitations*, III, ii, 175; *Little Red Book*, II, 227.

154 5 Malory, I, 278.

155 6 See *M. E. Sermons*, p. 180; *Acta Sanct.*, Aug. IV, 258, col. 1; Aug. I, 562, col. 2; Guerin, IV, 216.

155 7 *AR.*, ed. Morton, p. 288; *Jacob's Well*, p. 263.

155 8 *MG.*, p. 202.

156 9 *ibid.*, p. 116.

156 10 *ibid.*, pp. 216–217.

158 11 *MG*, p. 120; cf. *Fables*, ed. Jacobs, II, 298–299.

158 12 Caxton, *Chesse*, p. 170; see also Batman, fol. 356.

159 13 *MED.*, sv. chasten: 3 (c).

161 14 See Van, *ChauR*, III, 74. Van also suggests that there is word-play on *boon* and *boone* (2609).

161 15 Schoeck, *Bridge*, II, 239–255.

161 16 Steadman, *N&Q*, CCI, 374–375; Donaldson, *Chaucer's Poetry*, p. 952; see also Kittredge, *Chaucer*, pp. 41, 49; Malone, *Chapters*, pp. 32–33; Baker, *SN*, xxx, 20; Grennen, *MLQ*, xxv, 131–139; Carson, *ChauR*, I, 157–160.

NOTES TO THE TEXT

page

162   17 *AR.*, p. 130; *Jacob's Well*, pp. 86–87; Lydg. *Minor Poems*, 11, 814; cf. Skeat, *Proverbs*, p. 49.

163   18 Campbell, *Masks*, p. 423; Skeat (ed). *Astrolabe*, ii, 3, 28; R. P. Knight, *Symb. Lang.*, pp. 115–116.

164   19 Burriss, *Class. Phil*, xxx, 35; Henderson, *Folk-lore*, p. 45; Hopf, *Thierorake* , pp. 58, 59, 70.

Bibliography of References Cited[1]

I. Printed texts, records, dictionaries

Acta Sanctorum, ed. J. B. Sollerius et al. Vols. XXXV, XXXVIII. Paris and Rome, 1867.

Aelian. *De natura animalium*, ed. F. Jacobs. 2 vols. Jena, 1832.

Alanus de Insulis. 'Contra haereticos.' *Patrologia Latina*, ed. J.-P. Migne. Vol. CCX. Paris, 1855.

————— 'De Planctu naturae.' *Ibid.*

Albertus Magnus. *De animalibus libri*, XXVI, ed. Hermann Stadler. *Beiträge zur Geschichte der Philosophie des Mittelalters*. Vols. XV, XVI. Munster, 1916, 1921.

Albricus, *Liber ymaginum deorum*. See Liebeschütz, *Fulgentius . . .*, pp. 53–64.

Aldrovandi, Ulisse. *De quadripedibus digitalis viviparis*. Bonn, 1645.

Alfric's Colloquies. *A Volume of Vocabularies*, ed. Thomas Wright. London, 1857.

'Allegoriae in sacram scripturam, *Patrologia Latina*, ed. J.-P. Migne. Vol. CXII, Paris, 1878.

St Ambrose. 'Hexaemeron.' *Patrologia Latina*, ed. J.-P. Migne. Vol. XIV. Paris, 1882.

Pseudo-Ambrose. 'De trinitate tractatus.' *Patrologia Latina*, ed. J.-P. Migne. Vol. XVII. Paris, 1879.

Ancient Laws and Institutes of Wales, ed. A. Owen. 2 vols. London, 1841.

The Ancrene riwle, The English text of, ed. Mable Day. Early English Text Society, original series, 225. London, 1952. [AR]

The Ancren riwle, ed. J. Morton. London, 1853. [AR. ed. Morton]

An Anglo-Saxon Dictionary, ed. J. Bosworth and T. Northcote Toller. Oxford, 1898.

Anstey, H., ed. *Munimenta academica*. 2 vols. London, 1868.

Apuleius. *Metamorphoses. Opera omnia*, ed. F. Oudendorp. Leipzig, 1842.

Aristotle. *De animalium generatione. Opera omnia*, ed. A. Firmin Didot. Vol. III. Paris, 1854.

————— *Historia animalium. Opera omnia*, ed. A. Firmin Didot. Vol. III. Paris, 1854.

Artemidorus Daldianus. *Onirocriticon*, ed. Rudolph Hercher. Leipzig, 1864.

Avianus. *The Fables of Avianus*, ed. Robinson Ellis. Oxford, 1887.

St Augustine. 'Contra mendacium.' *Patrologia Latina*, ed. J.-P. Migne. Vol. XL. Paris, 1887.

————— 'De anima et eius origine.' *Patrologia Latina*, ed. J.-P. Migne. Vol. XLIV. Paris, 1865.

————— 'De moribus ecclesiae.' *Patrologia Latina*, ed. J.-P. Migne. Vol. XXXII. Paris, 1877.

Dan Michel's Ayenbite of Inwyt, ed. R. Morris. Early English Text Society, original series, 23. London, 1866.

Bacon, Roger, *Opus Maius*, ed. J. H. Bridges. 3 vols. Oxford, 1897–1900.

Bardenhewer, M. O. *Hermetis Trismegisti de castigatione animae libellum*. Bonn, 1873.

Bartholomew the Englishman. See Trevisa, Batman, Berthelet.

Batman vppon Bartholome, his Booke De Proprietatibus Rerum. London, 1582.

Berakoth. *The Babylonian Talmud, Zera 'im I*, ed. I. Epstein. London, 1948.

Berchorius. *Ovid moralisé. Reductorium morale*, bk. XV: *De fabulis poetarum*. Bruges, 1484.

Bernard Silvestris. *Commentarius super sex libros Eneidos Virgilii*, ed. G. Riedel. Greifswald, 1924.

[1] Editions listed in the bibliography are editions actually used. Where no special edition was used, reference to the works of well-known authors has been omitted.

BIBLIOGRAPHY

Berthelet, T. *De proprietatibus rerum* (Bartholomew the Englishman). London, 1535.

'Blessid god.' *Religious Lyrics of the XV Century*, ed. Carleton Brown. Oxford, 1939.

Blount, Thomas. *Fragmenta antiquitatis: ancient tenures of land*. London, 1679.

Blundeville, Thomas. *Fowre Cheifest Ofyces belong yng to Horsemanshippe*. London, 1565.

Boer, C. de, ed. *Ovide moralisé*. Amsterdam, 1936.

The Boke of Curtasye. *Early English Meals and Manners*, ed. F. J. Furnivall. Early English Text Society, original series, 32. London, 1868.

Boke of Nurture. Ibid.

Bond, E. A. 'Extracts from the Liberate Rolls, relative to loans supplied by Italian merchants to the Kings of England in the 13th and 14th Centuries,' *Archaeologia*, XXVIII (1840), 261–326.

The Book of St. Albans, introd. William Blades. London, 1881.

Bozon, Nicole. *Les contes moralisés de Nicole Bozon*, ed. Lucy Toulmin Smith and Paul Mayer. Paris, 1889.

Brabrook, E. W. 'The Will of Sir Gerard de Braybrooke,' *Essex Archaeological Society*, V (1895), 305.

Bromyard. *Summa Predicantium*. Nüremburg, 1485.

Capgrave, John. *The Chronicle of England*, ed. F. C. Hengeston. London, 1858.

—— *The Life of St. Katharine of Alexandria*, ed. C. Horstmann. Early English Text Society, original series, 100. London, 1893.

Carmody, F. J., ed. 'Physiologus Latinus Versio Y,' *University of California Publications in Classical Philology*, XII (1941), 95–134.

Catholicon Anglicum, ed. S. J. Herrtage. Early English Text Society, original series, 75. London, 1881.

Caxton's *Game and Plays of the Chesse*, introd. William E. A. Axon. London, 1883.

Champier, Symphorien. *Dyalogus in magicarum artium destructionem*. Lyons, *c.* 1500.

Chaucer Life Records, ed. M. M. Crow and C. C. Olson. Oxford, 1966.

Chester Plays, ed. Hermann Deimling. Vol. 1. Early English Text Society, extra series, 62. London, 1893.

Child, F. J., ed. *The English and Scottish Popular Ballads*. 5 vols. New York, 1962.

Chrestoleros. Seven bookes of epigrames written by T.B. London, 1598.

Cicero. *De natura deorum*, ed. C. F. W. Mueller. Vol. II. Leipzig, 1878.

Claudian. *In Rufinum. Opera*, ed. E. Doullay. Vol. II. Paris, 1845.

Clement of Alexandria. 'Stromatum.' *Patrologia Graeca*, ed. J.-P. Migne. Vol. IX. Paris, 1890.

'Colin Blowbol's Testament.' *Nugae Poeticae*, ed. J. O. Halliwell. London, 1844.

Conseil d'Amour. Notice sur la vie et les ouvrages de Richard de Fournival. Vol. II. Paris, 1840–1841.

Cook, Albert S., ed. *The Old English Elene, Phoenix and Physiologus*. Yale, 1899.

Cursor Mundi, ed. Richard Morris. Early English Text Society, original series, 62. London, 1876.

Dan Michel's Ayenbite of Inwyt, ed. R. Morris. Early English Text Society, original series, 23. London, 1866.

De deorum imaginibus libellus. Publ. in Liebeschütz. *Fulgentius* . . . , pp. 117–128.

'The Debate between the Body and the Soul,' ed. W. Linow. *Erlanger Beiträge*, I (1889), 25–65.

Dio Cassius. *Epitome. Historia Romana*, ed. Ludovic Dindorf. Vol. III. Leipzig, 1864.

Dunbar, William. 'The Flyting of Dunbar and Kennedie.' *The Poems of William Dunbar*, ed. W. Mackay Mackenzie. London, 1932.

Durham. *Extract from the account rolls of the Abbey of Durham*, ed. C. Fowler. Durham, 1901.

Edward I. *Wardrobe Account: Liber quotidianus contrarotulatoris garderobae*, ed. J. Topham. London, 1787.

Edward II. *Household Ordinances, Life Records of Chaucer*, II, ed. F. J. Furnival. London, 1900.

Encyclopaedia Britannica, 11th ed. New York, 1910–1911. [EB]

Eranos Archive. At the Warburg Institute, London.
Examiner, ed. Leigh Hunt, DCLXIV (Sept. 17, 1820).
The Fables of Aesop, ed. Joseph Jacobs. 2 vols. London, 1889.
Farinator, Mattias. *Lumen animae*. Augsburg, 1477.
Le Fèvre. See Matheolus.
Fitzherbert. *Book of Husbandry by Master Fitzherbert*, ed. W. W. Skeat. London, 1882.
Fitzstephen, William. *Materials for the history of Thomas à Beckett*, ed. James Craigie Robertson. 7 vols. London, 1875–1885.
France, Marie de. *Die Lais der Marie de France*, ed. K. Warnke. *Bibliotheca Normannica*. Halle, 1900.
Froissart. *Chroniques de Jehan Froissart*, ed. Kervyn de Lettenhove. 25 vols. Brussels, 1863–1877.
———— *The Chronicle of Froissart*, trans. Sir John Bourchier, Lord Berners, introd. W. P. Ker. 5 vols. London, 1901–1903.
Furnivall, F. J., ed. *The Harleian MS* 7334. London, 1884.
Gervase of Tilbury. *Otia Imperialia. Scriptores rerum Brunsvicensium*, ed. G. Leibnitz. Vols. I and II. Hanover, 1707.
Gesta Romanorum, ed. Hermann Oesterley. Berlin, 1871.
Gesta Romanorum, ed. S. J. Herrtage. Early English Text Society, extra series, 33. London, 1879.
Giraldus Cambrensis. *Topographia Hibernica* in *Opera*, ed. J. F. Dimock. Vol. V. London, 1867.
———— *Itinerarium Kambriae* in *Opera*, ed. J. F. Dimock. Vol. VI. London, 1868.
Gollancz, Israel. *The Caedmon MS*. Oxford, 1927.
Gower, John. *The Complete Works: Mirour de l'omme* (Vol. I). *Confessio amantis* (Vols. II, III). *Vox clamantis* (Vol. IV). Ed. G. C. Macaulay. Oxford, 1899–1902.
Guerin, Paul. *Les petites bollandistes vies des Saints*. Vol. IV. Paris, 1880.
Guillaume d'Auvergne. *Opera*. London, 1674.
Havelok, ed. W. W. Skeat. Revised K. Sisam. Oxford, 1915.
Hazlitt, W. C., ed. *Fragmenta antiquitatis*. London, 1874.
———— ed. *English Proverbs and Proverbial Phrases*. London, 1907.
Heinrich, F., ed. *Ein Mittelenglisches Medizinbuch*. Halle, 1896.
Helinand. 'De cognitione sui.' *Patrologia Latina*, ed. J.-P. Migne. Vol. CCXII. Paris, 1865.
Hervieux, Leopold, ed. *Les Fabulistes Latins*. 5 vols. Paris, 1884–1899.
Higden. *Polychronicon Ranulphi Higden together with the English translation of John Trevisa*, ed. C. Babington. 9 vols. London, 1865–1886.
St Hildegard of Bingen. 'De animalibus.' *Patrologia Latina*, ed. J.-P. Migne. Vol. CXCVII. Paris, 1882.
Hilton, Walter. *The Scale of Perfection*, ed. Evelyn Underhill. London, 1923.
Holcot, Robert. *Super librum ecclesiasti*. Venice, 1509.
———— *In librum sapientiae*. Basel, 1586.
Hugh of St Victor. 'De sacramentis fidei Christianae.' *Patrologia Latina*, ed. J.-P. Migne. Vol. CLXXVI. Paris, 1880.
———— *Didascalion*, ed. C. H. Buttimer. Washington, D.C., 1939.
Pseudo-Hugh of St Victor. 'De bestiis et aliis rebus.' *Patrologia Latina*, ed. J.-P. Migne. Vol. CLXXVII. Paris, 1879.
Ipomydon. Metrical Romances, ed. Henry Weber. Vol. II. Edinburgh, 1810.
Isidore of Seville. *Etymologiarum sive originum libri XX*, ed. W. M. Lindsay. Oxford, 1911.
The Issues of the Exchequer, Henry III–Henry IV inclusive, ed. Frederick Devon. London, 1837.
Jacob's Well, ed. Arthur Brandeis. Pt. I, Early English Text Society 115. London, 1900.
The Exempla of Jacques de Vitry, ed. T. F. Crane. London, 1890.
St Jerome. 'Commentaria in Isaiam Prophetam.' *Patrologia Latina*, ed. J.-P. Migne. Vol. XXIV. Paris, 1865.

BIBLIOGRAPHY

———— 'Adversus Jovinianum.' *Ibid.* Vol. xxiii, Paris, 1883.

———— 'Liber Isaiae Prophetae.' *Ibid.* Vol. xxviii. Paris, 1889.

Johannes de Trokelowe et *anon. Chronica et annales,* ed. H. T. Riley. London, 1866.

John of Gaunt, Duke of Lancaster. *John of Gaunt's Register,* ed. Sidney Armitage-Smith. 2 vols. London, 1911.

John of Salisbury. *Policratici, sive, De nugis curialium et vestigiis philosophorum libri VIII,* ed. Clemens C. I. Webb. 2 vols. Oxford.

King Horn, Floriz and Blauncheflur, ed. J. R. Lumby. Early English Text Society, original series, 14. London, 1866.

Kirk, Robert. *The Secret Commonwealth,* 1691, ed. A. Laing. Stirling, 1933.

Knighton, Henry, Canon of Leicester. *Chronicon Henrici Knighton,* ed. J. R. Lumby. 2 vols. London, 1889–1895.

Kyng Alisaunder, ed. G. V. Smithers. Early English Text Society, 227. London, 1952.

La Tour-Landry, The Book of the Knight of, ed. Thomas Wright. Early English Text Society, original series, 33. London, 1868.

Lactantius. 'Epitome divinarum institutionum.' *Patrologia Latina,* ed. J.-P. Migne. Vol. vi. Paris, 1844.

Lady Caroline Kerrison. *A Commonplace Book of the Fifteenth Century,* ed. Lucy Toulmin Smith. London, 1886.

'Lai d'Aristote.' *Recueil général et complet des fabliaux des XIIIe et XIVe siècles,* ed. Anatole de Montaiglon. Paris, 1872–1890.

'Lai du Trot.' *Lai d'Ignaurés,* ed. Louis J. N. Monmerqué and Francisque Xavier Michel. Paris, 1832.

Langland. *The Vision of William Concerning Piers the Plowman Together with Richard the Redeless,* ed. W. W. Skeat. 2 vols. Oxford, 1961. [P.Pl.]

Latini, Brunetto. *Li livres dou trésor,* ed. P. Chabaille. Paris, 1863.

Laȝamon's Brut, or *chronicle of Britain,* ed. F. Madden. London, 1847.

A Leechbook, or *collection of medical recipes of the fifteenth century,* ed. W. R. Dawson. London, 1934.

Leechdoms, Wort. *Cunning and Starcraft,* ed. O. Cockayne. Vol. ii. London, 1864–1866.

Liber Albus, Munimenta Gildhallae Londoniensis, ed. H. T. Riley. London, 1859.

Liber exemplorum ad usum praedicantium, ed. A. G. Little. Aberdeen, 1908.

Life-records of Chaucer. Parts i and iii, ed. W. D. Selby; Part ii, ed. F. J. Furnivall; Part iv, ed. R. C. Kirk. London, 1900.

The Little Red Book of Bristol, ed. F. B. Bickley. 2 vols. Bristol, 1900.

Le livre de Mellibee et Prudence. See *Sources and Analogues,* pp. 568–614.

Li livres de santes (Aldebrand of Sienna) in *Le régime du corps,* ed. Louis Landouzi and Roger Pepin. Paris, 1911.

'Love god, and drede.' *Twenty-six Political and other Poems,* ed. J. Kail. Early English Text Society, original series, 124. London, 1904.

Ludus Coventriae, ed. K. S. Block. Early English Text Society, extra series, 120. London, 1922.

Luther, Martin. *Tischreden oder colloquia . . . ,* ed. J. Aurifaber. Eisleben, 1566.

Lydgate. *The pilgrimage of the life of man,* ed. F. J. Furnivall. Early English Text Society, extra series, 77, 83, 92. London, 1899, 1901, 1904.

———— *The Minor Poems of John Lydgate,* ed. H. N. MacCracken. Early English Text Society, extra series 107, original series 192. London, 1911, 1934.

MD of Canada, ed. F. Marti-Ibáñez. Vol. iv. Westmount, Quebec, 1963.

Machaut, Guillaume de, Oeuvres de, ed. E. Hoepffner. Vols. i–iii. Paris, 1908, 1911, 1921.

Malone, Kemp. *Chapters on Chaucer.* Baltimore, 1951.

Malory, Sir Thomas, The works of, ed. Eugene Vinaver. 3 vols. Oxford, 1947.

Mandeville's Travels, ed. P. Hamelius. Early English Text Society, original series, 153–154. London, 1919–1923.

Manly, J. M., and Rickert, Edith, eds. *The Text of the Canterbury Tales*. 8 vols. Chicago, 1940.

The Manners and Household Expenses of England in the Thirteenth to Fifteenth Centuries, ed. B. Botfield. London, 1841.

Manning, Robert. *History of England*, ed. F. J. Furnivall. London, 1887.

Map, Walter. *De nugis curialium* in *Anecdota Oxoniensis*, ed. M. R. James. Oxford, 1914.

—— *The Latin Poems commonly attributed to Walter Mapes,* ed. Thos. Wright. London, 1841.

Martial. *De Spectaculis, Epigrammata*, ed. M. E. Lemaire, et al. Vol. I. Paris, 1825.

The Master of Game by Edward, Second Duke of York, ed. Wm. A. and F. Baillie-Grohman. London, 1909. [MG]

Matheolus, Les lamentations de, ed. A. G. Van Hamel. 2 vols. Paris, 1892–1905.

Mélanges d'archéologie, ed. Charles Cahier and Arthur Martin. 4 vols. Paris, 1848–1856.

Merlin, ed. H. B. Wheatley. Early English Text Society, original series, 10, 21, 36. London, 1865–1869.

Le Meunier et les. II. Clers, see *Sources and Analogues*, pp. 126–147.

Middle English Dictionary, ed. Hans Kurath and Sherman M. Kuhn. Ann Arbor: University of Michigan, 1952. [MED]

Middle English Sermons, ed. Woodburn O. Ross. Early English Text Society, original series, 209. London, 1940.

Millar, E. G. *English Illuminated MSS X–XIII Centuries*. Paris, 1926.

Mirk's Festial: *A collection of homilies by Johannes Mirkus*, ed. T. Erbe. Early English Text Society, extra series, 96. London, 1905.

Mustanoja, T. F., ed. *How the good wife taught her daughter*. Helsinki, 1948.

Neckam, Alexander. *De naturis rerum et de laudibus divinae sapientiae*, ed. Thomas Wright. London, 1863.

A New English dictionary on historical principles. 10 vols. Oxford, 1888–1928. [NED]

The Non-Cycle Mystery Plays, ed. O. Waterhouse. Early English Text Society, extra series, 104. London, 1909.

Norwich. *Records of the city of Norwich*, II, ed. J. C. Tingey. Norwich, 1910.

Odo of Ceriton. *Fabulae et parabolae. Les Fabulistes Latins*, ed. Leopold Hervieux. Vol. IV. Paris, 1896.

St Odo of Cluny. 'Prolegomena.' *Patrologia Latina*, ed. J.-.P. Migne. Vol. CXXXIII. Paris, 1881.

The Ormulum, ed. R. Holt. Oxford, 1878.

Paideia, ed. W. W. Jaeger, tr. Gilbert Highet. Oxford, 1939.

Palladius on Husbondrie, ed. Rev. Barton Lodge. Early English Text Society, original series, 52. London, 1873.

The Parlement of the thre ages, ed. I. Gollancz. London, 1915.

Pausanias. *Descriptio Graeciae*, ed. H. C. Schubart. 2 vols. Leipzig, 1862–1870.

'The Payne and Sorowe of Evyll Maryage' (Bodleian Digby MS 181, fol. 7). *The Latin Poems commonly attributed to Walter Mapes*, ed. Thos. Wright, London, 1841.

Peraldus, Guiliemus. *Summa Vitiorum*. Basel, 1497.

St Peter Damian. 'Opusculum XIX.' *Patrologia Latina*, ed. J.-P. Migne. Vol. CLXV. Paris, 1867.

Peter Idley's Instructions to his Son, ed. C. D'Evelyn. MLA Monograph 6, 1935.

Philippe de Thaon. *Le Bestiaire de Philippe de Thaün*, ed. Emmanuel Walberg. Paris and Lund, 1900.

Philo Judaeus. 'De Agricul.,' *Opera Omnia*, ed. G. E. Richter. Leipzig, 1828.

Physiologus of S. Ephanius of Cyprus, ed. Ponce de Leon. Antwerp, 1588.

Pierre de Beauvais. 'Bestiaire en prose de Pierre le Picard,' ed. Charles Cahier and Arthur Martin. *Mélanges d'archéologie*, II (1851), 85–100, 106–232; III (1853), 203–288; IV (1856), 57–87.

BIBLIOGRAPHY

Pliny. *Naturalis historiae libri* XXXVII, ed. Carl Mayhoff. 5 vols. Leipzig, 1892–1909.

Plutarch. 'De Iside et Osiride.' *Opera*, ed. J. G. Hutten. Vol. IX. Tübingen, 1797.

—— *Moralia. Opera*, ed. J. G. Hutten. Vol. VII. Tübingen, 1796.

Political Poems and Songs Relating to English History, ed. T. Wright. 2 vols. London, 1859–1861.

The Political Songs of England from the reign of John to that of Edward II, ed. T. Wright. London, 1839.

Polychronicon. See Higden.

Porphyry. 'Vitae Pythagorae.' *Opuscula selecta*, ed. Augustus Nauck. Leipzig, 1886.

Processus contra Templarios, Publ. in Dupuy. *Histoire* . . .

Promptorium Parvulorum, ed. A. Way. London, 1843–1865.

'Prosalegenden,' ed. Carl Horstmann. *Anglia*, VIII (1885), 102–196.

Le régime du corps, ed. Louis Landouzi and Roger Pepin. Paris, 1911.

Reinaert. *Willem's Van den vos Reinaert*, ed. E. Martin. Paderborn, 1874.

A Relation or rather a true account of the Island of England, tr. C. A. Sneyd. London, 1847.

Reliquiae Antiquae, ed. T. Wright and J. O. Halliwell. 2 vols. London, 1841–1843.

'Reply of Friar Daw Topias.' *Political poems and songs*, ed. T. Wright, II, 39–114.

Revelationes Caelestes (Saint Bridget). Munich, 1680.

The Revelations of Saint Birgitta, ed. W. P. Cumming. Early English Text Society, original series, 178. London, 1929.

Rhys, E., ed. *Giraldus Cambrensis: The Itinerary through Wales and the Description of Wales*. London, 1908.

Richard Coeur de Lion. Weber's Metrical Romances. Vol. II. London, 1810.

Richard the Redeless. See Langland.

Riley, Henry Thomas. *Memorials of London and London Life in the XIIIth, XIVth, and XVth Centuries.* 2 vols. London, 1868.

Robbins, Rossell Hope, ed. *Secular lyrics of the XIVth and XVth Centuries.* Rev. ed. Oxford, 1955.

—— *Historical Poems of the XIVth and XVth Centuries.* New York, 1959.

Robinson, F. N., ed. *The Works of Geoffrey Chaucer.* Boston, 1957. [All quotations and line references are from this edition.]

Le Roman de la rose, ed. Ernest Langlois. 5 vols. Paris, 1920–1924.

Li roumans de Berte aus grans piés, ed. Auguste Scheler. Brussels, 1874.

Ruiz, Juan, Arcipreste de Hita. *Libro de buen amor*, ed. Julio cejador y Frauca. Madrid, 1960.

Salter, H. E., ed. *Records of Mediaeval Oxford.* Oxford, 1912.

'Schole-house of Women.' *Remains of the Early Popular Poetry of England*, ed. W. Carew Hazlitt. Vol. IV. London, 1864–1866.

Scot, Reginald. *The Discoverie of Witchcraft.* London, 1886.

Secreta Secretorum, three prose versions, ed. R. Steele. Early English Text Society, extra series, 74. London, 1898.

Shoreham. *The Poems of William of Shoreham*, ed. M. Konrath. Early English Text Society, extra series, 86. London, 1902.

A Short Treatise of Hunting by Sir Thomas Cockaine, introd. W. R. Halliday. London, 1932.

Sir Beues. *The Romance of Sir Beues of Hamtoun*, ed. E. Kölbing. Early English Text Society, extra series, 46, 48, 65. London, 1885–1886, 1894.

Skeat, W. W., ed. *The Complete Works of Geoffrey Chaucer.* 7 vols. Oxford, 1944.

—— ed. *Early English Proverbs.* Oxford, 1910.

—— ed. *A Treatise on the Astrolabe.* Early English Text Society, extra series, 16. London, 1872.

Skelton, John. *Magnyfycence. The Poetical Works of John Skelton*, ed. Alexander Dyce. Vol. II. London, 1843.

La Somme le roy, ou livre des vices et des vertus. See *Sources and Analogues*, pp. 759–760.

Sources and Analogues of Chaucer's Canterbury Tales, ed. W. F. Bryan and Germaine Dempster. New York, 1958.

The South English Legendary, ed. Charlotte d'Evelyn and Anna J. Mill. Early English Text Society, 235, 236. London, 1956.

Sowdone of Babylone, ed. E. Hausknecht. Early English Text Society, extra series, 38. London, 1881.

Stow, John. *A Survey of the cities of London and Westminster.* London, 1710.

Strabo. *Rerum Geographicarum,* ed. Is. Casaubon. Vol. 1. Amsterdam, 1707.

Stratman, F. H., ed. *A Middle-English Dictionary,* rev. H. Bradley. Oxford, 1891.

Suetonius. *Nero,* ed. C. L. Roth. Leipzig, 1871.

Testamenta Eboracensia, ed. J. Raine. Vol. 11. Durham, 1855.

Theobaldus. *Physiologus of Theobaldus. An old English miscellany,* ed. R. Morris. Early English Text Society, 49. London, 1872.

Theodore. *Liber Poenitentialis. A Contemporary Narrative of the proceedings against Dame Alice Kyteler,* ed. T. Wright. London, 1843.

Toulmin Smith, Lucy, ed. *Expedition to Prussia and the Holy Land made by Henry, Earl of Derby, in the years 1390–1 and 1392–3.* London, 1894.

The Towneley Plays, ed. G. England and A. W. Pollard. Early English Text Society, extra series, 71. London, 1897.

'A Tretyse of Gostly Batayle.' *Yorkshire Writers: Richard Rolle of Hampole and his Followers,* ed. Carl Horstman. New York, 1896.

Trevisa, John. Trevisa's Englishing of Bartholomaeus *De proprietatibus rerum, libri XVIII,* printed by Wynken de Worde, 1495.

—— See Higden.

Turberville, George. *The Noble Art of Venery or Hunting,* 1576. Oxford, 1908.

Turner, Dawson. *An Account of a Tour in Normandy,* 2 vols. London, 1820.

Tusser, Thomas. *Five Hundred Pointes of Good Husbandrie* (1590). London, 1878.

La Vénerie de Twiti, ed. Gunnar Tilander. Uppsala, 1956.

Villon, François. *Poésies,* pref. Ch. M. Des Granges. Paris, n.d.

Vincent de Beauvais. *Speculum historiale. Opera.* Douai, 1624.

—— *Speculum naturale. Ibid.*

Pseudo-Vincent de Beauvais. *Speculum Morale. Ibid.*

Visitations of Religious Houses in the Diocese of Lincoln, ed. A. H. Thompson. London, 1919–1927.

Wace, *Roman de Brut,* ed. Ivor Arnold. 2 vols. Paris, 1938–1940.

Walsingham, Thomas. *Historia Anglicana,* ed. H. T. Riley. 2 vols. London, 1863–1864.

The Wars of Alexander, ed. W. W. Skeat. Early English Text Society, extra series, 47. London, 1886.

White, T. H. *The Bestiary.* New York, 1960.

Wilkins, David. *Concilia Magnae Britanniae et Hiberniae.* 4 vols. London, 1737.

William of Malmesbury. *De gestis pontificium Anglorum libri quinque,* ed. N. E. S. A. Hamilton. London, 1870.

Wills. *The fifty earliest English Wills,* ed. F. J. Furnivall. Early English Text Society, original series, 78. London, 1887.

Wright, T., ed. *A Contemporary narrative of the proceedings against Dame Alice Kyteler.* London, 1843.

—— ed. *A Volume of Vocabularies.* London, 1857.

Wyclif, John. *The English Works of Wyclif,* ed. F. D. Matthew. Early English Text Society, 74. London, 1880.

—— *Select English Works of John Wyclif,* ed. T. Arnold. Oxford, 1869–1870. [Cited under Arnold.]

—— *Tractatus de civili dominio,* ed. Reginald Lane Poole and Johann Loserth. 4 vols. London, 1885–1904.

—— *The Lantern of li3t*, ed. L. M. Swinburn. Early English Text Society, 151. London, 1917.

II. Principal Manuscripts

'Arundel Psalter.' London, British Museum. MS 83.

'Bedford Book of Hours.' London, British Museum. Ad. MS 18850.

Bestiaries. London, British Museum. Ad. MS 11283, fols. 1–41. Early XII century.

—— Cambridge, University Library. MS Ii.4.26, fols. 1–74. XII century.

—— London, British Museum. Royal MS 12 C.XIX, fols. 1–94. Late XII century.

—— London, British Museum. Harleian MS 4751, fols. 1–74v. Late XII century.

—— London, British Museum. MS 12F, XIII, fols. 1–141. XII–XIII century.

—— Cambridge, FitzWilliam Museum, MS 254, fols. 1–48. Early XIII century.

—— London, British Museum. Harleian MS 3244, fols. 1–74v. Early XIII century.

—— London, British Museum. Sloane MS 278, fols. 44–57. XIII century (Preceded by Aviarum).

—— London, British Museum. Sloane MS 3544, fols. 1–44. XIII century.

—— London, Sion College. MS L $\frac{40.2}{L\ 28}$ fols. 73–116. XIII century (Preceded by Aviarum).

—— London, Westminster Abbey. MS 22, fols. 1–54. XIII century (Followed by Aviarum).

—— London, British Museum. Cotton Vespasian MS A VII, fols. 4–33. XIV century.

—— Oxford, Bodleian. MS Douce 132, fols. 63–81v. XIV century.

Froissart. *Des croniques de France, dangleterre, descoce.* London, British Museum. Royal MS 18 E.i.

'Gorleston Psalter.' C. W. Dyson Perrins MS 13.

'Holkham Bible Picture Book.' London, British Museum. Ad. MS 47682.

Le Livre de la chasse. Paris, Bibliothèque Nationale. MS fr. 616.

'Luttrell Psalter.' London, British Museum. Ad. MS 42130.

'Ormesby Psalter.' Oxford, Bodleian Library. MS Douce 366.

La Pelerinage de la vie humaine. London, British Museum. Ad. MS 38120.

Pepysian Sketchbook. Magdalen College, Cambridge. MS 1916.

Prudentius. *Psychomachia.* London, British Museum. Cotton Cleo MS CVIII.

'Queen Mary's Psalter.' London, British Museum. Royal MS 2 B. VII.

'Romance of Alexander.' Oxford, Bodleian Library. MS 264.

'Smithfield Decretals.' London, British Museum. Royal MS 10 E. IV.

La Somme le Roy, ou Livre des Vices et des Vertus. London, British Museum. Royal MS 19.c.11.

'The Taymouth Horae.' London, British Museum. Yates Thompson MS 13.

'Tenison Psalter.' London, British Museum. Ad. MS 24686.

III. Studies

Abraham, Claude K. 'Myth and Symbol: The Rabbit in Medieval France,' *Studies in Philology*, LX (1963), 589–597.

Agnel, Emile. *Curiosités judiciaires et historiques du moyen âge.* Paris, 1858.

Allen, J. Romilly. 'The Norman Doorways of Yorkshire,' *Reliquary* I, new series (1888), 224–228.

Anderson, M. D. *The Mediaeval Carver.* Cambridge, 1935.

—— *Animal Carvings in British Churches.* Cambridge, 1938.

—— *Looking for History in British Churches.* London, 1951.

—— *Misericords.* Harmondsworth and Baltimore, 1954.

—— *Drama and Imagery in English Medieval Churches.* Cambridge, 1963.

Armitage-Smith, Sydney. *John of Gaunt.* London, 1904.

Baker, Donald C. 'Imagery and Structure in Chaucer's *Book of the Duchess,*' *Studia Neophilologica,* XXX (1958), 17–26.

—— 'The Parliament of Fowls' in *Companion to Chaucer Studies,* ed. Beryl Rowland. Toronto, 1968, pp. 355–369.

Bannerman, David A. *The Birds of the English Isles.* 9 vols. Edinburgh, 1953–1961.

Barclay-Smith, Phyllis. *British Birds.* London, 1939.

Barrett-Hamilton, G. E. H. *A History of British Mammals.* 3 vols. London, 1910.

Baum, Paull F. 'The Mare and the Wolf,' *Modern Language Notes,* XXXVII (1922), 350–353.

—— 'Chaucer's Puns: A Supplementary List,' *Publications of the Modern Language Association of America,* LXXIII (1958), 167–170.

Beichner, Paul E. 'Absolon's Hair,' *Mediaeval Studies,* XII (1950), 222–233.

Bennett, J. A. W. *The Parlement of Foules: An Interpretation.* Oxford, 1957.

—— *Chaucer's 'Book of Fame'.* Oxford, 1968.

Bentley, Joseph. 'Chaucer's Fatalistic Miller,' *South Atlantic Quarterly,* LXIV (1965), 247–253.

Biggins, D. '*Canterbury Tales* X (I) 424: "The hyndre part of a she-ape in the fulle of the moone",' *Medium Aevum,* XXXIII (1964), 200–203.

Birney, Earle. 'The Inhibited and the Uninhibited: Ironic Structure in the *Miller's Tale,*' *Neophilologus Mitteilungen,* XLIV (1960), 333–338.

—— 'Structural Irony within *The Summoner's Tale,*' *Anglia,* LXXVIII (1960), 204–218.

Bloomfield, Morton W. *The Seven Deadly Sins.* Michigan, 1952.

Boase, T. S. R. *English Art* 1100–1216. Oxford, 1953.

'Bombadier,' 'Chaucer, Ornithologist,' *Blackwood's Magazine,* CCLVI (1944), 125.

Bond, Francis. *Wood Carvings in English Churches.* 2 vols. London, 1910.

Boone, Lalia P. 'Chauntecleer and Partlet Identified,' *Modern Language Notes,* LXIV (1949), 78–81.

Bourke, J. G. *Scatologic Rites of all Nations.* Washington, D.C., 1891.

Bowden, Muriel. *A Commentary on the General Prologue to the Canterbury Tales.* New York, 1960.

Braddy, Haldeen. 'Chaucer's Bawdy Tongue,' *Southern Folklore Quarterly,* XXX (1966), 214–222.

—— 'The Oriental origin of Chaucer's Canacee—Falcon Episode.' *Modern Language Review,* XXXI (1936), 11–19.

Brand, J. *Observations on Popular Antiquities.* Newcastle, 1777.

Brehm, Alfred. *Brehm's Tierleben.* 4 vols. Leipzig, 1926.

Brewer, Derek S. *Chaucer.* London, 1963.

Brieger, Peter. *English Art* 1216–1307. Oxford, 1957.

Broes, Arthur T. 'Chaucer's Disgruntled Cleric: The *Nun's Priest's Tale,*' *Publications of the Modern Language Association,* LXXVIII (1963), 156–162.

Bronson, Bertrand H., 'The Book of the Duchess reopened.' *Publications of the Modern Language Association of America,* LXVII (1952), 863–881.

—— *In Search of Chaucer.* Toronto, 1960.

Burriss, Eli Edward. 'The Place of the Dog in Superstition as revealed in Latin Literature,' *Classical Philology,* XXX (1935), 32–42.

BIBLIOGRAPHY

Busch, H., and Lohre, B. *Romanesque Sculpture*. London, 1962.

Campbell, J. *The Masks of the Gods*. New York, 1959.

Carr, Harvey A. *The Behaviour of Pigeons*. Washington, 1919.

Carson, M. Angela, O.S.U. 'The Easing of the "Hert" in *The Book of the Duchess*,' *The Chaucer Review*, I, No. 3 (1967), 157–160.

Carus-Wilson, E. M., and Coleman, O. *England's Export Trade, 1275–1547*. Oxford, 1963.

Cave, C. J. P., and Borenius, T. 'The Painted Ceiling in the nave of Peterborough Cathedral,' *Archaeologia*, LXXXVII (1937), 297–309.

Chambers, E. K. *The Mediaeval Stage*. 2 vols. Oxford, 1903.

Christie, A. G. I. *English Medieval Embroidery*. Oxford, 1938.

Chronicon Novaliciense. ed. G. H. Pertz. Hanover, 1846.

Clayton, P. B. 'The Inlaid tiles of Westminster Abbey,' *Archaeological Journal*, LXIX (1912), 36–73.

Coghill, Neville. *The Poet Chaucer*. London, 1949.

Collins, Arthur Henry. *Symbolism of Animals and Birds represented in English Church Architecture*. London, 1913.

Cook, Albert S. 'The Historical Background of Chaucer's Knight,' *Transactions of the Connecticut Academy of Arts and Sciences*, XX (1916), 166–238.

Coulton, G. G. *Life in the Middle Ages*. Cambridge, 1930. Vol. IV.

Cox, G. W. *The Mythology of the Aryan Nation*. 2 vols. London, 1870.

Cox, Marian Roalfe. *An Introduction to Folk-lore*. London, 1897.

Craik, T. W. *The Comic Tales of Chaucer*. London, 1964.

Cuvier, Georges. *The Animal Kingdom*. 16 vols. London, 1827–1835.

Crisp, Frank. *Mediaeval Gardens*. 2 vols. London, 1924.

Curry, Walter Clyde. *Chaucer and the Mediaeval Sciences*. London, 1960.

Dahlberg, Charles. 'Chaucer's Cock and Fox,' *Journal of English and Germanic Philology*, LIII (1954), 277–290

Dalyell, J. G. *The Darker Superstitions of Scotland*. Glasgow, 1835.

Daniel, W. B. *Rural Sports*. 2 vols. London, n.d.

Dean, Christopher. 'Imagery in the *Knight's Tale* and in the *Miller's Tale*,' *Mediaeval Studies*, XXXI (1969), 149–163.

Delasanta, Rodney. 'Christian Affirmation in *The Book of the Duchess*,' *Publications of the Modern Language Association*, LXXXIV (1969), 245–251.

——— 'The Horsemen of the *Canterbury Tales*,' *The Chaucer Review*, III, No. 1 (1968), 29–36.

Dent, A. A., and Goodall, Daphne Machin. *The Foals of Epona*. London, 1962.

Dent, A. A. 'Chaucer and the Horse,' *Proceeds of the Leeds Philosophical and Literary Society*, IX (1959), 1–12.

Donaldson, E. T. *Chaucer's Poetry*. New York, 1958.

——— 'Idiom of Popular Poetry in the *Miller's Tale*,' *Essays in Criticism, 1950*. New York, 1951.

Donovan, Mortimer J. 'The Moralite of the *Nun's Priest's Sermon*,' *Journal of English and Germanic Philology*, LII (1953), 498–508.

Drabble, Phil. *A Weasel in My Meat Safe*. London, 1958.

Drimmer, Frederick. *The Animal Kingdom*. 3 vols. New York, 1954.

Dronke, Peter. *The Medieval Lyric*. London, 1968.

Druce, G. C. 'Some Abnormal and Composite Human Forms in English Church Architecture,' *Archaeological Journal*, LXXII (1915), 135–186.

——— *Notebooks* (unpublished). At Society of Antiquaries. London.

Duchausson, Jacques. *Le Bestiaire Divin*. Paris, 1958.

Duncan, Thomas Shearer. 'The Weasel in Religion, Myth and Superstition,' *Washington University Studies (Humanistic Series)*. XII (1924), 33–66.

Dundas, K. R. 'The Wawanga and other tribes of the Elgon District, British West Africa,' *Journal of the Royal Anthropological Association*, XLIII (1913), 48.

Dupuy, Pierre. *Histoire de la Condamnation des Templiers*. 2 vols. Brussels, 1713.

Emerson, Oliver Farrar. 'Chaucer and Medieval Hunting,' *Romanic Review*, XIII (1922), 115–150.

Evans, E. P. *Animal Symbolism in Ecclesiastical Architecture*. New York, 1896.

Evans, Joan. *Nature in Design*. Oxford, 1933.

Fisher, John H. 'Chaucer's Horses,' *South Atlantic Quarterly*, LX (1961), 71–79.

Fraser, Allan. *Sheep Husbandry*. London, 1949.

Frazer, J. B. *The Golden Bough*. 11 vols. London, 1907–1915.

Freud, Sigmund. *Die Traumdeutung*. London, 1948.

Friedman, John Block. 'A Reading of Chaucer's *Reeve's Tale*,' *The Chaucer Review*, 11, No. 1 (1967), 8–19.

Gale, Samuel. 'An historical dissertation upon the ancient Danish horn kept in the Cathedral Church of York,' *Archaeologia*, 1 (1779), 187–202.

Garver, Milton. 'Symbolic Animals of Perugia and Spoleto,' *Burlington Magazine*, XXXII (1918), 156–160.

Gener, Pompeyo. *La muerte y el Diablo*. 2 vols. Barcelona, 1883–1885.

Gerould, Gordon Hall. *Chaucerian Essays*. New Jersey, 1952.

Ginsberg, L. *Legends of the Jews*. Vol. 1. Philadelphia, 1909.

Goldsmith, Oliver. *A History of the Earth and Animated Nature*. 2 vols. London, 1855.

Gossett, A. L. J. *Shepherds of Britain*. London, 1912.

Gras, N. S. B. *The Early English Customs System*. Cambridge, Mass., 1918.

———, and E. C. Gras. *The Economic and Social History of an English Village*. Cambridge, Mass., 1930.

Gray, Minna. 'St Mary-church Parish Church Font,' *Torquay Directory and South Devon Journal*. December 30, 1903, p. 5.

Grennen, Joseph E. 'Hert-Huntyng in *The Book of the Duchess*,' *Modern Language Quarterly*, XXV (1964), 131–139.

——— ' "Sampsoun" in the *Canterbury Tales*,' *Neuphilologische Mitteilungen*, LXVII (1966), 117–122.

Gutch, Mrs [Elizabeth], ed. *County Folk-lore*. Vol. II. London, 1901.

Guthrie, James Francis. *A world history of sheep and wool*. Melbourne, 1957.

Hadfield, J. A. *Dreams and Nightmares*. Harmondsworth, 1961.

Harrison, T. P. *They tell of Birds*. Texas, 1956.

Hartung, Albert E. 'Two Notes on the *Summoner's Tale*: Hosts and Swains,' *English Language Notes*, IV (1967), 175–180.

Henderson, William. *Folk-lore of the Northern Counties of England and the Borders*. London, 1879.

Hieatt, Constance B. *The Realism of Dream Visions: The Poetic Exploitation of the Dream Experience in Chaucer and His Contemporaries*. The Hague, 1967.

Hinckley, Henry Barrett. *Notes on Chaucer*. Northampton, 1907.

Hopf, L. *Thierorakelund Orakelthiere*. Stuttgart, 1888.

Hoskins, W. G. *Sheep farming in Saxon and Medieval England*. London, 1955.

Hotson, J. Leslie. 'Colfox vs. Chauntecleer,' *Publications of the Modern Language Association of America*, XXXIX (1924), 762–781.

Huppé, Bernard F., and D. W. Robertson, Jr., *Fruyt and Chaf: Studies in Chaucer's Allegories*. Princeton, 1963.

Jähns, M. *Ross und Reiter in Leben und Sprache*. 2 vols. Leipzig, 1872.

James, M. R. *The Lost Apocrypha of the Old Testament*. London, 1920.

Janson, Horts W. *Apes and Ape Lore in the Middle Ages and the Renaissance*, London, 1952.

Jenckes, Adaline. *The Origin, the organization and the location of the Staple of England*. Philadelphia, 1908.

Jewett, Llewellyn. 'Scolds and how they cured them in the good old times,' *Reliquary*, I (1860–1861), 65–78.

———— 'A note on some additional examples of branks, or scolds' bridles,' *Reliquary*, XIII (1873), 193–194.

Jones, Ernest. *On the Nightmare*. New York, 1959.

Jordan, Robert M. *Chaucer and the Shape of Creation*. Cambridge, 1967.

Kaske, R. E. 'The *Canticum Canticorum* in the *Miller's Tale*,' *Studies in Philology*, LIX (1962), 479–500.

Katzenellenbogen, A. E. M. *Allegories of the virtues and vices in mediaeval art*. Repr. New York, 1964.

Kirby, Thomas A. 'The General Prologue,' in *Companion to Chaucer Studies*, ed. Beryl Rowland. Toronto, 1968, pp. 208–228.

Kittredge, G. L. *Witchcraft in Old and New England*. New York, 1956.

———— *Chaucer and his Poetry*, Cambridge, Mass., 1956.

Knight, Richard Payne. *The Symbolical Language of ancient art and mythology*. New York, 1876.

Knowles, David (M.D.). *The Monastic Order in England*, 2 vols. Cambridge, 1949.

Koonce, B. G. 'Satan the Fowler,' *Mediaeval Studies*, XXI (1959), 176–184.

———— *Chaucer and the Tradition of Fame*. Princeton, 1966.

De Lamothe-Langon, E. L. B. *Histoire de l'Inquisition en France*. 3 vols. Paris, 1829.

Larwood, Jacob, and Camden, John. *History of Signboards*. London, 1867.

Lawlor, John. 'The Pattern of Consolation in *The Book of the Duchess*,' *Speculum*, XXXI (1956), 626–648.

Lenaghan, R. T. 'The Nun's Priest's Fable,' *Publications of the Modern Language Association*, LXXVIII, 300–307.

Lewis, E. A. 'The Development of Industry and Commerce in Wales during the Middle Ages.' *Transactions of the Royal Historical Society*, new series, XVII (1903), 121–173.

Ley, Willy. *The Lungfish, the Dodo and the Unicorn*. New York, 1948.

Liebeschütz, Hans. *Fulgentius metaforalis*. Leipzig-Berlin, 1926.

Loftie, W. J. *A History of London*. 2 vols. London, 1884.

Low, David. *Elements of practical agriculture*. London, 1847.

Lowes, John Livingstone. 'The Prologue to the *Legend of Good Women* as related to the French Marguerite Poems and to the *Filostrato*,' *Publications of the Modern Language Association of America*, XIX (1904), 593–683.

Lumiansky, Robert Mayer. 'The Meaning of Chaucer's Prologue to Sir Thopas,' *Philological Quarterly*, XXVI (1947), 313–320.

Lydekker, Richard, ed. *Library of Natural History*. 6 vols. New York, 1904.

———— *The Sheep and its Cousins*. London, 1912.

Magenta, G. C. *Il castello di Pavia*. 2 vols. Milan, 1883.

Mâle, Emile. *L'Art religieux de la fin du moyen âge en France*. Paris, 1908.

———— *L'Art religieux du 13me siècle en France*. Paris, 1925.

Manly, J. M. *Canterbury Tales*. New York, 1928.

Marckwardt, A. H. *Characterization in Chaucer's Knight's Tale*. Oxford, 1947.

Matthews, W. H. *Mazes and Labyrinths*. London, 1922.

Mayers, W. F. *The Chinese Reader's Manual*. Shanghai, 1924.

Maynard, Charles J. *Vocal Organs of Talking Birds*. West Newton, Mass., 1928.

McCall, John P. 'Chaucer's May 3,' *Modern Language Notes*, LXXVI (1961), 201–205.

———— 'Troilus and Criseyde,' in *Companion to Chaucer Studies*, ed. Beryl Rowland. Toronto, 1968, pp. 370–384.

McCulloch, Florence. *Mediaeval Latin and French Bestiaries*. North Carolina, 1960.

Miller, B. D. H. 'Dame Sirith: Three Notes,' *Notes and Queries*, CCVI (1961), 412–414.

———— 'A Primitive Punishment: Further Instances,' *Notes and Queries*, CCVIII (1963) 366–368.

Miller, Robert P. 'Allegory in the *Canterbury Tales*,' in *Companion to Chaucer Studies*, ed. Beryl Rowland. Toronto, 1968, pp. 268–290.

———— 'Chaucer's Pardoner, the Scriptural Eunuch and the Pardoner's Tale,' *Chaucerian*

Criticism, ed. R. J. Schoeck and J. Taylor, pp. 221–244. Reprinted from *Speculum*, xxx (1955), 180–199.

Mitchell, R. J., and Leys, M.D.R. *A History of the English People*. London, 1951.

Moore, C. B. *A Book of Wild Pets*. Boston, 1954.

Murisier, E. *Les maladies du sentiment religieux*. Paris, 1901.

Muscatine, Charles. *Chaucer and the French Tradition*. Berkeley, 1957.

Nork, F. *Mythologie der Volkssagen und Volksmärchen, Das Kloster weltlich und geistlich*, ed. J. Scheible. Vol. ix. Leipzig, 1848.

Oakeshott, Walter. *The Sequence of English Medieval Art*. London, 1951.

Olson, Paul A. 'Poetic Justice in the *Miller's Tale*,' *Modern Language Quarterly*, xxiv (1963), 227–236.

Opie, Iona and Peter, eds. *The Oxford Dictionary of Nursery Rhymes*. Oxford, 1951.

Owst, G. R. *Literature and Pulpit in Medieval England*. Oxford, 1961.

Pächt, O. 'Early Italian Nature Studies and the Early Calendar Landscape,' *Journal of the Warburg and Courtauld Institute*, xiii (1950), pp. 13–47.

Payne, Robert O. *The Key of Remembrance*. New Haven, 1963.

Pelham, R. A. 'The Distribution of sheep in Sussex in the early fourteenth century,' *Sussex Archaeological Collection*, lxxv (1934), 129–135.

Petersen, K. O. *The Sources of the Parson's Tale*. Radcliffe College Monograph 12, Boston, 1901.

Phipson, Emma. *Choir Stalls and their Carving*. London, 1896.

Poole, Austin Lane. *Medieval England*. Oxford, 1958.

Power, Eileen. *The Wool Trade*. London, 1941.

Price, M. R. *A Portrait of Britain in the Middle Ages*. Oxford, 1951.

Ramsay, Sir James H. *Genesis of Lancaster*. 2 vols. Oxford, 1913.

Ramsay, Vance. 'Modes of Irony in the *Canterbury Tales*,' in *Companion to Chaucer Studies*, ed. Beryl Rowland. Toronto, 1968, pp. 291–312.

Raven, Charles E. *English Naturalists from Neckam to Ray*. Cambridge, 1947.

Reiss, Edmund. 'The Symbolic Surface of the *Canterbury Tales*; The Monk's Portrait,' *The Chaucer Review*, ii, No. 4 (1968), 254–272; iii, No. 1 (1968), 12–28.

Richardson, Janette L. 'Irony Through Imagery.' Unpublished Ph.D. Dissertation for the University of California, Berkeley, 1962.

Robbins, Rossell Hope. *The Encyclopedia of Witchcraft and Demonology*. New York, 1965.

Robertson, D. W., Jr. *A Preface to Chaucer*. Princeton, 1963. (See also under Huppé.)

Rogers, J. E. Thorold. *A History of Agriculture and prices in England*. Vol. i. Oxford, 1866.

—— *Six Centuries of Work and Wages*. London, 1909.

Rose, Elliot. *A Razor for a Goat*. Toronto, 1962.

Ross, A. S. C. 'The Middle English Poem on the Names of a Hare,' *Proceedings of the Leeds Philosophical and Literary Society*, iii (1932–1935), 347–377.

Rowland, Beryl. 'Chaucer's She-Ape (*The Parson's Tale*, 424),' *The Chaucer Review*, ii, No. 3 (1968), 159–165.

Ruggiers, Paul. *The Art of The Canterbury Tales*. Madison, 1967.

Rutter, G. M. 'An Holy Jewes Shepe,' *Modern Language Notes*, xxxxiii (1928), 536.

Ryder, M. L. 'The Evolution of Domestic Sheep,' *Span*, vi (1963), 114–117.

Sabine, Ernest L. 'Butchering in Medieval London,' *Speculum*, viii (1933), 335–353.

Salter, Elizabeth. 'Medieval Poetry and the Visual Arts,' *Essays and Studies*, xxii (1969), 16–32.

Salzman, L. F. *English Life in the Middle Ages*. London, 1926.

Schoeck, Richard J., and Taylor, Jeremy. *Chaucer Criticism*. Vol. i, Notre Dame, Indiana, 1960.

Schoeck, Richard J. 'Chaucer's Prioress: Mercy and Tender Heart,' *ibid.*, pp. 245–258, reprinted from *The Bridge, A Yearbook of Christian Studies*, ii. New York, 1956, pp. 239–255.

Schweitzer, Edward C. 'Chaucer's Pardoner and The Hare,' *English Language Notes*, iv (1967), 247–250.

BIBLIOGRAPHY

Scott, Kathleen L. 'Sow and Bagpipe Imagery in the Miller's Portrait,' *Review of English Studies*, XVIII (1967), 287–290.

Sedgewick, G. G. 'The Progress of Chaucer's Pardoner, 1880–1940,' *Chaucerian Criticism*, I, ed. R. J. Schoeck and J. Taylor, 190–220, reprinted from *Modern Language Quarterly*, I (1940), 431–458.

Severs, J. Burke. 'The Tales of Romance,' in *Companion to Chaucer Studies*, ed. Beryl Rowland. Toronto, 1968, pp. 229–246.

—— 'Chaucer's Self Portrait in the *Book of the Duchess*,' *Philological Quarterly*, XLIII (1964), 27–39.

Seznec, Jean. *The Survival of the Pagan Gods*. New York, 1961.

Shaver, C. L. 'Chaucer's "Owles and Apes,"' *Modern Language Notes*, LVIII (1943), 105–107.

Shook, Laurence K. 'The House of Fame,' in *Companion to Chaucer Studies*, ed. Beryl Rowland, Toronto, 1968, pp. 341–354.

Silverstein, Theodore. *Visio Sancti Pauli*. London, 1935.

Silvia, Daniel S., Jr. 'Chaucer's Friars: Swans or Swains? (*Summoner's Tale*, D 1930),' *English Language Notes*, I (1964), 248–250.

Skeat, W. W. *A Student's Pastime*. Oxford, 1896.

Steadman, J. M. 'Chaucer's "Whelp"; a Symbol of Marital Fidelity?' *Notes and Queries*, new series, CCI (1956), 374–375.

Strange, William C. 'The *Monks Tale*: A Generous View,' *The Chaucer Review*, I, No. 3 (1967), 167–180.

Strutt, Joseph. *The Sports and Pastimes of the People of England*, ed. William Hone. London, 1833.

Strzygowski, Josef. 'Der Bilderkreis des griechischen Physiologus,' *Byzantinisches Archiv*, Heft 2. 1899.

Swainson, C. *Provincial Names and Folklore of British Birds*. London, 1885.

Teager, Florence E. 'Chaucer's Eagle and the Rhetorical Colors,' *Publications of the Modern Language Association*, XLVII (1932), 410–418.

Thiébaux, Marcelle. 'The Mediaeval Chase,' *Speculum*, XLII (1967), 260–274.

—— 'The Mouth of the Boar as a Symbol in Medieval Literature,' *Romance Philology*, XXII (1969), 281–299.

Thompson, Stith. *The Folktale*. New York, 1946.

Tucker, S. I. 'Sir Thopas and the Wild Beasts,' *Review of English Studies*, X (1959), 54–56.

Utley, F. L. 'Noah, his Wife and the Devil,' *Studies in Biblical and Jewish Folklore*, XVII, 59–91.

Van, Thomas A. 'Second Meanings in Chaucer's *Knight's Tale*,' *The Chaucer Review*, III, No. 2 (1968), 69–76.

Varty, K. 'Reynard the Fox and the Smithfield Decretals,' *Journal of the Warburg and Courtauld Institute*, XXVI (1963), 347–354.

Veale, E. M. *The English Fur Trade in the Later Middle Ages*. Oxford, 1966.

Walker, J., ed. *Animals of America*. New York, 1937.

Wall, J. C. *Mediaeval Wall Paintings*. London, n.d.

Welsford, E. *The Court Masque*. Cambridge, 1927.

West, D. J. *Homosexuality*. Harmondsworth, 1960.

West, Rebecca. *Black Lamb and Grey Falcon*. 2 vols. London, 1946.

White, Beatrice. 'Two Notes on Middle English,' *Neophilologus*, XXXVII (1953), 113–115.

Wildridge, T. Tindall. *The Grotesque in Church Art*. London, 1899.

Wilson, William S. 'The Eagle's Speech in Chaucer's *House of Fame*,' *Quarterly Journal of Speech*, L (1964), 153–158.

Wimberly, Lowry C. *Folklore in English and Scottish Ballads*. New York, 1959.

Wise, Boyd Ashby. *The Influence of Statius upon Chaucer*. Baltimore, 1911.

Witherby, H. E., et al. *The Handbook of British Birds*. 5 vols. London, 1943.

Wood, J. G. *Animate Creation*. 5 vols. New York, 1898.

Wood, D. T. B. 'Tapestries of the Seven Deadly Sins,' *Burlington Magazine*, xx (1911–12), 210–222; 277–289.

Wright, T. *A History of Domestic Manners and Sentiments in England*. London, 1862.

———— *The Worship of the Generative Power in Sexual Symbolism*, introd. Ashley Montague, New York, 1957.

Zavadovski, M., and Litvinova, N. 'The time of slaughtering Karakul lambs for skins,' *Animal Breeding Abstracts*, xiv (1946), 25.

Zeuner, F. E. *A History of Domesticated Animals*. London, 1963.

Zuckerman, S. *The Social Life of Monkeys and Apes*. London, 1932.

Index

INDEX